Paul Revere's

Boston:

1735-1818

Contributors to the Catalogue

Introduction by WALTER MUIR WHITEHILL

JONATHAN L. FAIRBANKS, *Curator*

WENDY A. COOPER, *Special Assistant*

ANNE FARNAM

BROCK W. JOBE

MARTHA B. KATZ-HYMAN

Distributed by New York Graphic Society, Boston

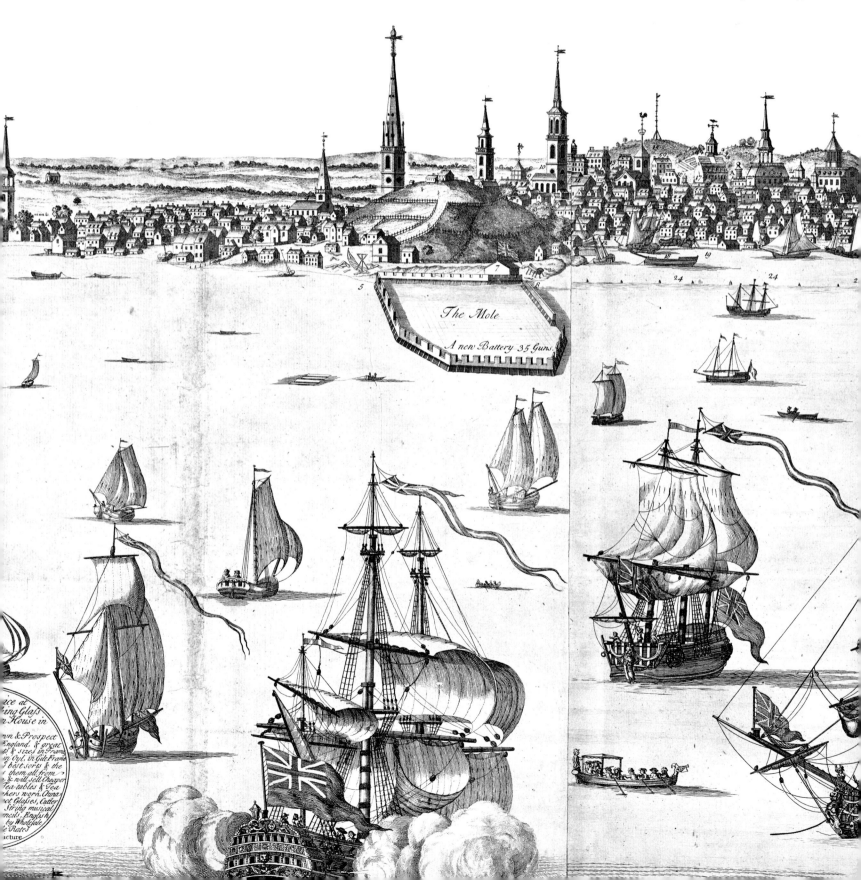

Paul Revere's Boston:

1735-1818

DEPARTMENT OF AMERICAN DECORATIVE

ARTS AND SCULPTURE

MUSEUM OF FINE ARTS, BOSTON

Shirley's Battery

This exhibition was organized with the cooperation of the Massachusetts Historical Society, Stephen T. Riley, Director.

This project is supported by a grant from the National Endowment for the Arts, a Federal Agency.

Library of Congress Catalog Card Number 74-21766
ISBN 0-87846-088-8

Typeset by Dumar Typesetting, Dayton, Ohio
Color separations by Techno-colour Co. Inc., Montreal
Printed by the Meriden Gravure Co., Meriden, Conn.
Designed by Carl F. Zahn

Dates of the exhibition:
April 18-October 12, 1975

PHOTOGRAPHY CREDITS

Richard Cheek: 26, 50, 51, 52, 61, 75, 88, 95, 101, 105, 107, 134, 136, 160, 181, 188, 189, 191, 216, 217, 221, 227, 231, 245, 257, 264, 279, 281-284, 286, 287, 306, 314, 315, 324, 326. Daniel Farber: 4, 11, 18, 21, 23, 65, 74, 76, 85, 93, 147, 149, 151, 154, 170, 179, 180, 200, 214, 215, 230, 240, 254, 262, 276, 307, 327, 331. Robert J. Steinberg: 13, 35, 80, 123, 124, 332-333, 338. George M. Cushing: 3, 30, 152, 158, 203. Israel Sack, Inc.: 43, 122, 258, 268, 277. Antiques Magazine: 135. E. Irving Blomstrann: 175, 177. The Brooklyn Museum: 298. Ginsburg & Levy, Inc.: 271. Harvard Theatre Collection: 232. Hayman Studio: 335. Cortlandt V. D. Hubbard: 266. Richard Merrill: 261. Metropolitan Museum of Art: 297. Museum of Fine Arts: 30, 113. Eric M. Sanford: 273. John Walton: 60.

Cover and title page:
Details from

23
WILLIAM BURGIS, active 1716-1741, and revised by WILLIAM PRICE, 1684-1771
JOHN HARRIS, active 1686-1740
A South East View of ye Great Town of Boston in New England in America
1743, Boston, line engraving, signed lower left: "W. Burgis Delin.," lower right: "I. Harris Sculp."; 23⅛ x 51⅛ in.
American Antiquarian Society, Worcester, Massachusetts

In 1743 William Price published this panoramic view of Boston harbor, revising William Burgis' 1725 edition. Price added ten landmarks to the fifty originally drawn and identified by Burgis and dedicated his version to Peter Faneuil, one of Boston's wealthiest and most prominent merchants. The harbor activity and urban concentration indicate the prosperity of pre-Revolutionary Boston as a port and commercial center.

William Price, an ambitious printseller and retailer at "the Kings Head and Looking Glass in Cornhill near the Town House," had been William Burgis' landlord in 1725 when the draughtsman Burgis issued the first state of this plate. The three copperplates used for the large view probably came into Price's hands in 1731 when Burgis suddenly left Boston, having depleted his wife's fortune.

Ref.: John W. Reps. "Boston by Bostonians: The Printed Plans and Views of the Colonial City by Its Artists, Cartographers, Engravers, and Publishers," in *Boston Prints & Printmakers 1670-1775*, Boston, Colonial Society of Massachusetts, 1973, pp. 3-56.

Contents

Preface

FOR EVERY AMERICAN, the patriot Paul Revere and the town in which he lived have a special meaning. And in this Bicentennial year, it is especially appropriate that he should serve as a focal figure to bring us a closer understanding of the Boston of his times. Paul Revere was a common man, a working craftsman, who through uncommon talents and traits became known at all levels of Boston society, from tradesmen and Masons to ministers and military men. Through his abundant energy and the variety of his occupations, he rose to economic success and finally to fame. His life spanned the final era of colonial rule, the years of the Revolution, and the building of a Federal city.

This exhibition reveals the taste and ideals of early Bostonians and their families, through a selection of their finest possessions both imported from England and made in the Colonies. In presenting the best surviving examples of art owned or made in Revere's Boston, we have been careful to choose works with well-documented histories. Only rarely have many of the objects been seen in public together. They are now assembled to recapture old relationships and establish new interpretations of the cultural history of early Boston.

Those who have helped produce this exhibition are many. Both public and private collectors have been generous in lending, and a grant from the National Endowment for the Arts assisted greatly in the exhibition's organization. In addition to the Museum staff, many others gave fully of their time and special knowledge of the period. To all of these and to those who have helped in countless ways, the Museum is sincerely grateful.

MERRILL C. RUEPPEL
Director

Lenders
to the Exhibition

Anonymous Lenders

American Antiquarian Society

Sheldon Arpad

The Art Institute of Chicago

Bortman-Larus Trust

The Boston Athenaeum

Boston Marine Society

Boston Public Library

Bowdoin College Museum of Art

Sargent Bradlee

The Brooklyn Museum

Mrs. Frances Brooks

Charles Bulfinch

Mrs. Charles L. Bybee

The Cleveland Museum of Art

Mr. and Mrs. Bertram D. Coleman

Colonial Williamsburg Foundation

Commonwealth of Massachusetts

The Connecticut Historical Society

Mr. and Mrs. Charles Crehore
Cunningham

The Currier Gallery of Art

Department of State, Diplomatic
Reception Rooms

The Detroit Institute of Art

Charles Devens, Jr.

Richard S. duPont

Peter W. Eliot

William A. Farnsworth Library and
Art Museum

Miss Eleanor Appleton Fayerweather

First and Second Church in Boston

Wilder Foote

Ginsburg & Levy, Inc.

The Grand Lodge of Masons in
Massachusetts

Mrs. Harlan P. Hanson

Harvard University

Mrs. John F. Higgins

Mr. and Mrs. Charles Fox Hovey

Mr. and Mrs. Edward C. Johnson III

Mr. and Mrs. George M. Kaufman

Miss Aimée Lamb

Lexington Historical Society

The Library Company of Philadelphia

Bertram K. and Nina Fletcher Little

Lodge of Saint Andrew

Mrs. Louis Long, Jr.

Augustus P. Loring

The Mariners Museum

Massachusetts Historical Society

Massachusetts Medical Society

Memorial Art Gallery of the University
of Rochester

The Metropolitan Museum of Art

Mrs. Charles G. Milham

Mrs. Grayson M. P. Murphy

National Gallery of Art

New England Historic Genealogical
Society

New York Public Library

Old South Church

Andrew Oliver

Oliver Family

Mrs. G. Gordon Olsen

Peabody Museum, Salem, Massachusetts

The Pilgrim Society

Miss Jane Pray

Reynolda House

Mrs. Edward Reynolds

Mrs. Walter B. Robb

Israel Sack, Inc.

David Saltonstall

Mrs. Ellery Sedgwick

Smithsonian Institution

The Society for the Preservation of New
England Antiquities

Mr. and Mrs. Lewis T. Steadman

Vernon Stoneman

Robert, David, and Edward Tappan

Miss Mary Thompson

Toms Memorial Collection

Mrs. Charles Townsend

Mr. and Mrs. Howland Warren

Dr. Richard Warren

Mrs. Clifford A. Waterhouse

Mr. and Mrs. Eric M. Wunsch

Yale University Art Gallery

Acknowledgments

PREPARATIONS FOR AN EXHIBITION usually begin several years before the proposed opening date. The concept of a Paul Revere exhibition during the Bicentennial was first suggested in the fall of 1972 by Jane Larus, a connoisseur of Revere silver and a devoted museum volunteer. The cooperation of the Massachusetts Historical Society and its director, Stephen T. Riley, led to the further development of the exhibition and its ultimate fulfillment. Full-time work on the focus and content of the exhibition, and the search for significant, interrelated objects began in August 1973. An exhibition of this breadth represents the work of many people. Museum curators, dealers, collectors, historians, researchers, designers, and editors are those responsible for the final product, from concept to execution. For over a year and a half many people have generously given of their knowledge, time, and energy. They have been unfailing in their advice and assistance with the numerous tasks that must be carefully completed in the production of an exhibition and a catalogue. To all who have been so generous and persistent, we express our most sincere gratitude.

The first laurels must go to the lenders to this exhibition, including both those listed in the catalogue and those who wished to remain anonymous. Without their unselfish willingness to share their treasured collections and inheritances with the public during this important Bicentennial year, there could not have been an exhibition of this magnitude.

As the search for objects began and the selection was finally made, invaluable assistance and direction was given by several professionals and scholars whose knowledge and judgment never ceases to amaze; to Kathryn C. Buhler, Senior Research Fellow in the Department of American Decorative Arts and Sculpture, Museum of Fine Arts; Charles Childs; Sinclair Hitchings, Keeper of Prints, Boston Public Library; Brock W. Jobe, Associate Curator of Exhibition Buildings, Colonial Williamsburg; Stephen T. Riley, Director, Massachusetts Historical Society; and Albert, Harold, and Robert Sack, we extend our deepest thanks for their cooperation, knowledge, and suggestions.

Further direction and advice was generously given during the preliminary stages of the exhibition by Louise Todd Ambler, Curator, Harvard University Portrait Collection; Rodney Armstrong, Director and Librarian, the Boston Athenaeum; Robert Beach, Grand Secretary, the Grand Lodge of Masons in Massachusetts; Ronald Bourgeault; Nicholas Bragg, Executive Director, Reynolda House; Georgia B. Bumgardner, Curator of Graphic Arts, American Antiquarian Society; Winifred Collins, Assistant Librarian, Massachusetts Historical Society; Clement Conger, Chairman, Fine Arts Committee, Department of State; Carl Crossman; Dean and Martha Gandy

Fales; Malcolm Freiberg, Editor of Publications, Massachusetts Historical Society; Benjamin Ginsburg; Dr. Richard Hale, Archivist, Commonwealth of Massachusetts; Roland Hammond; Roberta Hankemer, Librarian, the Grand Lodge of Masons in Massachusetts; D. Roger Howlett; Joseph Kindig III; Mr. and Mrs. Bertram K. Little; Marcus McCorison, Director, American Antiquarian Society; Peter Mooz, Director, Bowdoin College Museum of Art; Bettina Norton; Richard Nylander, Curator, the Society for the Preservation of New England Antiquities; Mrs. A. W. Smith; Diggory Venn; Walter Muir Whitehill; and Eric M. Wunsch.

The text and catalogue entries were written and compiled by Wendy A. Cooper, Jonathan Fairbanks, Anne Farnam, Brock Jobe, and Martha B. Katz-Hyman. The checklist was organized by Martha Katz-Hyman, who also capably assisted with numerous details during the preparation of the exhibition. Caroline Adams, Beth Carver, Eleuthera duPont, Susan Geib, Joyce Goldberg, Barbara Jobe, Myrna Kaye, Jane Larus, and Nancy Webbe all ably assisted in the preliminary research and preparation of the exhibition and catalogue.

Members of other departments at the Museum of Fine Arts were generous with their advice and help. Many thanks are due Laura Luckey, Lucretia Giese, and Sandra Emerson of the Department of Paintings. Robert Moeller and Judith Applegate of the Department of European Decorative Arts and Sculpture, Sue Reed of the Department of Prints and Drawings, and Barbara Lambert, Keeper of Musical Instruments, were most generous with their time in helping with the selection of objects. The curator of textiles, Larry Salmon, and his staff, assisted in the care, cataloguing and displaying of all textiles in the exhibition. Painting conservation was done by Elizabeth H. Jones and her assistant, Brigitte Smith, while preparation of prints and drawings was done by Frank Dolloff and his staff in the Department of Prints and Drawings. William Young and his staff in the Research Laboratory at the Museum of Fine Arts provided analytical assistance as well as object conservation. Repairs and restoration of furniture were performed by Vincent Cerbone, Robert Walker, and Luis Neri-Zagal. All of the complex details of loan agreements, transportation, and insurance were handled by registrars Linda Thomas and Allison Gulick. Design and installation of the exhibition were under the direction of Tom Wong, and Mary Ann Dulude. Carl Zahn deserves high praise for his design of this catalogue, and Lynn Salerno provided invaluable and much appreciated assistance and advice in editing this catalogue. Richard Cheek photographed many of the objects in the exhibition. Robert Steinberg photographed some of the silver and gold objects, while Daniel Farber generously donated his photographic services for several photographs appearing here.

Finally, we are most grateful to the National Endowment for the Arts for financial assistance which made this exhibition possible.

Jonathan L. Fairbanks Wendy A. Cooper
Curator Special Assistant

10

I Introduction

Walter Muir Whitehill

BICENTENNIAL VISITORS TO BOSTON will have to look hard to find buildings that existed during the American Revolution. The exterior of the old State House looks much as it did in 1775, but in 1805 Faneuil Hall was enlarged out of all resemblance to its original state. Two out of the three eighteenth century Anglican churches—Christ Church and King's Chapel—are still in use, but only one of the Congregational churches—the Old South—has survived, and it is preserved as an historic monument. A handful of dwellings, three burying grounds, and Boston Common are all that remain of the 1775 town scene. Even the landscape has been altered by the leveling off of most of the hills to fill in coves. Only through the collections of the Museum of Fine Arts and the Massachusetts Historical Society can one get a sense of what Boston was like during the American Revolution. As the Historical Society is essentially a research library, and cannot accommodate large numbers of general visitors, it welcomes the opportunity to display some of its greatest treasures in this exhibition at the museum, together with objects generously lent from many public and private collections. In *Paul Revere's Boston, 1735 - 1818,* the Museum of Fine Arts offers a unique picture of the town during the eighty-three years of the patriot's life.

Most Americans know Revere's name, not because of his accomplishments as a goldsmith, entrepreneur, and innovator, but because of a ride that he took on the evening of April 18, 1775, to give warning of the movement of British troops to Lexington and Concord. Revere owes this disproportionate fame to Henry Wadsworth Longfellow's "Paul Revere's Ride," which was the first of his *Tales of a Wayside Inn,* published in 1863. Through this poem, Christ Church, in Salem Street, where signal lanterns were hung in the belfry to inform patriot watchers which route the British were taking to Concord, has acquired the nickname of the "Old North Church." Just as Longfellow converted an accomplished craftsman into a mounted messenger, so the signal lanterns that flickered for a few minutes on the night of April 18, 1775, have obscured the fact that Christ Church, Salem Street, built in 1723, is a handsome piece of architecture and the oldest surviving church in Boston, having been in continuous use for more than two and a half centuries. Longfellow, however inaccurate he may have been in historical details and however lacking in biographical perspective, gives proof that the power of the poet to influence people has not diminished since the Homeric age. When a 1954 hurricane blew down the steeple of Christ Church, it was promptly replaced, thanks to the gifts of many readers of "Paul Revere's Ride." The Wayside Inn in Sudbury, Massachusetts, was equally promptly restored after a disastrous fire a few years later, because it had been the scene of Longfellow's *Tales*. These examples are the basis of Whitehill's Law for Historic Preservation: "Catch a poet whose rhymes are easily remembered."

Oddly enough the oldest building in Boston owes its preservation to the fact that Paul Revere bought it in 1770 and lived in it for a few years thereafter. This wooden house in North Square, built soon after the great fire of November 27, 1676, is the only surviving example of the almost medieval timber houses that abounded in the seventeenth century town. In 1770, when Paul Revere bought the house, a third story had been added, and many of the original details modified. Nevertheless when the Paul Revere Memorial Association was organized in 1907 to preserve the building, the architect Joseph Everett Chandler restored it to the form it had when it was built in the seventeenth century, rather than to its appearance a century later when Revere owned it. Thus its clapboarded facade, with an overhanging second story, has the leaded glass casement windows and other characteristics of the time of its construction. There is a large room on each of the two floors, and a smaller one in an ell that juts out at the rear. Visitors frequently wonder where Paul Revere stowed his sixteen children in so modest a dwelling. He didn't, for during his ownership the house had another story. Although the ghost of Paul Revere, were it to walk in North Square, would not recognize the house as his own, it is nevertheless worthy of preservation as a unique example of a Boston dwelling of the last quarter of the seventeenth century.

The life and work of Paul Revere are well documented, for, in addition to the numerous examples of his work in the Museum of Fine Arts, his papers are preserved in the Massachusetts Historical Society. His services as a patriot make him the obvious focus for the chief Bicentennial exhibition at the Museum of Fine Arts. Moreover, his long life spanned several very different aspects of Boston's history, as well as important changes in artistic taste. When he was born, in 1735, Boston was the largest town in the British North American colonies. When he died, in 1818, it was the capital of the Commonwealth of Massachusetts in the United States of America. Although New York and Philadelphia had long since outstripped Boston in population, the town had grown to a point that rendered government by selectmen and town meeting impractical; four years after Revere's death Boston was incorporated as a city. During almost all of Paul Revere's life, Boston was a seaport, depending for its life upon maritime commerce; only in his old age did maritime capital venture into the new field of large-scale textile manufacturing. Revere himself made the transition from hand-craftmanship to manufacturing, for he cast bells and cannon and established copper-rolling mills at Canton Dale.

Seventeenth century Bostonians became shipbuilders, seamen, and merchants through necessity, not choice; there was little else that would gain them a livelihood. Moreover, the peninsula on which Boston stood was at the head of a sheltered deep-water harbor; its extensive shoreline provided ample space for wharves and shipyards only a few minute's walk from any part of the peninsula. This seaport was an English town, a microcosm of the city of London, for close ties of family and trade linked Boston and London. Many Boston houses, like the Paul Revere House, were small, with overhanging upper stories and numerous gables, in the crowded late-medieval English tradition. Yet the great three-story, free-standing brick house built by Peter Sargeant in 1679, which in 1716 became the residence of the governors of the Province of Massachusetts Bay, is eloquent testimony to the success of trade. Built only forty-nine years after the first settlement of Boston, it was a house that an English gentleman would not have been ashamed to live in.

It was, indeed, the growing prosperity of Boston trade that caused the authority of the crown to be definitely established in 1686 in the person of Sir Edmund Andros, first royal governor of the Province of Massachusetts Bay. With him came the Church of England. In 1689 a modest King's Chapel was opened for Anglican worship in the center of the town. The growth of the Church of England is indicated by the establishment of two new parishes —Christ Church in the North End in 1723 and Trinity Church in the South End a decade later—and by the need in 1750 of replacing the first King's Chapel by the present stone church, designed by Peter Harrison.

By the eighteenth century, the Puritan clergy no longer ruled the roost without competition. Bostonians with money in their pockets behaved much as Englishmen might at home. Thus Daniel Neal in his *History of New England,* published in London in 1725, suggested that a *"Gentleman from London would almost think himself at home at Boston when he observes the numbers of people, their Houses, their Furniture, their Tables, their Dress and Conversation, which perhaps, is as splendid and showy, as that of the most considerable Tradesmen in London."* When John Adams arrived for the first time in London on October 26, 1783, he remarked of his quarters in Osborne's Adelphi Hotel: *"The Rooms and Furniture are more to my Taste than in Paris, because they are more like what I have been used to in America."*

In Paul Revere's youth, Boston merchants with pretentions to style ordered their finest household furnishings and carriages from London, although there was no scarcity of competent craftsmen near home. *Boston Furniture of the Eighteenth Century,* a book resulting from a conference arranged by Jonathan Fairbanks for the Colonial Society of Massachusetts in 1972, included a list of some 560 eighteenth century Boston craftsmen engaged in some aspect of furniture-making. On occasion a gentleman who had an English chair that he liked might engage a Boston craftsman to copy it and create a set, just as the merchant Charles Apthorp might commission Paul Revere to make a single tablespoon, using Apthorp's English spoon as a model, to replace a lost or stolen spoon. In other instances Boston craftsmen would embrace a detail, like the blockfront form, and use it longer and more generally than it survived in London fashion.

Reticence and understatement had not become Boston virtues in the middle of the eighteenth century. Sitters to John Singleton Copley invariably were commemorated in their best clothes, and sometimes against a background of baroque architecture and drapery that existed only in the painter's imagination. Thomas Hancock's house on Beacon Hill was splendid for its time and place, yet Copley portrayed Hancock in a setting more appropriate to a European nobleman than to a Boston merchant. Such a standing full-length portrait was clearly designed to impress. Robert Feke's likeness of Charles Apthorp was more modest, yet when the subject died his widow and fifteen surviving children sent to Sir Henry Cheere in London for a memorial tablet with a sonorous Latin inscription, characterizing the deceased as PATERFAMILIAS PRUDENS ET LIBERALIS, MERCATOR INTEGERRIMUS, INSIGNI PROBITATE CIVIS. As this elegant creation, surmounted by a plump cherub, weeping beside an urn, was placed on a wall in King's Chapel, Apthorp was further characterized as INTER HUIUS AEDIS INSTAURATORES PRAECIPUE MUNIFICUS, SINCERA FIDE ET LARGA CARITATE CHRISTIANUS. Such a rich mercantile scene provided lively activity for makers or importers of furniture and of the decorative objects appropriate for elegant use or display, although Copley complained sourly in 1767 that his craft of painting was regarded as *"no more than any other usefull trade, as they sometimes term it, like that of a Carpenter, tailor or shew maker."*

The American Revolution, which began in Massachusetts, rudely interrupted the life of Boston. The town was in a state of siege for nine months, at the end of which many Loyalists left with the British troops, never to return. But as the scene of military operations moved southward, the Bostonians who remained picked up the threads of life. While the war continued, some men were looking ahead to a new national civilization. Through the efforts of John Adams, the American Academy of Arts and Sciences was incorporated on May 4, 1780, with James Bowdoin as its president. Within the year the new academy organized an expedition to Penobscot Bay to observe a total eclipse of the sun. The ideal site was within territory still controlled by the British. Although the scientific party traveled in the galley *Lincoln,* lent by the Commonwealth of Massachusetts, the officer in command of the British garrison permitted the vessel to enter the enemy-held Penobscot Bay, while the commanding officer of HMS *Albany* made himself especially helpful.

For all such high-minded efforts, there was no getting around the fact that Boston's maritime trade had been developed while it was a British colony; with independence, Bostonians became foreigners in the harbors of the Empire. The port's survival in an independent postwar period depended upon finding wholly new channels of trade. So in the early years of peace, Boston ships for the first time pushed into the Pacific, and went to the Northwest coast, the Hawaiian Islands, and on to China. The China trade, which raised Boston to greater prosperity than it had hitherto known, was largely the accomplishment of new men, many of whom had moved in from Essex

County to fill Loyalist shoes. Direct contact with the Far East also brought about new tastes in household decoration.

In Charles Bulfinch Boston had a remarkable architect to guide the great changes that soon took place in the physical appearance of the town. A grandson of Charles Apthorp, he had the property and leisure to embark on a grand tour of Europe in 1785, during which he came under Thomas Jefferson's wing in Paris, and had in Bordeaux, Rome, and London the opportunity to see buildings that were a far cry from the Boston of his youth. On returning home, he was, he stated, *"warmly received by friends, and passed a season of leisure, pursuing no business but giving gratuitous advice in architecture, and looking forward to an establishment in life."* Bulfinch brought back with him firsthand knowledge of the neoclassical architecture that was sweeping Europe. In 1793 he created in Franklin Street a crescent of sixteen connected brick houses, of an elegance recalling the work of the Adam brothers in London or the symmetries of Bath. Bulfinch proved a better designer than a businessman, for the building of the Tontine Crescent led him into bankruptcy in 1796. From the comfortable situation of a gentleman concerned with architecture he turned to a laborious life of architectural practice and public service. From the 1790's until 1818, when he moved to Washington to become architect of the Capitol, Bulfinch was not only personally responsible for the design of most of the new public and private buildings in Boston but, as the perennial chairman of the board of selectmen and superintendent of police, he was the competent head of the town government. Although many of his finest buildings fell before nineteenth century *"progress,"* the State House, the three houses that he built for Harrison Gray Otis, St. Stephen's Church in Hanover Street, and other survivors testify to the extent to which he imposed a new style on Federalist Boston.

The neoclassical style came to prevail over the decorative arts as Bulfinch had made it predominate in architecture. The new Bostonians were painted by Gilbert Stuart rather than by Copley, who had gone to London in 1774, never to return. They imported little from London but bought a great deal from British-born cabinetmakers like John and Thomas Seymour, who settled in Boston in 1794. Paul Revere and other craftsmen who had long been in Boston cheerfully took up the new styles.

This exhibition presents not only works of art and craftsmanship bearing upon the American Revolution; it throws equal light upon the social life and taste of Boston in the decades preceding and following that conflict. It elucidates Paul Revere's part in the Revolution as well as illustrating his development as a craftsman and an innovator. By presenting objects of known provenance whenever possible, it helps bring the dead to life. It is, moreover, a proof that in recreating a segment of the past, paintings and objects of decorative art are quite as legitimate historical documents as books and manuscripts.

Paul Revere – The Man

3

SHEM DROWNE, 1683-1774
Indian weathervane
Ca. 1716-1720, Boston, gilded copper;
H. 54½ in., w. 47½ in.
Massachusetts Historical Society, Boston

From 1629 an Indian with outstretched bow and arrow was the symbol of the Massachusetts Bay Colony. In 1716 the Province House became the residence of the royal governors, and from that time on or shortly thereafter, this symbolic Indian weathervane surmounted the cupola. With its curious amber glass eye, it witnessed the history of colonial Boston. Hammered out of copper and gilded, this unusual weathervane was made by Deacon Shem Drowne, Boston's most noted tinplate worker. Drowne made numerous other weathervanes about town, including the famed grasshopper atop Faneuil Hall and the cockerel on the steeple of the New Brick Church on Middle Street, the church that the Revere family attended. A deacon of the First Baptist Church of Boston, and father of ten children, Drowne was a respected and prosperous craftsman who owned much property including a mansion house on Cornhill that he left to his son, Thomas, the only one of his children who continued in the trade of tinplate worker.

Refs.: Leroy L. Thwing, "Deacon Shem Drowne — Maker of Weather-vanes," *The Chronicle of the Early American Industries Association* 2 (September 1937), 1-2, 7. American Antiquarian Society, *A Society's Chief Joys,* Worcester, Mass., 1969, no. 270.

THE LEGENDARY PAUL REVERE lives in our national memory as an image composed of fact and fantasy. As with most enduring folk heroes, he represents the common man whose reputation rests on his good sense and extraordinary actions. But we have much more than the oral tradition and written history of the career of Paul Revere the patriot to bring us a truer picture of his life. His material achievements as a goldsmith, engraver, and business entrepreneur in the copper industry remain today, reminding us of his skills and ceaseless energy. In churches, museums, libraries, and on original sites, precious handwrought silver, elaborate engravings of many subjects, and cast bells and cannons survive as evidence of his varied and productive career. In an era of transition when hand craftsmanship was giving way to industrial production, Revere seems to have adjusted to the economic and technical changes with ease. During his lifetime, Boston grew from a colonial port, dependent on English trade, to a self-reliant city after the Revolution, when it became a center of manufacturing and international trade in the newly independent country.

Through the years the images of Revere the man and Revere the myth have increasingly diverged as millions of Americans have learned by heart Henry Wadsworth Longfellow's poem of Revere's famous midnight ride in *Tales of a Wayside Inn:*

> *Listen, my children, and you shall hear*
> *Of the midnight ride of Paul Revere,*
> *On the eighteenth of April, in Seventy-five;*
> *Hardly a man is now alive*
> *Who remembers that famous day and year.*[1]

Written in 1860, Longfellow's poem promoted Revere to the legendary realms that often surround patriotic acts of daring and courage. Yet during Revere's lifetime few would have viewed his messenger's ride on the evening of April 18, 1775, as his first claim to immortality. Those who knew his work or who encountered him in the business, political, or social worlds of Boston would have remembered him as *The Boston Intelligencer* did when it recorded his death in May 1818:

> *On Sunday last Paul Revere Esq. aged 83. In the death of Col. Revere, the community, but especially the extensive circle of his own connection, have sustained an irreparable loss. Every person, whose whole life, when considered in regard to the public, or to its private transactions*

1. Henry Wadsworth Longfellow, *Tales of a Wayside Inn* (Boston: Tichnor and Fields, 1863), p. 18.

has been spent in active exertions, in useful pursuits, in the performance of acts of disinterested benevolence or general utility, or in the exercise of the best affections of the heart & most practical qualities of understanding, has an undoubted title to posthumous panegyric. Such was Col. Revere. Cool in thought, ardent in action, he was well adapted to form plans, and to carry them into successful execution — both for the benefit of himself & the service of others.[2]

"The extensive circle of his own connections," the artistic currents and the personalities of Boston during Revere's lifetime are the main concerns of this exhibition and catalogue.

Paul Revere was a first-generation American of French Huguenot descent. His father, Apollos Rivoire (1702-1754), was born in Riaucaud, France, not far from Bordeaux, where French Catholic persecution of the French Protestant minority was intense. Rivoire was sent by his parents first to the Isle of Guernsey to escape religious intolerance, but he later came to Boston as a young boy in about 1716. Apollos was apprenticed to John Coney, the leading goldsmith of early eighteenth century Boston. The goldsmith's trade was important in an era when wealth was transformed into precious, durable commodities, and a goldsmith worked in all precious metals known, especially gold and silver. Lodging with the master, in the North End near Dock Square, Apollos succeeded another apprentice in the shop, John Burt (1693-1745). Both men later had sons, Paul Revere II and Benjamin Burt, who vied with each other for success as the leading goldsmiths in Boston during the second half of the eighteenth century.

After Coney's death in 1722, Apollos purchased what remained of his debt as an apprentice and became an independent goldsmith. In 1729, the émigré Rivoire married Deborah Hitchbourn, who came from an old New England family, and about that time anglicized his name to Paul Revere. Today, to distinguish him from his more famous son, historians separate the two generations, identifying the father as Paul Revere I and the son as Paul Revere II.

Paul Revere II was born December 31, 1735, the second child, first son. At this time the family probably lived on North Street (now Hanover), opposite Clark Street, for in 1730 Paul Revere I announced in *The Weekly News Letter* for May 21 that he had *"Removed from Capt. Pitt's, at the Town Dock, to the North End over against Col. Hutchinson's."*[3] Paul II attended the North Grammar School, where he learned reading and writing, before he was apprenticed to his father. When Paul's father died, in 1754, the young apprentice was not yet of age, but he aided his mother in his father's goldsmith's shop, when she continued the trade according to colonial custom.

As a young man of twenty-one, Revere left his widowed mother briefly in 1756, when he was commissioned a second-lieutenant in the infantry and

5
JOHN SINGLETON COPLEY, 1738-1815
Paul Revere II, 1735-1818
Ca. 1768-1770, Boston, oil on canvas;
35 x 28½ in.
Museum of Fine Arts, gift of Joseph W., William B., and Edward H. R. Revere. 30.781

Paul Revere appears in a workingman's linen shirtsleeves and vest. On the table are engraving tools (burin and needle), and in his left hand is a silver teapot. Revere's next step would be to engrave the teapot, rotating it on the leather pad on which his hand rests. This is one of the few paintings that shows a colonial American craftsman at work.

Both Revere and Copley were well established in their long and successful careers when this painting was made. As contemporaries in pre-Revolutionary Boston, the two men led varied lives in the renaissance spirit of the eighteenth century. Revere, craftsman, patriot, Mason, entrepreneur, was a man who related to many levels of society. Copley, artist and portraitist to the wealthy and elegant merchant princes of Boston, moved to England on the eve of the Revolution, in search of broader artistic horizons. Married into the wealthy Tory merchant family of Richard Clarke, Copley was unable to deal with the problems generated by the popular defiance of royal authority of which Revere was so much a part.

Refs.: Museum of Fine Arts, Boston, *American Paintings in the Museum of Fine Arts, Boston,* Boston, 1969, p. 70, no. 279. Jules David Prown, *John Singleton Copley,* 2 vols. Cambridge, Mass., Harvard University Press, 1966, vol. 1, p. 266, fig. 272.

2. *Boston Intelligencer,* May 16, 1818, in Elbridge Henry Goss, *The Life of Colonel Paul Revere* (Boston: Joseph George Cupples, 1891), vol. 2, pp. 611-613.
3. *Weekly News Letter,* 1730, in Kathryn C. Buhler, *American Silver, 1655-1825, in the Museum of Fine Arts, Boston* (Boston: Museum of Fine Arts, 1972), vol. 1, p. 181.

sent to Crown Point, New York, to fight during the French and Indian War. By November 1756, he had returned to Boston, and in 1757 he was working as a master goldsmith with his younger brother, Thomas, as his apprentice. In August 1757, Paul married Sara Orne, and in April 1758, the first of their eight children was born. Several years later, Revere recorded in his daybook on November 2, 1762, that *"This Day I hired a house of Doc*[r]*. Clark Esq*[r]*. Joyning to M*[r]*. Cocran at Sixteen Pounds Lawfull Money a year."* By 1770 he had accumulated enough capital to purchase a house in North Square (that known today as the Paul Revere House) for £ 213:6:8, with a mortgage of £ 160. His wife, Sara, died in 1773 shortly after the birth of her eighth child, and in October of the same year Revere married Rachel Walker, who also bore eight children.

Revere's career as a goldsmith and engraver began in the late 1750's and early 1760's at a time when the intricacies of the rococo style were being introduced into the arts of the colonies. Design books, prints, and actual pieces of silver, furniture, ceramics, and glass were imported from England and the continent. Local craftsmen, such as Revere, finding it necessary to compete with stylish imported goods, adopted their form and ornament, often with skill and a keen eye for design and proportion. From 1761 until 1797, Paul Revere II kept his business accounts spasmodically in two daybooks[4] which provide a valuable source of information about this production and his many activities and associations.

Among the merchants for whom Revere worked before the Revolution were Thomas Brattle, Edmund Quincy III, Epes Sargent, Zachariah Johonnot Esq., Andrew Oliver, and Captain Joseph Goodwin. It was for Goodwin that Revere made his largest tankard (no. 13), the sole known survivor today of several pieces fashioned for Goodwin. Perhaps one of the most exotic orders Revere recorded was that for Andrew Oliver in 1764: *"To Making a Sugar Dis out of an Ostrich Egg / To Silver . . . £ 4:0:0."* The largest single order that he ever filled was for Dr. William Paine, who in 1773 gave his bride the following pieces of silver: coffee pot, teapot, tankard, pairs of canns, butterboats and porringers, twelve large spoons and eighteen teaspoons, tea tongs and salt spoons, and a creampot.[5]

During the 1760's a number of entries show Revere working for the artist John Singleton Copley. Revere sold him gold bracelets and gold and silver frames and cases, probably for miniatures. Revere's daybooks showed that Copley owed Revere about £ 12 and this may be why Copley painted Revere's portrait around 1768-1770 (no. 5). Paul Revere and Nathaniel Hurd are the only two craftsmen painted by Copley, and it is difficult to imagine either of these men commissioning such portraits at the start of their careers.

Among the entries in the daybooks can be found a number of instances when Revere actually did work for other goldsmiths, including Nathaniel

4
Carved plaque of royal arms
Eighteenth century, Boston, carved and painted wood; 31 x 36½ in.
Massachusetts Historical Society, Boston

The carved royal arms hung over the doorway of the Province House, residence of the royal governors of the Massachusetts Bay from 1716 until the Revolution. As an emblem of the royal presence in the colonies, the painted and gilt plaque symbolized the royal governors' control and power over Englishmen several thousand miles from the mother country.

Refs.: Nina Fletcher Little, "Winthrop Chandler," *Art in America* 35 (April 1947), 110-111. James H. Stark, *Antique Views of ye Towne of Boston,* Boston, James H. Stark, 1901, pp. 221-222.

4. The daybooks are now with the Revere Papers at the Massachusetts Historical Society.
5. Most of this extensive order is now in the Worcester Art Museum.

Hurd, John Coburn, Nathaniel Austin, Samuel Minott, Jonathan Trott, Benjamin Green, Jacob Perkins, and Cox and Berry. As an engraver he recorded names of several prominent printers for whom he worked, including Isaiah Thomas, Joseph Greenleaf, and Edes and Gill.

It is not known how or when Revere was trained as an engraver, but his competence by the early 1760's was such that he was engraving copperplates for a variety of purposes: certificates, bookplates, illustrations in books and periodicals, single prints for mass distribution, trade cards (no. 18) and currency for the colony of Massachusetts. Revere's designs for copperplates were largely derivative, for many plates were direct copies of English prototypes, but he was an excellent copyist, and that seems to have been all that was required.

Revere engraved a wide variety of illustrative material for songbooks (no. 136), a cookbook, a treatise on hemp-husbandry by Edmund Quincy, a history of King Philip's War (no. 20), a volume of Captain Cook's voyage, and maps for Bernard Roman's *Concise Natural History of East and West Florida*. He supplied extensive illustrations for *The Royal American Magazine,* published monthly from January 1774 to March 1775 (nos. 21, 170).[6] A number of the prints that Revere engraved were issued as single sheets to be sold possibly as popular revolutionary propaganda material, or simply for profit. Several of these prints are known to be direct copies of English prints published previously, such as *A View of the Year 1765* (no. 149).

A few prints show some originality on Revere's part, the most notable single engraving probably being *A View of the Obelisk Erected under Liberty-Tree in Boston on the Rejoicings for the Repeal of the Stamp Act 1766* (no. 152).

Of the smaller engraving tasks for which Revere was commissioned, such as bookplates, trade cards, and billheads, few examples survive today. He is known to have made eleven bookplates (no. 11), all for clients who also ordered silver. His trade cards were usually ornamented with elaborate rococo motifs, and several are known to be copied from English models.

In many ways Revere's professional, social, and political lives were interconnected. Before the Revolution he joined a number of organizations, including the Freemasons. In 1760 at the age of twenty-five he became a member of the Lodge of Saint Andrew; later he was the secretary, then Master of the Lodge, and finally he served as Grand Master of the Grand Lodge of Massachusetts from 1795 to 1797. He engraved notices of meetings and Masonic certificates, and he also made silver jewels for a number of lodges.

The Sons of Liberty was primarily a political organization about whose formation, organization, and revolutionary activities little is known. Revere was a member of this group along with John Hancock, Moses Gill, Benjamin Church, Joseph Warren, Martin Brimmer, Joshua Brackett, Josiah Flagg, and Josiah Quincy. While it is not certain that he belonged to the little-known Long Room Club, another political organization that met

6. For a complete description of Revere's engravings, see Clarence S. Brigham, *Paul Revere's Engravings,* rev. ed. (New York: Atheneum, 1969).

above the printing office of Edes and Gill, he did belong to the political lobby group known as the North End Caucus. This group numbered about sixty active citizens, mostly from the North End of Boston, and at a meeting in March of 1772 the following men were among those present: Sam Adams, John Adams, Nathaniel Barber, Benjamin Burt, Perez Morton, Benjamin Edes, Gabriel Johonnot, Dr. Benjamin Church, James Swan, and John Winthrop.

Political organization, discussion, and thought led to political, and later military, activity on Revere's part. On several occasions, including the evening of April 18, 1775, he rode as a messenger for the Massachusetts Committee of Correspondence. In 1776 he was commissioned a major and later that year a lieutenant colonel of the artillery. For several years during the Revolution Revere was in command of Castle William, a fortress in Boston Harbor, and in 1779 he led the artillery forces in the ill-fated Penobscot Expedition. A miserable failure, the mission resulted in the court martial of Revere for insubordination, a charge of which he was exonerated by 1782.

After the Revolution, Revere resumed his profession of goldsmith, becoming interested also in the casting of iron and brass. By 1788 he and his son, Joseph Warren Revere, had established an air furnace and foundry on Lynn Street, and in 1792 they cast their first bell. Revere's curiosity about the properties of certain metals and their potential maleability drew him into a number of business ventures, the most successful of which was the establishment of copper-rolling mills at Canton, Massachusetts, after 1800. Copper from these mills was used to bottom the Frigate *Constitution* and to cover the dome of the new State House designed by Charles Bulfinch in 1797.

More than a summary view of the life of Paul Revere II is beyond the scope of this catalogue, but it will be seen that he was a superior craftsman, skilled in technique, though not always original in design. He was also a patriot and political leader and a moving force in the fight for the independence of his country from colonial rule. He was a competent businessman who shaped his career according to the changing demands of the times.[7]

Three portraits, all in the collection of the Museum of Fine Arts, provide the visitor to this exhibition with an opportunity to study the face of Revere as he appeared to different artists at different periods in his life. The first, by Copley (no. 5), shows the goldsmith before the Revolution, holding a teapot, seemingly pondering his next step in ornamenting its surface. The second is a profile drawing on toned paper by St. Memin (no. 305), showing the tradesman Revere as he appeared during his adventure with foundry and copper-rolling mills. The third, by Gilbert Stuart in 1813 (no. 314), five years before Revere's death, shows him as an elderly, successful entrepreneur at the end of his career. Taken together, these three portraits show the person of Paul Revere II better than any other Colonial craftsman.

11

PAUL REVERE II, 1735-1818
Bookplate of Gardiner Chandler
Ca. 1760-1770, Boston, line engraving, signed lower right: "P Revere Sculp"; 3 3/8 x 2 3/4 in.
Private collection

Revere's heraldic engraving was not limited to his work on silver, for he is known to have engraved copperplates for at least eleven bookplates. In several instances he engraved clients' arms on silver as well as copper, as he did for the Chandler family as well as the Sargents and Mortons. The Chandler arms seen on this bookplate are identical to those Revere engraved on Lucretia Chandler's silver in 1761. Although the motif for this bookplate seems to have been adapted from Nathaniel Hurd's design of an earlier bookplate for John Chandler, Jr., Revere's work for John's brother Gardiner is more elaborate and distinctly Revere's own interpretation.

Ref.: Clarence S. Brigham, *Paul Revere's Engravings,* New York, Atheneum, 1969, p. 158, pl. 51.

7. The bibliography on Revere's life is extensive, beginning with Elbridge H. Goss, *The Life of Colonel Paul Revere,* 2 vols. (Boston: Joseph George Cupples, 1891), and continuing to the present with Esther Forbes, *Paul Revere and the World He Lived In* (Boston: Houghton Mifflin, 1969), and Clarence S. Brigham, *Paul Revere's Engravings* (New York: Atheneum, 1969).

7

PAUL REVERE II, 1735-1818
Teapot
Ca. 1770, Boston, silver with wooden handle, marked: "·REVERE" in rectangle on bottom, engraved with Parsons arms on pourer's side, inscribed on other side, not by Revere: "TSP/ to/SP"; H. 6¾ in., DIAM. (base) 3⅛ in. Museum of Fine Arts, bequest of Mrs. Beatrice Constance (Turner) Maynard in memory of Winthrop Sargent. 61.1160

This fine teapot made by Paul Revere may well be the piece he was preparing to engrave when Copley painted his image. With its pear-shaped form and cast pineapple finial, it was fashioned in the newest rococo style. The surface ornament demonstrates Revere's skill as an engraver with its elaborately embellished cartouche and rim ornament.

Ref.: Buhler, *American Silver in the Museum of Fine Arts,* vol. 2, p. 412, no. 359.

8, 9

PAUL REVERE II, 1735-1818
Creampot and sugar bowl
1761, Boston, silver, both marked: "·REVERE" and script "PR" on bottom, sugar bowl marked with script "PR" at base of finial, both engraved with Chandler coat of arms and crest; creampot: H. 4⅜ in.; sugar bowl: H. 6½ in., DIAM. (base) 3¼ in., DIAM. (rim) 4¼ in. Museum of Fine Arts, Pauline Revere Thayer Collection. 35.1782 and 35.1781

The epitome of Revere's rococo decoration on silver can be seen in the combination of engraved and embossed decoration on this finely proportioned sugar bowl and creampot. Apparently made in 1761 as a wedding gift to Lucretia Chandler from Benjamin Greene, her brother-in-law and a little-known silversmith, the sugar bowl is inscribed under the foot "B. Greene to L. Chandler." According to Revere's accounts, he did not charge Greene for this "sugar dish" until March 11, 1762. These two pieces of silver are among Revere's early works and display his complete command of the craft at the age of twenty-six.

Ref.: Buhler, *American Silver in the Museum of Fine Arts,* vol. 2, pp. 394-395, pl. 344.

13
PAUL REVERE II, 1735-1818
Tankard
1769, Boston, silver, marked: "•REVERE" in
rectangle, engraved with Goodwin coat of arms
on side and inscribed "Joseph Goodwin" on
scrolls below, engraved with Goodwin crest on
cover; H. 8⅞ in., DIAM. (base) 6¼ in., DIAM.
(lip) 2¾ in.
Private collection

This tankard, the largest ever recorded by
Revere in his daybooks, weighs 44 oz. 10 dwt.
Its fabrication and the engraving of arms cost
Joseph Goodwin £ 12. The name of Goodwin,
one of Revere's more affluent patrons, appears
frequently in the daybooks, indicating that he
was a steady client. In 1764 Goodwin ordered
a complete tea service, an unusually large order,
since it is the only one to be charged at one time
in Revere's daybooks until the 1790's.

14
PAUL REVERE II, 1735-1818
Sauceboat
1760-1770, Boston, silver, marked: "•REVERE"
in rectangle on slant below initials, inscribed on
bottom "z^{I}E"; H. 5⅛ in., L. 8 in.
Museum of Fine Arts, Pauline Revere Thayer
Collection. 35.1771

Revere made this pair of sauceboats, or butter
boats or cups, as he called them in his daybooks,
for Zachariah Johonnot, Sr., elder member of a
prominent Huguenot family in Boston. It seems
quite natural that Revere, of Huguenot descent
himself, should have filled orders for at least
six members of the Johonnot family. He made a
similar pair of sauceboats with cherubs' heads
adorning the terminals of the scroll handles for
Francis and Mary Johonnot, who were married
in 1752. In addition, various family members
purchased everything from buckles and polished
teaspoons to a baptismal basin and flagon given
to the Hollis Street Church by Zachariah.

Ref.: Buhler, *American Silver in the Museum of
Fine Arts*, vol. 2, p. 405, no. 354.

18

PAUL REVERE II, 1735-1818
Trade card of Joseph Webb
1765, Boston, line engraving, signed lower right:
"Paul Revere Sculp"; 7⅜ x 5⅞ in.
American Antiquarian Society, Worcester,
Massachusetts

Revere is known to have engraved at least a
dozen trade cards or business advertisements in
his career, including this one for Joseph Webb.
Eighteenth century business cards reveal merchant and manufacturing activity and indicate
the breadth of an individual's economic scope,
both in word and illustration. Joseph Webb was
a fellow Mason with Revere and a member of
the Lodge of Saint Andrew in Boston. He became Grand Master of the Lodge of Massachusetts in 1765-1766. Revere also made use of
the same rococo border of this trade card on the
Lodge of Saint Andrew's Notification, which he
engraved as early as 1767.

Ref.: Clarence S. Brigham, *Paul Revere's Engravings,*
New York, Atheneum, 1969, p. 174, pl. 54.

21

PAUL REVERE II, 1735-1818
History of Lauretta
1775, Boston, line engraving, signed lower right:
"P Revere Sc"; 6¼ x 3½ in.
Private collection

Of twenty-two full-page illustrations that
appeared in the fifteen month run (1774-1775)
of *The Royal American Magazine* Paul Revere
is known to have produced seventeen. Frequently his plates, such as this for the "History
of Lauretta," were copies of English prints that
accompanied a text also derived directly from
English publications. *The Royal American
Magazine* was one of many colonial periodicals
that had a short and eventful life. During its run
it had two publishers, Isaiah Thomas and
Joseph Greenleaf. It ceased with the beginnings
of war activities in April 1775.

Ref.: Clarence S. Brigham, *Paul Revere's Engravings,* New York, Atheneum, 1969, pp. 130-135, pl. 45.

III Boston before the Revolution

IN EIGHTEENTH CENTURY BOSTON, nearly everyone was affected in some way by the sea. The sea was the vital connection between English ports and Boston's sweeping mile-long harbor, lined with wharves, shops, houses, and public buildings. The voyage to Boston was shorter by several days than to any other major port in colonial North America. At a time when shipboard supplies of food and water were severely limited, this difference was critical. With a good harbor, and a location between the New England hinterlands and the mother country, Boston naturally developed into a mercantile town (nos. 23, 27, 30).

Ships brought manufactured goods to supply the needs of the colonists. Clothing, tools, nails, pins, buttons, glass, prints, paper, tableware, and cooking implements were but a few of the many indispensable items only partly supplied by native production. Importation and distribution of these goods was the business of merchants, a class that from the late seventeenth century rose to wealth and influence as the population and thus also the need for manufactured goods increased. In eighteenth century Boston, merchants controlled the economic, political, and social scene as the old-style Calvinist leadership waned.

Before the Revolution, a few merchant families dominated the town, among whom the Amorys, Bowdoins, Faneuils, Hutchinsons, Hancocks, Apthorps, and Winslows were the most important. Through their purchases, their London connections, and their luxurious style of living, these families set the fashion. Together with the governing officials, the merchants and their commerce broadened the horizons of provincial townfolk and changed the culture of Cotton and Increase Mather's time into a more liberal and luxurious world, abounding in gardens, mansions, silver, and furniture. Revere's Boston was unexcelled among colonial cities for refinement of worldly goods and pleasures.

Most responsible for changes in Boston were the merchants, whose travel to other colonies, to island ports, and abroad to England and Europe enlarged their cultural and economic worlds. The trading system through which they operated seemed, on the surface, logical and beneficial to both the mother country and her colonies. The mercantile system was based on the theory that manufactured goods from the mother country would be needed by colonists, who would in turn be able and willing to complete the cycle, returning ships filled with raw materials from the new world to the manufacturing source, England. Although the theory had flaws in practice, it worked in part for a few who became wealthy. For colonial craftsmen, like Revere, the mercantile system was restrictive and competitive, for it yielded

JOHN SMIBERT, 1688-1751
Peter Faneuil, 1700-1742/43
Ca. 1742, Boston, oil on canvas; 49 x 39 in.
Massachusetts Historical Society, Boston

A benevolent merchant of French Huguenot descent, Peter Faneuil inherited his great fortune from his uncle, Andrew Faneuil. When Peter died a bachelor in 1743, he was reputed to be the richest man in Boston. His inventory included a total of 1400 oz. of plate (solid silver), "6 lignum vitae chocolate cups lin'd with silver," and a "Prospect of Boston," which may have been William Price's recently published print, dedicated to him. Faneuil was also well known for his civic generosity. In September 1742, the townspeople of Boston recorded at a town meeting their thanks to Faneuil for his most magnanimous public gift, Faneuil Hall. At "a very great expense, [he] erected a noble structure ... [containing] not only a large and sufficient accommodation for a market place, but a spacious and most beautiful town hall over it."

Faneuil patronized the Scottish immigrant painter John Smibert not only as an artist but also as an architect, for Smibert designed the hall that Faneuil gave to Boston. Smibert had trained in London and come to Boston in 1729, via Newport, Rhode Island. He painted more than two hundred portraits in Boston between 1730 and 1750. In 1730 he held the first art exhibition in Boston at his studio. He was Boston's major painter before Robert Feke's arrival in 1748 and Joseph Blackburn's in 1755.

Ref.: John Smibert, *The Notebook of John Smibert*, Boston, Massachusetts Historical Society, 1969.

only indirect benefits by increasing the purchasing power of the merchants who became their customers.

Boston merchants came from a variety of family backgrounds. Their presence gave Boston a sophistication unmatched in the colonial period in any other city. *"As to politeness and humanity,"* wrote Alexander Hamilton in his diary in 1744, the colonies are *"much alike except in the great towns where the inhabitants are more civilized, especially att Boston."*[1] These more civilized were the great merchant families — the Bowdoins, Faneuils, Hutchinsons, and especially the two most successful merchants of their day, Thomas Hancock and Charles Apthorp. They were the elite in wealth and social standing of Revere's Boston. It is worth studying their careers in some detail to understand how they transformed the city.

Thomas Hancock's biography is one of the great success stories of the eighteenth century (nos. 37, 41). Born in 1703, the son of a Lexington minister, he was a fourth-generation New Englander with a modest family background. After serving an apprenticeship to a Boston bookseller, young Hancock opened his own shop about 1724 at the Sign of the Bible and Three Crowns. At the beginning of his career he gained the trust of several merchants and stationers. One of these, Daniel Henchman, offered him English stationery goods on credit as well as a marriageable daughter, Lydia. By 1730 Hancock had become Henchman's son-in-law and occasional partner.

During the 1730's Hancock rapidly expanded his stationery business into a wholesale dry goods firm with a wide variety of imported merchandise for sale. He purchased ships, established a network of mercantile connections throughout the Atlantic community, and by 1740 had developed a thriving overseas trade. He augmented his fortune by securing government contracts to supply food and equipment to British troops and vessels during wartime. With three maritime wars and twenty-two years of conflict between 1739 and 1763, these contracts offered lucrative livelihoods for Hancock and a small number of his friends.

With his newly achieved fortune secure, Hancock quickly began to assume the trappings of Boston's foremost merchant prince. In 1737 he erected an imposing stone mansion on Beacon Hill near the Common. The two-story edifice, which was ornamented with a balcony, dormers, and quoins, became a well-known landmark of the local scene. It was often shown in drawings and paintings and is pictured in a unique needlework scene of the Common (no. 102). The granite blocks for the facade came from Braintree, Massachusetts, the sandstone trim from Middletown, Connecticut, and the window glass from London. For the interiors Hancock purchased English marble hearths, fireplace tiles, and wallpapers. Hancock described one paper as bright red decorated with green flockwork (finely chopped wool); another showed country scenes and a variety of birds.[2]

1. Carl Bridenbaugh, ed., *Gentleman's Progress, the Itinerarium of Dr. Alexander Hamilton 1744* (Chapel Hill: University of North Carolina Press, 1948), p. 199.
2. W. T. Baxter, *The House of Hancock, Business in Boston 1724-1775* (Cambridge, Mass.: Harvard University Press, 1945), p. 68. This is the best account of Hancock's life.

To the Merchants of Boston this View of the LIGHT HOUSE is most humbly presented By their Humble Serv. W.*m Burgis*

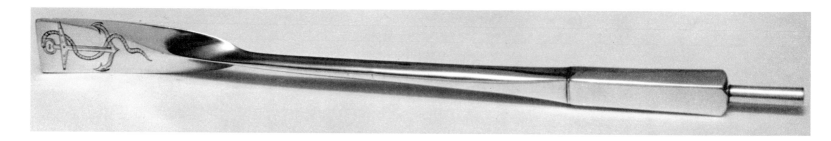

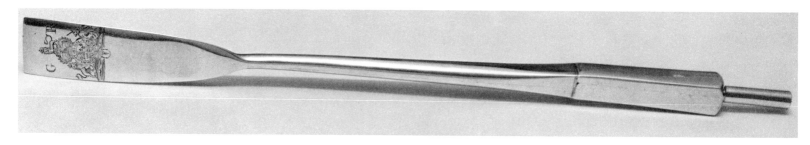

27

WILLIAM BURGIS, active ca. 1716-1731
View of the Lighthouse
1729, Boston, line engraving, signed lower right under picture: "W. Burgis del et fecit";
9⅞ x 12⅜ in.
The Mariners Museum, Newport News, Virginia

Constructed in 1716, the Boston light was the first beacon of its kind in an American port, and its importance to the merchants of Boston cannot be overemphasized. Its constant light safely guided hundreds of ships, laden with imported goods, into the port.

When the draughtsman and artist William Burgis issued this print in 1729, it was the first maritime print and the second mezzotint published in America. It is the only known print that Burgis appears to have engraved as well as drawn. Today there are only two remaining copies known. A similar view of the lighthouse was chosen by the Boston Marine Society, organized in 1742, which was cut into the silver seal Nathaniel Hurd made for the society in 1754.

Ref.: Richard B. Holman, "William Burgis," in *Boston Prints & Printmakers 1670-1775*, Boston, Colonial Society of Massachusetts, 1973, pp. 57-81.

30

JACOB HURD, 1702/3-1758
Admiralty oar
1740-1750, Boston, silver, marked: "HURD" in small rectangle on blade, engraved with royal arms on one side, admiralty anchor on other;
L. 23¼ in.
Massachusetts Historical Society, Boston

As a symbol of judicial authority in the British high court of admiralty in Boston, this piece of ceremonial silver fashioned in the shape of an oar was carried as a mace when the court was in session. The engraved emblems of royal authority on both sides indicated Britain's rule of the seas and her control of mercantile activity through the admiralty courts.

While Jacob Hurd did not make this oar until the 1740's, the Boston admiralty court must have had a similar mace in 1704 when the account of the execution of Quelch, a pirate, in that year noted that the condemned man was "allowed to walk on Foot through the Town . . . the Silver Oar being carried before them . . ."

Ref.: Martha Gandy Fales, *Early American Silver for the Cautious Collector,* New York, Funk and Wagnalls, 1970, p. 145.

Like many of his friends in Boston, Hancock ordered his finest furnishings from England. In a letter to his agent in London in 1738, he requested: *"the favour of you to procure for me & Send with my Spring Goods a Handsome Chiming Clock of the newest fashion, works neat & Good with a Good black Walnutt-Tree Case veneer'd work, with Dark lively branches, on the Top instead of Balls let me have three handsome Carv'd figures Gilt with burnish'd Gold, I'd have the Case without the figures to be 10 foot Long the price 15 not to Exceed 20 Guineas as its for my own use."*[3] He also obtained from London carved gilt looking-glasses, a mahogany card table, a settee, and a chariot. *"As to the Chariot,"* he wrote, *"You know M^rs. Hancock is none of the shortest smallst folks, tho I'd prefer as light a one as possible to her size."*[4] Complementing the imported furniture were a number of less elaborate but skillfully constructed local examples made of walnut and mahogany. A handsome Boston drop-leaf table is one of the few pieces of Hancock furniture to survive (no. 43). Its diminutive proportions and subtly curved legs certainly identify it as the product of a highly proficient local craftsman.

His silver collection, a mixture of English and American objects, contained several Henchman family pieces, including a superb spout cup by Jeremiah Dummer of Boston as well as fashionable Georgian and rococo forms imported from Europe. A pierced cake basket by William Plummer is characteristic of the quality of his London plate (no. 124). Hancock's fondness for cilver even extended to his counting house, where he placed his *"Crest & Arms in Silver & fixt to Ivory."*[5]

On several acres of land behind his grand home, Hancock laid out magnificent gardens filled with flowers and trees of all varieties. Mulberry, cherry, pear, plum, peach, nectarine, apricot, and gooseberry trees were imported from England and an English gardener was hired to maintain the grounds. Hancock carefully attended to his garden, and indeed nothing angered him more than the arrival of dead trees and seedlings from Europe. *"All the seeds,"* he irately reminded one London friend, *"(Except the Asparrow grass) was not worth one farthing. Not one of them Came up They cost me £6:8:2 . . . to Send so far pay dear and be Imposed upon at such a Rate is hard to Bare & he must Return me the money or Send me the same Sortment of Seeds that are Good."*[6] Such problems never disheartened Hancock for long. He took great pride in his grounds, even boasting that *"the Kingdom of England don't afford so fine a Prospect as I have."*[7]

Thomas Hancock amassed a fortune of approximately £100,000, much of which passed at his death in 1764 to his nephew John Hancock, the

3. Thomas Hancock Letterbook, 1735-1740, December 20, 1738, p. 91, Baker Library, Harvard University.
4. Thomas Hancock Letterbook, 1745-1750, September 10, 1748, p. 310, Massachusetts Historical Society.
5. Quoted in W. T. Baxter, *The House of Hancock, Business in Boston 1724-1775* (Cambridge, Mass.: Harvard University Press, 1945), p. 69.
6. Ibid., p. 68.
7. Ibid., p. 67.

Revolutionary leader.[8] Thomas, however, was also liberal in his bequests to the public. He presented large donations to several churches, including £100 to the Brattle Street Church, which was used to purchase silver communion plates (no. 42). He also gave generously to the Linen Manufacturing Society, an agency to provide work for Boston's poor, and to a home for the mentally disturbed. His largest gift, totaling £1000, went to Harvard College to establish a chair in Oriental languages.[9]

In the short span of one generation Thomas Hancock climbed to the height of the mercantile world. Though many of his fellow tradesmen sought to emulate his rise from petty tradesman to wealthy entrepreneur, they rarely duplicated even a part of his achievements. Hancock's portrait by John Smibert portrays him at the beginning for his career (no. 37), a modish upstart with a bright future. John Singleton Copley's portrait (no. 41), painted as a memorial to Hancock around 1765, depicts him in grand scale as one of the merchant princes of Boston. Obviously proud of his accomplishments, the Hancock portrayed by Copley seems nevertheless ungainly in his new luxurious environment.

Much more comfortable in his surroundings is Charles Apthorp, Hancock's friend and rival in business.[10] A portrait of Apthorp by Robert Feke (no. 44), the Newport artist, reveals him to be a sophisticated individual with a cosmopolitan air. Certainly his family background would indicate that he looked more to England than to Boston as his home. The scion of a prosperous English family, Charles was born outside London in 1698 and educated at Eton. He immigrated to Boston at the start of his career and in 1726 married Grizzel, daughter of John and Grizzel Eastwick, an influential Jamaican family who had moved to Boston in 1716.

With connections in England and the West Indies, Apthorp developed an extensive Atlantic trade by which he supplied textiles, hardware, and other goods to many of Boston's shopkeepers, upholsterers, and tradesmen. In 1739, for example, the japanner Robert Davis purchased from Apthorp a shipment of imported looking-glasses valued at over £600.[11] Samuel Grant, a prominent local upholsterer, acquired large quantities of textiles from Apthorp, one lot alone costing £1131 in 1738.[12] Unfortunately, few of Apthorp's business records have come to light, making it difficult to pinpoint the reasons for his success. One important factor, however, was his association with Governor William Shirley. A loyal friend of the governor throughout the political conflicts of the 1740's and 1750's, Apthorp was rewarded with numerous wartime contracts, and, like Hancock, he profited enormously from them. For the famous expedition against the French in Canada

8. Ibid., pp. 223-224. No inventory was taken of his estate, so this figure is an estimate.
9. Suffolk Probate Records, docket 1348.4.
10. No book-length treatment of Apthorp's life has appeared. For brief biographical sketches, see Wendell D. Garrett, *Apthorp House 1760-1960* (Cambridge, Mass.: Harvard University Press, 1960), pp. 4-8; James H. Stark, *The Loyalists of Massachusetts* (Boston: James H. Stark, 1910), pp. 351-352.
11. Suffolk Probate Records, docket 7326.
12. Samuel Grant Ledger, 1737-1760, August 24, 1738, p. 51, American Antiquarian Society.

31

ANONYMOUS ARTIST
Commodore Edward Tyng, 1683-1755
Ca. 1725-1750, probably Boston, oil on canvas;
49¾ x 40⅜ in.
Yale University Art Gallery, New Haven,
Connecticut, the Mabel Brady Garvan
Collection

The attributes of naval dress and a seascape
background in this portrait of Commodore
Edward Tyng indicate his prominence as a naval
officer and merchant in Boston. In 1740 he was
made captain of the batteries and fortifications
in Boston by Governor Jonathan Belcher. That
same year Belcher made him commander of the
province vessel *Prince of Orange,* a snow
recently built for the protection of the naviga-
tion and trade of the colony. During the
following decade Tyng became one of the
leading colonial naval officers and was most
successful in his protection of American ships
from cruising privateers.

at Louisburg in 1744, Apthorp, Hancock, and Nathaniel Sparhawk, son-in-
law of William Pepperell, the commander of the New England forces, pro-
cured the supplies. During the next war, the French and Indian conflict of
1755 to 1763, Shirley appointed Apthorp commissary and paymaster of the
Anglo-American forces, a lucrative post for which he received a five percent
commission on all transactions.[13]

13. Wendell D. Garrett, *Apthorp House 1760-1960* (Cambridge, Mass.: Harvard University Press,
    1960), pp. 5-6; James A. Schutz, *William Shirley, King's Governor of Massachusetts* (Chapel
    Hill: University of North Carolina Press, 1961), pp. 88-103, 123-124.

32

JACOB HURD, 1702/3-1758
Two-handled covered cup
1744, Boston, silver, marked: "HURD" in small
rectangle at lip and twice on bezel of cover, and
"Jacob Hurd" in two lines in cartouche on
bottom; inscribed in semiscript and block
letters on front: "To/EDWARD TYNG Esqr./
Commander of ye SNOW/Prince of Orange/As
an Acknowledgement of/his good Service done
the/TRADE in Taking ye First/French Privateer/
on this Coast the 24th of June/1744 This Plate
is presented BY Several of ye Merchts./in Boston
New/England"; H. 15⅛ in., W. 13¾ in.,
DIAM. (base) 6¼ in., DIAM. (lip) 7¾ in.
Yale University Art Gallery, New Haven,
Connecticut, the Mabel Brady Garvan
Collection

During the eighteenth century the British and
American ships that sailed the high seas between
England, the West Indies, and America on the
triangle route were fair game for French and
Spanish privateers. The illegal capture of a ship
laden with cargo for the colonies or London
often turned a handsome profit for the daring
pirate and a tremendous loss to the owners and
merchants who were the intended recipients of
the cargo.

The merchants of Boston demonstrated their
gratitude to Commodore Edward Tyng for
taking the first French privateer in 1744 by
presenting him with this handsome, massive
silver cup weighing 96 oz. 5 dwt. Two days
later, on June 26, 1744, the town of Boston, by
a special vote, offered its appreciation to Tyng
for the capture of a sloop that had cruised the
coast for several days, threatening the mercantile fleet.

Ref.: Kathryn C. Buhler and Graham Hood,
*American Silver, Garvan and Other Collections in
the Yale University Art Gallery,* New Haven, Conn.,
Yale University Press, 1970, vol. 1, p. 133, no. 157.

33

JOSEPH BADGER, 1708-1765
James Bowdoin, 1676-1747
1746-1747, Boston, oil on canvas;
51⅛ x 40⅛ in.
The Detroit Institute of Arts, Gibbs-Williams
Fund

James Bowdoin was the son of the French
Huguenot refugee, Pierre Baudouin, who came
to America in 1686, first settling in Maine and
later moving to Boston, in 1689. James was a
merchant who assembled an enormous fortune
during his life—his estate at his death in 1747
totaled £82,875. According to one document,
on a busy summer day in 1737 Bowdoin trans-
acted over £5,000 of business.

This portrait of the first James Bowdoin was
painted by Joseph Badger, possibly shortly after
Bowdoin's death. Badger, the son of a poor
Charlestown tailor, was Boston's first native-
trained painter during the colonial period. He
was apprenticed to a house painter at an early
age, and in 1733 he married and moved to
Boston, where he performed a wide variety of
jobs, including the painting of houses, coaches,
and coats of arms, and the glazing of windows.
Around 1740 Badger may have studied with
John Smibert, and from that time onward he

enjoyed popularity as a portrait painter,
although throughout his life he had to compete
with talents greater than his own. Smibert, Feke,
Greenwood, Blackburn, and finally the young
Copley were more skillful than he in depicting
the colonial gentry in an English manner in the
splendor of their imported silks and satins.
Badger died, insolvent, in 1765.

Ref.: Lawrence Park, "An Account of Joseph
Badger, and a Descriptive List of His Work," *Proceedings of the Massachusetts Historical Society* 51
(1917-1918), 158-201.

34
ROBERT FEKE
James Bowdoin, II
(see p. 38)

35
CHARLES-LOUIS SPRIGMAN
Covered tureen with liner
(see p. 38)

34

ROBERT FEKE, active 1741-1750
James Bowdoin II, 1726-1790
1748, Boston, oil on canvas, signed and dated
lower left: "R F Pinx 1748"; 50 x 40 in.
Bowdoin College Museum of Art, Brunswick,
Maine, bequest of Mrs. Sarah Bowdoin
Dearborn

James Bowdoin II, like his father, proved to be
a man of talent and intelligence. A graduate of
Harvard in 1745, he became the executor of
his father's estate in 1747, inheriting an ample
sum to start his career. He added to this
inheritance in 1748 through his marriage to
Elizabeth Erving, a daughter of the wealthy
merchant John Erving. "The money, my dear
Scott," Bowdoin wrote to a brother-in-law on
the subject of marriage some years later, "you
know is the primum mobile of most matches."
The Bowdoins knew how to spend their
fortunes in splendid style, as is indicated by the
extent of a 1774 inventory of their household
goods.

Bowdoin enjoyed an important political career
from his election to the General Court in 1753
to his position as governor of the Commonwealth from 1785 until his death in 1790. He
remained in commerce, also speculating in
Maine land, investing in mines, paper mills, and
the China trade. At his death he left an estate
of over £15,000. Bowdoin's portrait was
painted in 1748 by a young artist from Newport,
Robert Feke, about the time of his marriage.
The portrait demonstrates Feke's ability as a
colorist. In contrast to the flat, linear rendering
of Bowdoin's father by Joseph Badger just one
year before, the painting by Feke shows a
greater attention to modeling and surface detail.

Refs.: Marvin Sadik, *Colonial and Federal Portraits
at Bowdoin College,* Brunswick, Maine, Bowdoin
College Museum of Art, 1966, pp. 40-49. R. Peter
Mooz, "Colonial Art," in *The Genius of American
Painting,* edited by John Wilmerding, London,
Weidenfeld and Nicholson, 1973, pp. 25-79.

35

CHARLES-LOUIS SPRIGMAN, active ca. 1776-1783
Covered tureen with liner
1775, Paris, France, silver, marked on cover,
tureen and liner with maker's marks; engraved
with Bowdoin crest; H. 10¼ in., L. 15¼ in.,
W. 8½ in.
Bowdoin College Museum of Art, Brunswick,
Maine, gift of Miss Clara Bowdoin Winthrop
for the children of Mr. and Mrs. Robert C.
Winthrop, Jr.

Silver imported from France and the Continent
in general was not common in the Colonies prior
to the Revolution. The Bowdoin family's early
roots in France provide a logical reason for
their ownership of French silver. Family tradition relates that James Bowdoin's son, James III,
brought this tureen back from Paris in 1774-
1775 when he went abroad for an extended
journey. A large oval silver tray with a similar
mark has also descended in the Bowdoin family.
While the two pieces do not appear to be a set,
they may have been used together.

Apthorp's life style was characterized by opulence and generosity. He amply provided for each of his fifteen children: he established three of his sons in business; he sent one son to England to study at Jesus College, Cambridge; his daughters married into the best families of Boston; and one daughter married his business partner in London. Charles Apthorp himself, a staunch Anglican, was probably chiefly responsible for the construction of King's Chapel in Boston. He contributed over £1000 to a building fund and arranged for his close friend Peter Harrison of Newport to be appointed architect.[14]

His three-story town house on King Street near the State House was one of Boston's finest mansions. Fitted with every eighteenth century convenience, the house contained an entryway, two parlors, business office, back room, and kitchen on the first floor and four chambers, a dining room, and "*ye Ironing Room*" with baskets and "*fold^g bords*" on the second floor. In the best parlor Apthorp hung six family portraits along with a large looking-glass, another glass over the mantel, two brass sconces, and three pictures — no doubt a crowded assemblage for one room. Yellow window curtains matched by chairs with yellow seats added color to the scene. In an adjoining parlor Apthorp kept a spinet, a tall clock, mahogany pier tables, "*4 Philosophers heads,*" and a "*Mohogony Beauro with Glass doors.*"[15] The "*Beauro*" is one of the few pieces of Apthorp furniture to survive. A massive chest-on-chest of English origin, the piece is in the early Georgian style popularized by designers such as William Kent and probably dates from between 1745 and 1750 (no. 49).

The dispersal of Apthorp's possessions to his many children has made it difficult to trace other family objects. A set of English silver tablespoons and teaspoons, along with a pair of English silver sauceboats, both with the Apthorp crest, have descended in the family and together with the chest-on-chest suggest that Charles Apthorp, like other Boston merchants with London connections, imported his best household goods from abroad.

At his death in 1758 Apthorp bequeathed an estate of over £23,000 to his widow and fifteen children.[16] In addition to his King Street residence, he left eleven other houses, four warehouses, part of a distillery, and immense tracts of land in Kennebec and on Long Island. His fortune matched that of Thomas Hancock; however, his interests and background were far different. Hancock, the son of a Congregational minister, always remained a native New Englander in outlook. Apthorp, on the other hand, was an Englishman living in a foreign environment who continued to maintain close ties with his friends and relatives in England. He imported many of his furnishings from his homeland, he sent his children to England as often as he could, and he himself returned to London several times. In Boston he supported the King's church, and indeed it is inside King's Chapel that we

14. Henry Wilder Foote, *Annals of King's Chapel,* 2 vols. (Boston: Little, Brown, 1896), vol. 1, pp. 142-144.
15. Suffolk Probate Records, docket 11871.
16. Ibid.

JOHN SMIBERT, 1688-1751
Thomas Hancock, 1703-1764
Ca. 1730, Boston, oil on canvas; 30 x 25 in.
Museum of Fine Arts, gift of Miss Amelia
Peabody. 65.1712

Thomas Hancock's career as a merchant was
one of success and steady accumulation of
wealth. In 1730 Hancock and Smibert, the subject and artist of the portrait, were both starting
their careers in Boston. The half-length portrait
format was Smibert's most successful.

As part of his artistic career, as well as to help
support himself, Smibert maintained a shop and
gallery in his house on Queen street. There he
sold "all Sorts of Colours, dry or ground, with
Oils, and Brushes, Fans of Several Sorts, the best
Mezotints, Italian, French, Dutch and English
Prints, in Frames and Glasses, or without, by
Wholesale or Retail at Reasonable Rates . . ."
When he died in 1751, his wife, Mary Smibert,
continued his business.

Refs.: Henry Wilder Foote, *John Smibert, Painter*,
Cambridge, Harvard University Press, 1950, p. 76.
Museum of Fine Arts, Boston, *American Paintings
in the Museum of Fine Arts, Boston*, 2 vols. Boston,
1969, vol. 1, p. 236, no. 887.

41
JOHN SINGLETON COPLEY, 1738-1815
Thomas Hancock, 1703-1764
1764-1766, Boston, oil on canvas;
95⅝ x 59½ in.
Harvard University Portrait Collection

By the time of his death in 1764, Thomas
Hancock had amassed a fortune of about
£100,000, much of which was inherited by his
nephew, John Hancock, the Revolutionary War
leader. This ambitious full-length portrait by
Boston's finest colonial artist, John Singleton
Copley, was commissioned by young John
Hancock shortly after his uncle's death in 1764.
Copley had painted a miniature portrait of the
wealthy merchant some years before, which
seems to have been the source of this posthumous portrait. In 1766 John Hancock presented the portrait to Harvard College, thus
establishing a precedent for a series of large
portraits of Harvard's major benefactors, including Thomas Hollis, Governor Francis
Bernard, and Nicholas Boylston. On his death
Thomas Hancock bequeathed £1,000 sterling
to the president and Fellows of Harvard College
for the purpose of creating a professorship of
Hebrew and Oriental languages.

Ref.: Jules David Prown, *John Singleton Copley*,
2 vols. Cambridge, Mass., Harvard University Press,
1966, vol. 1, p. 217, fig. 154.

42
JOHN COBURN, 1725-1803
Communion dish
1764, Boston, silver, marked: "J. COBURN" on
bottom at center point and upside down on rim
in left wing framing cherub; engraved with
Hancock arms and crest, and inscribed in semi-
script and block letters on rim: "The Gift of the
Hon[ble] THOMAS HANCOCK ESQ[R]/to the CHURCH
in Brattle Street Boston 1764"; DIAM. 13¼ in.
Museum of Fine Arts, gift of the Benevolent
Fraternity of Churches. 13.394

Thomas Hancock's generosity at the time of his
death extended to his church, to Harvard
College, and to his nephew, John, as well as
others. In 1764 he bequeathed £100:0:0 to the
Church in Brattle Street for "two silver Flaggons
for the Communion Table." Apparently the
church needed dishes more than drinking
vessels, for the £100 was used for six communion dishes instead. The commission was
divided between two Boston silversmiths, John
Coburn and Samuel Minott, who each fashioned
three dishes. All six dishes are engraved with the
Hancock coat of arms and a winged cherub's
head and are similarly inscribed.

During the seventeenth and eighteenth centuries
it was customary for the wealth of churches to
be held in the form of "plate," or silver. Individual pieces or whole sets of communion silver
were commissioned by church members as tribute, or many acted as Hancock did, bequeathing
a sum of money to be turned into silver.

Ref.: Buhler, *American Silver in the Museum of
Fine Arts,* vol. 1, p. 316, no. 272.

find the most visible symbol of Apthorp's bond to England. On the north
wall is an elegant memorial plaque in his honor. Rather than a stiff New
England death's head, the tablet bears a grandiloquent Latin inscription and
is surmounted by a beautifully sculpted urn and teary-eyed cherub. This
superb monument, executed by the London artist Sir Henry Cheere (1703-
1781), serves as a testimony to Apthorp's relationship with England.[17]

The merchant families — the Bowdoins, Faneuils, Hutchinsons, Hancocks, and Apthorps — through their purchases, both foreign and domestic,
served as style-setters for the rest of the townspeople in Boston and its
environs. Joined by a scattering of other prominent Massachusetts families
and the governing officials, they broadened the horizons of a provincial
town and created a sophisticated, urban environment unexcelled in colonial
North America.

17. Foote, *Annals of King's Chapel,* vol. 1, p. 146; Walter Muir Whitehill, *Boston's Statues* (Barre,
 Mass.: Barre Publishers, 1970), pp. 10-12.

44

Robert Feke, active 1741-1750
Charles Apthorp, 1698-1758
1748, Boston, oil on canvas, signed and dated
lower right: "R F 1748"; 50 x 40 in.
The Cleveland Museum of Art, gift of the
John Huntington Art and Polytechnic Trust

Charles Apthorp, born in London, maintained
his English connections in business and pleasure
throughout his life. A sophisticated and cosmopolitan merchant, he was at times a partner,
a friend, and a rival to Thomas Hancock. He
participated in the lucrative trade routes between London, the West Indies, and America,
supplying many of Boston's shopkeepers and
tradesmen.

The Apthorps' three-story mansion on King
Street near the State House was lavishly
equipped with both English and American
furnishings. Probably his portrait and that of
his wife, Grizzel, were among the "6 Family
Pictures" located "In the best Parlour" and
valued at £32:10:00 in the inventory taken of
his estate at his death in 1758.

Refs.: Wendell D. Garrett, *Apthorp House
1760-1960*, Cambridge, Mass.: Harvard University
Press, 1960, pp. 3-8. Inventory of Charles Apthorp,
Suffolk County Probate Records, Boston, January,
1759, docket 11871.

49

Linen press

1745-1760, England, mahogany with oak and deal; H. 97 in., w. 46¾ in., DEPTH 25½ in. Museum of Fine Arts, gift of Albert Sack. 1971.737

Of great importance as the possible design source for the American bombé form, this English chest-on-chest was once owned by Charles Apthorp and could easily have been the means by which the bombé or swelled base was introduced to Boston cabinetmakers. This furniture form had been popular in England since around 1730. Since it was adopted in the Colonies exclusively by Massachusetts cabinetmakers, English imports provide the obvious key to preference for this form in Boston.

In Apthorp's 1759 estate inventory, the "Great Parlour" contained among its furnishings "a Mohogony Beauro with Glass doors . . . £32:0:0," and in the "Dining Room up Stairs" there was "a Mohogony Cabinet with glass doors . . . £30:0:0." Either of these expensive pieces of furniture may have been the chest-on-chest with glass doors illustrated here.

Ref.: Gilbert T. Vincent, "The Bombé Furniture of Boston," in *Boston Furniture of the Eighteenth Century,* Boston, Colonial Society of Massachusetts, 1974, pp. 137-196.

50

BENJAMIN FROTHINGHAM, SR., 1708-1765, or
JR., 1734-1809
Desk and bookcase
1753, Charlestown, Massachusetts, mahogany
with red cedar and white pine, inscribed in
pencil in four places, including date and "Dº
Sprage" twice and "Benjª Frothingham" once;
H. 97⅜ in., W. 44½ in., DEPTH 24⅝ in.
Department of State, Diplomatic Reception
Rooms, Washington, D.C.

Magnificently patterned mahogany, superb
architectural detailing and proportions, and
flawless workmanship make this Boston desk
and bookcase one of the masterpieces of
American furniture. Signed and dated in 1753
by Benjamin Frothingham and an unidentified
"Dº Sprage," this desk and bookcase is the
earliest known dated bombé piece of furniture
made in America. Three generations of Frothinghams worked as cabinetmakers in Boston
and Charlestown, and this signature may be
that either of Benjamin Sr. (1708-1765) or of
Benjamin Jr. (1734-1809). The desk, though
capped by a typical New England swan's neck
pediment, displays the same massive features
and straight-sided drawers of the Apthorp chest.
Frothingham also applied a beaded molding,
now missing, around the upper drawer of the
desk section, a common characteristic of
English cabinetwork. In 1754 Thomas Chippendale, the London cabinetmaker, published a
design for a clock case with the same bombé
base and foot. Thus the Frothingham desk and
bookcase was in the mainstream of London
furniture design.

Ref.: Richard H. Randall, Jr., "Benjamin Frothingham." *Boston Furniture of the Eighteenth Century,*
Boston, Colonial Society of Massachusetts, 1974,
pp. 223-249.

THE CRAFTSMEN in Revere's Boston had the real problem of competition from goods imported from England by merchants, but in many ways their economic life was not as restricted as in the mother country, where a strict guild system regulated the crafts. The scarcity of skilled labor made opportunity almost unlimited for the person with special training, talent, and ambition. To meet the demand for specialized goods craftsmen diversified their production. Some cabinetmakers also made soap or buttons, or turned their hand to tavern- or shop-keeping or iron manufacturing, as did Philadelphia's most outstanding cabinetmaker, Benjamin Randolph. Paul Revere's own career certainly illustrates the many facets of an eighteenth century craftsman. He was involved in many different endeavors, often simultaneously: goldsmith, engraver, soldier, dentist, wholesaler, industrialist. The goal of financial success and independence is implicit in such diversification.

In 1750, James Birket, a visitor from the West Indies, found Boston filled with artisans and craftsmen: *The Artificers in this Place Exceed Any upon ye Continent And are here also Most Numerous as Cabinet Makers, Chace & Coach Makers, Shoe Makers, Taylors Peruke Makers Watchmakers, Printers, Smiths, &C &C.*[18] Almost half the adult males were employed in shops spread throughout the town. Boston's large craft community was spawned and shaped by its vigorous mercantile economy. Prosperous merchants and governing officials with close ties to England supported hundreds of skilled furniture craftsmen, silversmiths, engravers, and specialty tradesmen and influenced the products that they made. Furniture imported by merchants, for example, probably provided the major design source for local craftsmen to keep up with the latest mode.

The English mahogany chest-on-chest (no. 49) owned by Charles Apthorp could easily have been the means by which the bombé, or swelled base, was introduced to Boston cabinetmakers. Popular in England as early as 1730, the form appears locally in a desk and bookcase signed by Benjamin Frothingham and an unidentified *"D° Sprage,"* dated 1753 (no. 50). Three generations of Frothinghams worked as cabinetmakers in Boston and Charlestown and were influential in the growth of a school of Boston cabinetmaking. The bombé form, clearly identifiable as a Boston style preference, remained fashionable and prestigious for over half a century. A chest-on-chest made by John Cogswell in 1782 demonstrates the refinement of shape, with a lighter, more graceful character, which later cabinetmakers perfected in the bombé.[19]

Colonial craftsmen often preferred certain fashions and forms over others. Though a wide range of stylistic possibilities existed, they usually adopted a particular English form, refined and perfected it over a lengthy period, and then continued to produce it for several decades, even after it

51
Double chairback settee
1740-1750, England, mahogany, secondary woods unexamined; H. 39½ in., W. 55¼ in., DEPTH 28½ in.
American Antiquarian Society, Worcester, Massachusetts

This English settee traditionally has had a provenance of Hancock family ownership and may have been purchased by Thomas Hancock around 1740 and inherited by John Hancock. The double chairback settee is a furniture form produced almost exclusively by Massachusetts cabinetmakers with apparent inspiration from both English design sources and actual imported pieces. The carved masks on the knees and the hairy paw feet on this settee are features found on both English and Irish furniture and only occasionally on Massachusetts rococo furniture.

Ref.: Wendell D. Garrett, "Furniture Owned by the American Antiquarian Society," *Antiques* 97 (March 1970), 402-407.

18. *Some Cursory Remarks Made by James Birket in His Voyage to North America, 1750-1751*, edited by Charles M. Andrews (New Haven, Conn.: Yale University Press, 1916), p. 24.
19. Joseph Downs, "John Cogswell, Cabinetmaker," *Antiques* 61 (April 1952), 322-324. See also Gilbert T. Vincent, "The Bombé Furniture of Boston," *Boston Furniture of the Eighteenth Century* (Boston: Colonial Society of Massachusetts, 1974), pp. 178-182.

52

Double chairback settee
1770-1780, Boston, mahogany with maple and pine; H. 37½ in., W. 63 in., DEPTH 21¾ in.
Private collection

Less than a dozen American Chippendale-style chairback settees are known today, and six are of Massachusetts origin. The finely made crest rail with symmetrical shells and molded ears, the typical Massachusetts leafy carved knees with central punched motif, and the serpentine front seat rail combine to make this settee an exciting and successful piece of furniture. With a firm history of ownership by Thomas Melville (1751-1832), a Boston merchant and Revolutionary War patriot, this settee may have been made at the time of his marriage to Priscilla Scollay in 1774. Two matching side chairs have also descended through the Melville family as part of a set. Melville's estate inventory, December 24, 1832, listed "1 old Settee 2 $" in the "Front Entry."

had long passed from fashion in London. The block-front form, for example, appeared in English furniture, often on dressing stands and desk interiors, during the early eighteenth century. However, the form did not sustain its popularity as long in London as it did in Boston. Soon after the blocked facade was introduced into Massachusetts, cabinetmakers decided to extend it across the entire front of large case pieces. Such monumental blocking rarely appeared in English furniture, suggesting the artisans in the Boston area first experimented with the form before adapting it to suit their tastes. The earliest dated example of monumental blocking in Boston is a desk and bookcase made by Job Coit and Job Coit, Jr., in 1738.[20] While the Coits seem to have had difficulty mastering the new form, later craftsmen were able to standardize it into two types composed of either rounded or flat blocks. A handsome walnut dressing stand of about 1745 demonstrates the diminutive use of rounded blocks in a manner quite similar to English precedents (no. 60). A later example of flattened blocking is the desk made for John Amory, a merchant, about 1775 (nos. 63, 64). In this case the craftsman, rather than using the typical slant lid, employed a slightly sloping top and a writing surface that slides out. Pieces of furniture in the block-front style were constructed throughout the 1780's and in all likelihood until as late as 1800.[21]

Boston chairs, sofas, and settees also owed much to English design. The estate inventories of Boston's wealthier residents are sprinkled with references to imported chairs. Edward Clarke, a local merchant, owned "*8 Mahogony Chairs (English)*" which were appraised at a higher sum than any other chairs in his home.[22] Several English settees with Boston histories are known. Thomas Hancock imported one in the 1740's for his Beacon Hill house (no. 51); Josiah Quincy purchased another at about the same time. While it is not known that Boston chair-makers copied either English settee line for line, they did employ the form. Thomas Melville, a well-to-do merchant and Revolutionary leader, owned a settee in the Chippendale style that was made about 1775 (no. 52). Its tightly carved splat, composed of two strapwork volutes, is repeated on several other Boston settees of this type and countless chairs. While all were made in the Boston area, the basic design source was not native.

A greater diversity of form existed in silver than in furniture, and imported English silver had an equally strong impact on Colonial taste. The ease in importing silver enabled many wealthy persons to own foreign examples and provided an abundance of forms for native silversmiths to copy. Imported coffee pots, teapots, cruet stands, pierced baskets, two-handled covered cups, were all items that demonstrated prestige and status

20. R. Peter Mooz, "The Origins of Newport Block-Front Furniture Design," *Antiques* 99 (June 1971), 882-113. See also Nancy Goyne Evans, "The Genealogy of a Bookcase Desk," in *Winterthur Portfolio* 9 (Charlottesville: University Press of Virginia, 1974), pp. 213-222.
21. Margaretta Markle Lovell, "Boston Blockfront Furniture," *Boston Furniture of the Eighteenth Century* (Boston: Colonial Society of Massachusetts, 1974), pp. 79, 111.
22. Suffolk County Registry of Probate, Boston, docket 14656.

53

Side chair

1765-1785, England, mahogany with beech,
stamped on back seat rail and front corner
brace: "T. HOOPER"; H. 37¼ in., W. (front)
23¼ in., DEPTH 19¼ in.

Museum of Fine Arts, gift of Mrs. Joshua Crane
in memory of her husband. 30.726

This English chair was brought to America
about 1750 and was owned by William Phillips
of Boston during the eighteenth century. With
its leafy carved crest rail, interlaced splat
design, stopped-fluted rear stiles, and exceptional asymmetrical leaf carving on the knees,
the chair is a good example of an English object
imported and later directly copied by chair-
makers on this side of the Atlantic. The estate
inventories of Boston's wealthier residents often
contain references to imported chairs. In 1765,
the widow of John Spooner, Esquire, received
as part of her legacy "6 London made black
Walnut Chairs" and "6 London made Carvd
Mahogany Chairs."

Ref.: Mary Ellen Hayward Yehia, "Ornamental
Carving on Boston Furniture," in *Boston Furniture
of the Eighteenth Century,* Boston, Colonial Society
of Massachusetts, 1974, pp. 197-222.

54

Armchair

1765-1785, probably Boston, mahogany with soft maple and birch; H. 37¾ in., W. 24¾ in., DEPTH 19⅝ in.

Yale University Art Gallery, New Haven, Connecticut, gift of Maria Trumbull Dana

The characteristic English splat and crest rail of this Boston-made armchair shows how American chair-makers adapted designs from English sources. The English-derived asymmetrical leaf carving on the knees relates this chair to a small group of furniture with similar carving made or owned in Boston, including several card tables, an upholstered settee, and other armchairs and side chairs. While this chair comes from a set originally owned by Governor Burnet and later by Governor Belcher of Massachusetts, an almost identical set of chairs was once owned by Elias Hasket Derby of Salem.

56

GEORGE WICKES, active 1721-1742
Two-handled covered cup
Ca. 1740, London, silver, maker's marks on bottom with date letter missing; engraved on front with impaled Hancock-Henchman coat of arms; H. 10⅞ in., W. 10½ in., DIAM. (base), 4½ in., DIAM. (lip) 6⅛ in.
Museum of Fine Arts, gift of the heirs of Samuel May (1723-1794). 30.437

Monumental two-handled silver covered cups were occasionally presentation pieces, as in the case of cups presented during the eighteenth century to Edward Tyng and Richard Spry by groups of Boston merchants, as well as that presented to Benjamin Pickman by the Province of Massachusetts. But Thomas Hancock's English cup purchased about 1740 has no inscription. It can only be assumed that it was a personal purchase. In 1765 Lydia Henchman Hancock, Thomas' wife, bequeathed this cup, along with a silver spout cup and silver bowl, to her nephew John Hancock; she left the rest of her silver to her mother.

in a public or ceremonial fashion. They also represented solid investments in precious metal in an age of constantly fluctuating currency.

In 1743 the painter John Smibert ordered a silver teapot for his wife from his London agent, Arthur Pond. Smibert enclosed a sketch of his coat of arms to be engraved on the teapot and cautioned that the top of the pot should not be hinged to the body, but left the style to his agent, who was undoubtedly aware of London fashions.[23] On March 24, 1743/4, Smibert reported to Pond that the teapot had arrived and met with his satisfaction. Smibert inserted in the letter a request from his nephew that attests to the popularity of the English teapot: *"Sir: — I hope youl excuse the trouble I now give you, occasioned by the Tea Pott you sent which is admired by all the Ladies and so much that in behalf of one of them (who I assure you has great merit) I Must beg the favour of you to send such another one of the same fashion and size only the top to have a neat hinge, for the payment of it the silver is appropriated."*[24]

Numerous examples of silver with Boston histories help to document the ties between England and Massachusetts. Thomas Hancock ordered a two-handled cup from London about 1740 (no.56). Three other Boston made examples closely correspond to it in proportion and design: The Tyng cup (no. 32), a cup made for the merchant John Rowe, and one owned by Henry Hope. Two of these cups were made by Jacob Hurd. A fourth-generation New Englander, Hurd never traveled to England and must have gained knowledge of the latest styles through imported silver.

Boston's population demanded other artisans besides cabinetmakers and silversmiths, and it is in the careers of the specialty tradesmen that the economic complexities of the eighteenth century enterpreneurs can best be seen. Like all provincial societies isolated to some degree from the mother country, Boston developed with each generation into a more distinctive, more individualistic cultural and economic center. Walking along the major thoroughfares of Boston toward the center of town in 1750, one would pass as he neared the State House the shops of specialty tradesmen— japanners, engravers, portrait painters, and print- and looking-glass sellers. William Price at the sign of the King's Head and Looking-Glass in Cornhill, Thomas Johnston at the Golden Lyon in Ann Street, James Buck at the Spectacles in Queen Street, and Stephen Whiting at the Rose and Crown in Union Street, among others, were clustered around the town center.

Although few in number, the influence of these specialists multiplied with each object they sold or picture they painted. On the one hand, they served as disseminators of knowledge and popularizers of ideas; working with Boston's many printers they published navigational charts, trade cards, handbills, broadsides, political cartoons, newspapers, and magazines to inform the public and, during the Revolutionary period, to sway popular opinion. They also fulfilled a second role. Through the importation of art

23. Henry Wilder Foote, *John Smibert, Painter* (Cambridge, Mass.: Harvard University Press, 1950), p. 86.
24. Ibid., p. 88.

58

WILLIAM SHAW and WILLIAM PRIEST, active
in partnership 1749-1758
Coffee pot
1751, London, silver with wooden handle,
maker's marks on right side of handle, engraved
with Faneuil coat of arms on pourer's side and
with Faneuil crest on the other; H. 10⅝ in.,
DIAM. (base) 4⅞ in.
Museum of Fine Arts, gift of General John P.
Hawkins in the name of Jane Bethune Craig
Hawkins. 13.2857

Although this silver coffee pot bears the inscription "Peter Faneuil Born June 20 1700
His Pot," it was made in London eight years
after Peter's death, and the inscription must be
attributed to inaccurate family history. Actually
the coffee pot was ordered by Peter's brother
Benjamin, in 1751, who was possibly familiar
with the Hancock's English coffee pot ordered
in 1745-1746 from the goldsmith Thomas Rush.
The Boston silversmith John Coburn must have
seen one of these English pots, for between 1750
and 1760 he fashioned a handsome silver coffee
pot for the Symmes family of Boston that
rivaled the English workmanship and design.

Refs.: Kathryn C. Buhler, "Gifts of Faneuil Silver,"
Bulletin of the Museum of Fine Arts 37 (June 1939),
51-53. Buhler, *American Silver in the Museum of
Fine Arts,* vol. 1, p. 308, no. 263.

59

SAMUEL WOODS, active 1733-1773
Cruet stand
1745, London, silver with glass bottles, marked
on back foil of each caster; lion and maker's
mark on bezel of casters and handle, engraved
with Faneuil coat of arms on plaque of stand
and front of each caster, and with Faneuil crest
on cylindrical top of each bottle; H. (stand)
8⅛ in., H. (caster) 6¼ in.
Museum of Fine Arts, gift of Faneuil Suydam
and Henry Bethune Weisse. 36.1651

Benjamin Faneuil ordered his cruet stand from
London about 1746. The Apthorps ordered an
almost identical stand from Woods two years
later. While there are no Boston cruet stands
of this early date known to exist, in 1781 Paul
Revere recorded making a "silver frame for
casters."

60

Dressing stand

Ca. 1735-1760, Boston, mahogany with white pine; H. 31¼ in., W. 18¾ in., DEPTH 11⅝ in.
Mr. and Mrs. Eric M. Wunsch

The introduction of blocking across the front of American case furniture is usually associated with the region around Newport, Rhode Island, yet it was frequently used on Massachusetts furniture and is now thought to have originated in this country first in Boston.

The rounded blocking of this handsome early dressing stand is reminiscent of its English precedents. Original brasses, the carved and gilt inner edge of the frame, and the delicate turned and carved acorn finials are added refinements on this masterful, diminutive piece of Boston blockfront furniture. Its original ownership by the Russell family is further evidence of its Boston origin.

from abroad or the creation of native art, they became transmitters of taste. In their lifelike portraits, well-crafted mezzotints, ornate gilt-framed looking-glasses, and exotic japanned furniture, they brought elegance to Colonial Boston homes.

Versatility and interdependence were crucial to the success of these tradesmen. Although often trained in particular crafts, these men found it necessary to develop a variety of talents. Thomas Johnston, Boston's Da Vinci, worked as a painter, japanner, looking-glass seller, engraver, church singer, publisher of song books, and organ builder. By such a diversified career, he accumulated a respectable estate, including a large home on Brattle Street. Only John Singleton Copley, whose popularity as a painter brought him ample patronage, became wealthy by mastering a single craft.

Just as Boston's cabinetmakers and silversmiths closely followed London models, so did these specialty tradesmen. Painters, engravers, and japanners borrowed details of landscape, costume, and composition from English prints. Copley, for example, copied engravings of European history paintings and modeled his portraits on English print sources. Paul Revere's engraving of the *Able Doctor, or America Swallowing the Bitter Draught* (no. 170), a political cartoon published in 1774, was taken from an English print of the same name. Japanners also seem to have adapted their whimsical and exotic decoration from prints; in 1745 John Smibert requested from his London agent "*10 to 15 Shill. worth of coloured prints slight and cheap for Japanning.*"[25]

The artistic climate in Boston was a curious blend of naïveté and sophistication. Many tradesmen developed their artistic skills as supplements to other occupations. Others became full-time professional artists who, as their abilities increased, came to recognize their isolation from the artistic center of London. Native artists had to depend on imported engravings and immigrant decorative painters for interpretation of the artistic trends abroad. Immigrants themselves were forced to rely on each other and the memory of the art world that they had left. Decorative art in Boston bowed to its cultural mother, England, but it developed uniquely from the isolation and mutual interdependence of its artists.

25. Ibid., p. 92.

61

Miniature chest of drawers
Ca. 1760-1790, Boston, mahogany with white pine; H. 9⅜ in., W. 14¼ in. (top), DEPTH 9⅛ in. (top)
Private collection

The rarity of miniature furniture makes this miniature blockfront bureau a particularly exciting piece of furniture. The date "1755" written on the bottom in ink could possibly be a contemporary inscription by the original owner. An early twentieth century note that accompanies the piece describes its provenance: "This little Bureau owned by Susannah Hayward Shaw—mother of Judge Lemuel Shaw Given to Elizabeth Shaw—wife of Herman Melville (daughter of Judge Shaw) Given by her to his daughter Elizabeth Melville when she was able to button her panties . . ."

63

Desk
1760-1775, Boston, mahogany with white pine; H. 39¼ in., W. 38¼ in., DEPTH 20⅝ in.
Museum of Fine Arts, the M. and M. Karolik Collection of Eighteenth Century American Arts. 39.85

The unusual form of this slant-top desk, with blockfront and movable writing slide, suggests that it was made to special order and for a specific space, possibly in an office or counting house. The desk, with its original large, bold brasses and side-mounted carrying handles, was originally owned by the Tory merchant John Amory. Since the eighteenth century it has descended through the Amory and Codman families. Only one other desk of identical form is currently known, and it has descended in the family of Chief Justice Peter Oliver.

Refs.: Edwin J. Hipkiss, *Eighteenth-Century American Arts, The M. and M. Karolik Collection*, Cambridge, Mass., Harvard University Press, 1950, p. 44, no. 26. *American Antiques from Israel Sack Collection*, vol. 1, p. 223.

64

JOHN SINGLETON COPLEY, 1738-1815
John Amory, 1728-1803
1768, Boston, oil on canvas; 50 x 40 in.
Museum of Fine Arts, the M. and M. Karolik
Collection of Eighteenth Century American
Arts. 37.37

John Amory, an Anglican and a Tory, was at the
height of his successful mercantile career in
1768 when John Singleton Copley painted this
portrait of him for £14. In the painting Copley
has bestowed on him all the attributes of success, from his confident air to the abundance of
gold buttons on his waistcoat. However, the
Queen Anne chair that Amory is casually lean-
ing on seems out of fashion at a time when the
Chippendale style was at the height of
popularity.

In 1757 Amory married Katherine Greene
(1731-1777), the daughter of Rufus Greene, a
Boston goldsmith. Because of Amory's extreme
Tory sentiments, they left Boston for London in
May of 1775, thus escaping patriot wrath.
Rufus Greene, a moderate Tory, stayed behind,
and his letters to his daughter in London are
vivid accounts of Boston during the British
occupation. Katherine died in England in 1777,
but John Amory later returned to America to
carry on his mercantile business with his
brother.

Ref.: Museum of Fine Arts, Boston, *American
Paintings in the Museum of Fine Arts, Boston*, 2
vols., Boston, 1969, vol. 1, p. 70, no. 278.

Harvard

THROUGHOUT REVERE'S LIFETIME two worlds struggled for dominion in the minds and hearts of most Bostonians: the material world versus the world of the spirit or intellect. The values of Revere's Boston clearly drifted toward greater and greater luxury, yielding to things earthly. But while the old Calvinist order waned, spiritual and intellectual matters were still important. In the Burgis view of Boston (no. 23), this is manifested in the overscaled steeples of churches, which vie for attention with the ships in the harbor. The fact that they are shown larger than life, out of proportion with the rest of the scene, confirms their importance not only as landmarks but also as cherished symbols of spiritual thought.

New England's churches required men of learning for their pulpits. For their schooling, Harvard College was founded across the Charles River in Cambridge. Determined not to have learning buried with their fathers, first-generation English colonists saw to it that Harvard College was established in 1636 by an act of the Great and General Court of Massachusetts and a grant of £400. Two years later, through the bequest of the Reverend John Harvard of Charlestown (a graduate of Emmanuel College, Cambridge, England), the fledgling college received a welcome endowment of £779:17:02 and about four hundred volumes.

Harvard's location in Cambridge and its intimate ties with Boston were extremely important throughout the eighteenth century for both religious and secular reasons. As the French traveler Jean Brissot observed in 1788[1]: *"The imagination could not fix on a place that could better unite all the conditions essential to a seat of education; sufficiently near to Boston to enjoy all the advantages of a communication with Europe and the rest of the world, and sufficiently distant not to expose the student to the contagion of licentious manners common in commercial towns."*

Harvard was the training ground for most of the Boston clergy. Many graduates served as tutors for several years at Harvard before obtaining posts as ministers of congregations in Boston. When ordained, they influenced both students and citizens with sermons and published works. Their portraits were painted, and copperplates for mezzotints were scraped so all who desired could adorn their walls with prints showing their favorite pastor. The ministers of Boston were the literary and imaginative backbone of society; they exerted a powerful force in Revere's time.

All Harvard presidents were men who had been pastors for many years.

75
Embroidered picture of Harvard Hall
First half eighteenth century, Boston area, silk, wool, and gilt-silver yarns on linen;
7¾ x 9⅞ in.
Massachusetts Historical Society, Boston

The woman who worked this small and fascinating architectural view of a building at Harvard College used both imagination and creativity. The building shown appears to be a composite with features from two of Harvard's early structures, Harvard Hall and Stoughton College. Two putti flank the central pediment and support a beehive surrounded by bees. The cherubs also hold a scroll on which is the mangled Latin phrase "EUCO. A PRAESEPIBUS RCEUT," which roughly translated means, "They keep drones from these premises."

Ref.: Samuel Eliot Morison, "Needlework Picture Representing a Colonial College Building," *Old Time New England* 24 (October 1933), 67-72.

1. Lewis P. Simpson, "The Intercommunity of the Learned: Boston and Cambridge in 1800," *New England Quarterly* 23 (1950), 503. Samuel Eliot Morison, *Three Centuries of Harvard, 1636-1936* (Cambridge, Mass.: Harvard University Press, 1936), is the best general history of Harvard.

Cottonus Matherus
S. Theologiæ Doctor Regiæ Societatis Londinensis Socius.
& Ecclesiæ apud Bostonum Nov-Anglorum nuper Præpositus.
Ætatis Suæ LXV, MDCCXXVII.   P. Pelham ad vivum ... ab Origin Feci

65

PETER PELHAM, 1697-1751
Cotton Mather, 1663-1728
1728, Boston, mezzotint, signed lower right:
"P. Pelham ad vivum pinxt ab Origin Fecit";
14 x 10 in.
Massachusetts Historical Society, Boston

Cotton Mather, graduate of Harvard (A.B., 1678, M.A., 1681), noted clergyman, minister of the Second Church, was an influential religious and scientific scholar. His numerous discourses and publications, including his sentiments on smallpox inoculation and his most famous work, *Magnalia Christi Americana: or the Ecclesiastical History of New England from Its First Planting* (1702), had far-reaching influence in the eighteenth century.

Bostonians were pious people with great civic and spiritual pride that manifested itself in a devoted respect for clergymen. During the second quarter of the eighteenth century several artists capitalized on the popularity of the various ministers by producing and selling mezzotint portraits of them. These prints could be framed and hung and were sometimes varnished to protect them "against the injuries of Smoak & Flies."

Peter Pelham was an eminent English engraver who emigrated to Boston. This first mezzotint to be produced in America was announced early in 1728 by Pelham when he published his "Proposals for making a Print in Metzotinto, of the late Reverend Dr. Cotton Mather" in the *Boston Gazette* of February 26/March 4, 1727/28. The advertisement noted that the print would be issued by subscription. Since there were no painters in Boston capable of producing portraits to copy for mezzotint engraving, Pelham was forced to paint several of the preliminary portraits himself. From 1735 to 1750 Pelham, who was John Singleton Copley's stepfather, produced ten mezzotints of ministers, which were advertised and sold either singly or as a set.

Refs.: Andrew Oliver, "Peter Pelham (c. 1697-1751) Sometime Printmaker of Boston," in *Boston Prints and Printmakers 1670-1775,* Boston, Colonial Society of Massachusetts, 1973, pp. 133-169, pl. 63. George Francis Dow, *The Arts & Crafts in New England 1704-1775,* Topsfield, Mass., Wayside Press, 1927, pp. 17, 33.

Among the lists of Overseers of Harvard were prominent clergymen of Boston: Benjamin Colman, William Cooper, Joshua Gee, Thomas Prince, Cotton Mather, William Welsteed, Mather Byles, Jonathan Mayhew, and Charles Chauncey. The impact of these men in the life of the town went far beyond their theological disputes or sermons; science, politics, and poetry also engaged their attention more fully than one might expect of the clergy.

The growth of Harvard can be seen in a number of prints produced in the eighteenth century. The earliest view was drawn in 1726 by William Burgis (no. 74) and reissued in 1743 by William Price. This view shows three buildings: Harvard Hall (built 1676, burned 1764), Stoughton Hall (completed 1699), and Massachusetts Hall (completed 1720). Between 1741 and 1744 a new chapel was built, the gift of a lady and her daughter from London. The handsome new building was named Holden Chapel in honor of its benefactresses and with Massachusetts Hall still stands today. James Birket, a traveler from Antigua, described the college when he visited in 1750[2]: "*We went with a Couple of Country Clergymen, Conducted by [Belcher] Hancock one of the Tutors to See the College at Cambridge, Which Consists of three Separat Brik buildings which was Errected at different times . . . there is also a Small Chapell where the Students hear prayers twice every day.*" Birket also described the student population: "*They are About 100 in Number, and as likely well looking young men from about 15 to 20 years of age as any I have Seen, They have a Large & Commodious Library but the books are mostly Old and not kept in the Order One could wish, They have also Some Natural Curiositys but in no regularity nor do they know what many of 'em Are.*"

Certainly the scene that Birket viewed must have been impressive, but before the next recorded view of the college was engraved by Revere in 1767 (no. 76), there was a disastrous fire that entirely destroyed Harvard Hall in 1764.

Harvard's faculty consisted primarily of four tutors, and as the eighteenth century progressed, several specialized professors were added to the faculty as benevolent citizens endowed chairs. They were required to live in the college with the students and could not marry. Until 1767 each tutor was responsible for taking a class and teaching all subjects of the curriculum. But in 1767 it was decided that each tutor would specialize in a subject as well as be responsible for teaching rhetoric, elocution, and English composition. At the end of each school year, it was customary for the graduating class to give their tutor a gift, frequently a piece of silver — most likely engraved "*Ex dono pupillorum*" (nos. 78, 80).

While Harvard nurtured the serious pursuits of New England society in the eighteenth century, it also supplied the populace with an important traditional holiday, commencement. Crowds came from near and far, businesses closed in Boston, tents and booths lined the narrow streets

2. Albert Matthews, "A Glimpse of Harvard in 1750," *Harvard Graduates Magazine* 26, no. 104 (June 1918), 702-703.

The Rev.d JONATHAN MAYHEW. D.D.
Paſtor of the Weſt Church. Boston. N.E.
Ob.t JULY. 9.th 1766. Æ.t 46.

70

PAUL REVERE II, 1735-1818
The Revd Jonathan Mayhew. D.D., 1720-1766
1766, Boston, line engraving, signed lower right:
"P Revere sculp"; 5¾ x 4 in.
Prints Division, the New York Public Library,
Astor, Lenox and Tilden Foundations

From 1747 until 1766 the Reverend Jonathan
Mayhew was the pastor of the West Church in
Boston. His theology was well in advance of his
times, and he distinguished himself among other
clergy by being a staunch upholder of civil
liberty. An intimate of provincial leaders like
James Otis, Josiah Quincy, Samuel Adams, and
John Adams, he was a leading figure in the
formation of the ideology of the American
Revolution.

Revere may have been a great friend of Mayhew's. When Mayhew died in 1766, Revere
made this small engraving of him. The purpose
of this engraving is not known; it does not appear in any of the funeral orations published
after Mayhew's death nor in Mayhew's posthumous discourse, *The Snare Broken* of 1766.
As was typical of Revere, he copied his engraving from a larger mezzotint of Mayhew by
Richard Jennys, Jr., published by Nathaniel
Hurd a few days after Mayhew's death.

Ref.: Clarence S. Brigham, *Paul Revere's Engravings,* rev. ed. New York, Atheneum, 1969, pp. 32-35,
pl. 7.

around the college yard, and there was an overall atmosphere of a village fair. Even the governor and his council journeyed to Cambridge for commencement, which always occurred in July, on a Wednesday, but the entire week was taken up with celebration. President Quincy recorded in his history of Harvard that *"great excesses, immoralities, and disorders occurred about the period of Commencement."*[3] In fact, between 1720 and 1740 this event became so uncontrollable and boisterous that the Harvard Corporation endeavored to keep the day of its celebration a secret.

Harvard was extremely fortunate, for while it supplied the province with learned men and an annual amusement, numerous weathly Bostonians and Londoners took care of it in time of need. Thomas Hollis III of London was one of the college's greatest benefactors beginning in 1721 when he gave funds to create the first professorship, that of divinity.[4] In 1727 he founded a professorship of mathematics and natural philosophy, and he also supplied the college with regular shipments of books from London and scientific apparatus, including a telescope. Thomas Hancock, Nicholas Boylston, and Isaac Royall were among others who endowed chairs in the years to follow.

When Harvard Hall burned in 1764, not only the library but also the scientific apparatus used by the Hollis Professor of Mathematics and Natural Philosophy was lost. It did not take long, however, for a number of alumni to respond to the needs of the college with gifts of apparatus or funds for new equipment, like Jonathan Belcher of Nova Scotia, who gave money for an elegant pair of globes in mahogany stands in 1765 (no. 83). James Bowdoin gave money for an orrery in 1768, and it was promptly supplied by a London instrument-maker, Benjamin Martin. The rooms where all of this apparatus was kept were on the second floor of the new Harvard Hall, and judging from college records it was a handsomely appointed room. In 1766 the Corporation thanked Samuel Quincy of Boston for *"a large carpet for the Apparatus Chamber,"* and in 1772 John Hancock was thanked for *"carpets to cover the floors of the library, the Philosophy, and the Apparatus Chambers, and the walls of the Philosophy Chamber with paper hangings."*[5]

Dr. Benjamin Waterhouse, a professor of the recently formed medical school, described the Philosophy Chamber in 1799: *"It is ornamented with full length paintings of our principal benefactors . . . In the same room is placed a large orrery, made by Joseph Pope of Boston, which is particularly described in the second volume of* Memoirs of the American Academy of Arts and Sciences. *Adjoining this room is a smaller one filled with philosophical apparatus of English workmanship, by far the largest collection of the kind in the United States."*[6]

3. Josiah Quincy, *History of Harvard University*, 2nd ed. (Boston: Crosby, Nichols Lee, 1860), vol. 1, p. 43.

4. Thomas Hollis III must also be cited as an avid supporter of civil liberty. See Frank H. Somer III, "Thomas Hollis and the Arts of Dissent," in *Prints in and of America to 1850*, John D. Morse, ed. (Charlottesville: University Press of Virginia, 1970), pp. 111-159.

5. David P. Wheatland, *The Apparatus of Science at Harvard, 1765-1800* (Cambridge, Mass.: Harvard University Press, 1968), pp. 4-5.

6. Ibid., p. 6.

A Prospect of the Colledges in Cambridge in New England

Josh Chadwick. del—

A Westerly View of The Colledges in Cambridge New England

A *Harvard Hall*　B *Stoughton*　C *Massachusett*　D *Hollis*　E *Holden Chapel*

P Revere sculp

74

WILLIAM BURGIS, active ca. 1716-1731
A Prospect of the Colledges in Cambridge in New England
1726, Boston, hand-colored line engraving, signed: "W:Burgis" in cartouche at center bottom; 19 x 24⅝ in.
Massachusetts Historical Society, Boston

This print of Harvard, drawn by William Burgis in 1726 and probably engraved in England by an unknown hand, is the earliest and only copy of this eighteenth century print of the college that has survived. Prior to its discovery, a later version, engraved from the same copperplate and issued by William Price in 1743, was considered the earliest. The first issue was announced on July 14, 1726, in the *Boston News-Letter:* "This Day is Published a Prospect of the Colledges in Cambridge New England, curiously Engraved in Copper; and are to be sold at Mr. Prince's Print seller, over against the Town-House, Mr. Randal Japanner in Ann Street, by Mr. Stedman in Cambridge, and the Booksellers of Boston."

The discovery of this Burgis print is interesting. In 1795 Colonel William Scollay gave the Massachusetts Historical Society a print mounted on a wooden panel — the 1743 issue of this Harvard view by William Price. After many years, this print and its backing board became warped and cracked. In an attempt to save the print, it was carefully removed from the board, and beneath it the earlier 1726 print was discovered. The first owner had apparently updated his original print by pasting over it the second issue of the Harvard view when it came out in 1743.

Refs.: Richard B. Holman, "William Burgis," in *Boston Prints and Printmakers 1670-1775,* Boston, Colonial Society of Massachusetts, 1973, pp. 65-67. Massachusetts Historical Society, *Collecting for Clio,* Boston, 1969, p. 21. Hamilton Vaughan Bail, *Views of Harvard, a Pictorial Record to 1860,* Cambridge, Mass., Harvard University Press, 1949, pp. 16-35.

76

PAUL REVERE II, 1735-1818
JOSEPH CHADWICK, ca. 1721-1783
A Westerly View of the Colledges in Cambridge New England
1767, Boston, line engraving, signed lower right: "P Revere Sculp," signed lower left: "Josʰ Chadwick. del —"; 9¼ x 15¼ in.
Private collection

This pleasing view of Harvard College was engraved and printed in 1767 by Revere after a drawing made by Joseph Chadwick. It is among Revere's largest, rarest, and pictorially most successful engravings. It shows Harvard after the construction of three major new buildings. At the far left is Holden Chapel, completed in 1744. Next to the chapel is Hollis Hall, built in 1763, and adjoining Hollis is the third Harvard Hall, rebuilt shortly after the fire in 1764.

In the production of this print, Revere collaborated with a noted surveyor and engineer, Joseph Chadwick, and together they seem to have timed its production to coincide with the July commencement at Harvard. The cost of engraving and printing was apparently split between Chadwick and Revere, for recorded in Revere's daybook on July 6, 1767, is the entry: "Capt Josep Chadwick Dr/To one half of the Engraving a Plate. for a Perspective View of the Colleges/To Printing/4-0-0."

Refs.: Clarence S. Brigham, *Paul Revere's Engravings,* rev. ed. New York, Atheneum, 1969, pp. 39-42, pl. 9. Hamilton Vaughan Bail, *Views of Harvard; a pictorial Record to 1860,* Cambridge, Mass., Harvard University Press, 1949, pp. 43-59.

77

Attributed to JOHN GREENWOOD, 1727-1792
Henry Flynt, 1675-1760
Ca. 1750, Boston, oil on canvas; 29 x 24½ in.
Harvard University Portrait Collection

Though pictured here in clerical garb, Henry
Flynt never actually had a parish. He devoted
his life to educating young men at Harvard,
where he served the longest term of any tutor
(1699-1754). As a tutor, he remained a bachelor
all his life. He bequeathed to the college £700
Old Tenor for the benefit of future tutors and
£112:10 Old Tenor, or 50 Spanish Dollars, for
the benefit of one or more needy students. Although he was apparently liked by all, Flynt
could not escape the students' traditional jokes
and pranks. In good-humored reply to mis-
behavior Flynt commented that "wild colts
often make good horses."

Ref.: *Sibley's Harvard Graduates: Biographical
Sketches of Those Who Attended Harvard College,*
Boston, Massachusetts Historical Society, 1873-19—,
vol. 4, pp. 162-167.

78

JACOB HURD, 1702/3-1758
Teapot
1738, Boston, silver, marked: "Hurd" in semi-script in an ellipse on bottom, engraved with Flynt coat of arms, inscribed below: "Ex dono Pupillorum"; H. 5¾ in., DIAM. (base) 3¼ in. Museum of Fine Arts, Edward Jackson Holmes Collection, bequest of Mrs. Holmes. 65.385

At the end of each school year it was customary for the graduating class to give their tutor a gift. This silver teapot bears the legend "Ex dono Pupillorum," or "A gift from the students," inscribed beneath the Flynt coat of arms. It is one of numerous pieces of silver given to Flynt by students during his fifty-five years as a tutor.

Silver porringers, teapots, a covered cup, and candlesticks were among the silver given to Flynt by different classes. It is also recorded that one year a group of students asked Flynt what he would like as a gift. He replied that as he was a bachelor he really had no need for anything. The students, unwilling to accept this answer, proudly presented their beloved Tutor with a silver chamber pot on Commencement Day. On it was inscribed: "Mingere cum bombis Res est saluberrima lumbis."

Ref.: Walter Muir Whitehill, "Tutor Flynt's Silver Chamberpot," in *Publications of the Colonial Society of Massachusetts*, vol. 38 (1947-1951), pp. 360-363. Buhler, *American Silver in the Museum of Fine Arts*, vol. 1, p. 221, no. 182.

80

SAMUEL MINOTT, 1732-1803
Tankard
Ca. 1770, Boston, silver, marked: "M" in semi-script in a square above center point and "Minott" in semiscript in a rectangle below center point, inscribed on front: "HARVARDIN-ATIBUS/Anno Domini MDCCLXX initiatis/Tertium sub ejus tutela annum agentibus,/Hoc poculum acceptum/Refert JOSEPHUS WILLARD."; on bottom within guidelines: "Josephus Willard/Coll:Harv: tutor/Cal: Septembris electus fuit/Anno MDCCLXVI."; H. 8⅞ in., DIAM. (base) 5⅛ in., DIAM. (lip) 4 in.
Museum of Fine Arts, the Philip Leffingwell Spalding Collection. Given in his memory by Katherine Ames Spalding and Philip Spalding, Oakes Ames Spalding, Hobart Ames Spalding.
42.246

This handsome tankard, made by the Boston goldsmith Samuel Minott, is a piece of tutorial silver given to Joseph Willard when he was a tutor at Harvard between 1766 and 1772. Later, from 1781 to 1804, Willard served as president of Harvard. When translated, the Latin inscription engraved on this tankard reads: "Joseph Willard records that this tankard was received at the beginning of the year 1770 from the sons of Harvard entering the third year under his tutelage." The same class gave Willard a silver cann also made by Samuel Minott.

Ref.: Buhler, *American Silver in the Museum of Fine Arts,* vol. 1, pp. 365-367, no. 322.

82

Desk

1700-1750, Massachusetts, probably North Shore, painted white pine; signed in ink inside desk: "J. Gyles Merrill's Harvard College 1755" and "James G. Merrill's Desk Harvard College October 6, 1803"; H. 51¼ in., w. 32½ in., DEPTH 19¼ in.
Colonial Williamsburg Foundation, Williamsburg, Virginia

Gyles Merrill was from Salisbury, Massachusetts; he graduated from Harvard in 1759 and received an M.A. degree in 1762. He served as pastor of the North Church in Haverhill, Massachusetts, until his death in 1801. His son, James Merrill, graduated from Harvard in 1807 and received an M.A. degree in 1810. This plain piece, fitting for a student, represents the common sort of furniture of which little survives with documentation. Few pieces of furniture known to have been used by students at Harvard during the eighteenth century exist today. Originally this desk was painted or stained red. The light blue-grey paint that now covers it may date to the latter part of the eighteenth century. The sliding shelf is probably a nineteenth century addition, but all brasses and the butterfly hinges securing the lid are original. When raised, the slanted top reveals a simple, unpainted interior with two small drawers below a row of pigeonholes.

The desk was probably made in the area of eastern Massachusetts where Merrill lived and brought to Harvard upon his entrance. The elongated double-baluster and ring turnings of the legs indicate that it may have been made earlier than 1755, though as a country piece of furniture it could have been manufactured over a longer time period.

Ref.: Barry A. Greenlaw, *New England Furniture at Williamsburg,* Charlottesville, University of Virginia Press, 1974, pp. 112-113.

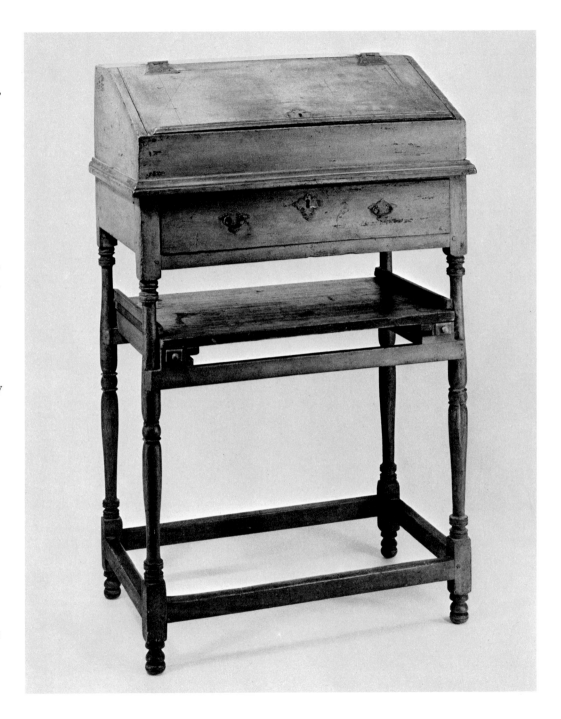

83

Benjamin Martin, 1704-1782
Celestial globe
Ca. 1765, London, paper-covered globe on
mahogany stand; H. 35 in., DIAM. (stand) 35½
in., DIAM. (globe) 26¾ in.
Harvard University Collection of Historical
Scientific Instruments, Cambridge, Mass.

When Harvard Hall was destroyed by fire in
1764, the college lost not only its library but
also all of the scientific apparatus that had been
accumulated for use by the Hollis Professor of
Mathematics and Natural Philosophy. It did not
take long for a number of concerned alumni to
respond to the need and give apparatus or funds
toward the purchase of new equipment.

In 1765 Jonathan Belcher, then a chief justice in
Halifax, Nova Scotia, bought the college a fine
pair of globes, one celestial and the other
terrestrial. The order was filled by Benjamin
Martin, one of the finest instrument-makers of
London, and by the autumn of 1765 he sent the
college "a pair of 28 Inch Globes in Mohogany
carv'd frames Silver'd & Laquer'd Meredians
&c . . ." This globe in its elegant and finely
carved frame is the only portion of this 1765
purchase to survive in original condition.

Ref.: David Wheatland, *The Apparatus of Science
at Harvard, 1765-1800,* Cambridge, Mass., Harvard
University Press, 1968, pp. 63-66.

JOSEPH POPE, ca. 1750-1826
Orrery
1787, Boston, mahogany stand, brass works, glass, cast brass gilded statuettes of Isaac Newton, Benjamin Franklin and James Bowdoin, inscribed around base of sun: "Joseph Pope fecit State of Massachusetts 1787"; H. 78 in., DIAM. 78 in., H. statuettes: Franklin and Bowdoin 12 in., Newton on plinth 14 in.
Harvard University Collection of Historical Scientific Instruments
(not in exhibition)

The Pope orrery is undoubtedly one of the greatest achievements of the eighteenth century by an American instrument-maker. It is not known what prompted Pope to begin making it around 1776, but by 1788 a group of Boston citizens tried to purchase it for Harvard through private subscription. This failed, and finally the money was raised by a public lottery and the orrery was acquired for the sum of £450. This magnificent piece of apparatus measures over six and a half feet in height and the same in diameter. Twelve cast brass gilded statuettes surround the mechanism, representing Benjamin Franklin, Isaac Newton, and James Bowdoin, each repeated four times. Bowdoin was probably included along with Franklin and Newton because of his great contributions to scientific experimentation and knowledge during his lifetime (no. 84).

Prominent Bostonians were always to be found among the members of the Harvard Corporation, and one citizen who must be mentioned is John Hancock. Like his uncle Thomas, who died in 1764 and left great sums to Harvard, Hancock was also very generous to his alma mater. In 1773 he was elected treasurer of the college, but much to the dismay of the Corporation, he carried all the college bonds and evidences of property to Philadelphia

84
CHRISTIAN GULLAGER, 1759-1826
James Bowdoin II, 1726-1790 (version B)
Ca. 1791, Boston, oil on panel; 10¾ x 8⅝ in.
Bowdoin College Museum of Art, Brunswick,
Maine, bequest of Sarah Bowdoin Dearborn

James Bowdoin II was not only a rich and
highly successful merchant and politician but
also one of Boston's leading intellectuals. A
graduate of Harvard in 1745, he was a constant
and generous supporter of the college. In the
eighteenth century tradition of a gentleman and
intellectual, he had a commodious library, well-
equipped with over 1,200 volumes and pieces of
scientific apparatus such as the globe on stand
depicted in this painting by Christian Gullager
done shortly after Bowdoin's death.

From 1750 onward Bowdoin enjoyed an intimate friendship with Benjamin Franklin, a
comrade in scientific curiosity and experimentation. In 1768, he gave £90 to Harvard for the
purchase of an orrery that Benjamin Martin of
London made for the college. In 1780 he became
the first president of the American Academy of
Arts and Sciences. On his death he left £400 to
Harvard for giving premiums of moderate
amount for the best dissertations on subjects to
be set by the officers of the college.

Ref.: Marvin S. Sadik, *Colonial and Federal Portraits at Bowdoin College,* Brunswick, Maine,
Bowdoin College Museum of Art, 1966, pp. 40-49,
92-103.

with him in 1774. Furthermore, he not only took away all the property but
also neglected to make out any annual account and refused either to perform
the duties of the office or to resign it. Finally in 1777 the Corporation did get
from him a statement of accounts, but they still had to send a special messenger to Philadelphia to retrieve their property. In that same year the
Corporation relieved Hancock of his responsibilities as treasurer, and
appointed Ebenezer Storer (A.B., 1747) as treasurer (no. 85). However,
Hancock's accounts were not fully adjusted, and the balance due from him
was not paid until after his death in 1793.

The proximity of Cambridge to Boston served both Harvard and the
town of Boston well. With intellectual critics nearby, Revere's Boston was
assured against becoming a mere trade center. The wealth generated by the
merchants happily benefited the college and its growing needs.

85

John Singleton Copley, 1738-1815
Ebenezer Storer II, 1730-1807
1767-1769, Boston, pastel on paper; 28 x 22 in.
Private collection

Ebenezer Storer II graduated from Harvard in
1747 and was soon apprenticed to his father, a
leading Boston merchant. By 1754 he was in
partnership with his father. Besides being a successful merchant, Storer also held a number of
responsible civic positions, including the post of
selectman of Boston and Overseer of the Poor.
In 1777 he succeeded John Hancock as treasurer
of Harvard College, and remained in that position until his death. Unlike Hancock, he was a
shrewd businessman and manager of finances.
His own life is testimony to the fact that he enjoyed and made optimum use of his wealth. Like
Bowdoin's, his mansion on the corner of Sudbury and Portland streets was lavishly furnished, and it included "A large apartment in
the second story devoted to a valuable library, a
philosophical apparatus, a collection of engravings, a solar microscope, a camera, etc."

Ref.: Alice Morse Earle, ed., *Diary of Anna Green
Winslow: A Boston School Girl,* Cambridge, Mass.,
Riverside Press, 1894, p. 96.

Domestic Pursuits

88

Chest of drawers

1765, Boston, mahogany with white pine; H. 30 in., W. 36 in., DEPTH 20 in.

Department of State, Diplomatic Reception Rooms, Washington, D.C.

Originally owned by Ebenezer Storer, this chest of drawers exemplifies the refined taste and rich life style of a wealthy Boston family. It is the best of a popular type of eighteenth century Boston furniture — the bombé, or swelled-base form. The excellence of its overall proportions, the subtle shaping of its serpentine front, and its swelled or bombé sides mark this as an outstanding piece of Boston cabinetmaking. The lively graining of the mahogany is patterned so as to move with the great swelling curves of the form itself. As a final complement to the piece, imported ormolu or fire gilt rococo brasses of the highest quality embellish the front.

BEFORE THE REVOLUTION most women did not receive a formal education. Their function within the family and household was an essential part of the economic, domestic, and social life of the colonies. Numerous women worked beside their husbands in shops and family businesses while continuing to raise large families, manage households, and still display social attributes. Many were expected to have some knowledge of literature, music, history, and perhaps a little French. One of the most acceptable and fashionable pursuits of women at leisure in the home involved needlework.

Born in 1744, Abigail Smith Adams (no. 93) grew up in the country town of Braintree, where educational and cultural offerings were more limited than in the urban area of Boston, but her remarks on education apply to most women of the time. In 1817 she reflected on her youth: *"My early education did not partake of the abundant opportunities which the present days offer, and which even our common country schools now afford. I was never sent to any school. I was always sick. Female education, in the best of families, went no further than writing and arithmetic; in some few and rare instances music and dancing."*[1]

In Boston there were five public schools by 1720 that offered a classical preparation as well as reading, writing, and mathematics, mainly for boys. Private academies and special tutors offered a varied curriculum to many, and girls had an increasing opportunity for education as the century went on.

Probably the earliest instruction received by any young girl was in needlework, at home, from age five through eight or ten. At that time she might work a sampler on canvas, learning the alphabet as she worked it in both capital and lower case letters, and also working the numerals as she learned to count. Then she would proudly spell out her name, sometimes her age, the date, and less frequently the place where she lived. More accomplished girls advanced to stitching verses on their samplers, or sometimes the Lord's Prayer, and surrounding the text with various decorative motifs or idyllic scenes. The educational value of these delightful works of art was twofold: while mastering her alphabet, numbers, and spelling, a young girl also learned a large repertoire of embroidery stitches that she could later use on other projects, whether utilitarian marking of linens or an elaborate embroidered scene based on a print or other pictorial source (no. 101).

Many young women received more advanced training outside their homes. Throughout the eighteenth century private instructors advertised that in addition to *"English, Writing & Arithmetic, both Vulgar and*

1. Alice Morse Earle, *Child Life in Colonial Days* (New York: Macmillan, 1899), p. 93.

JOHN GREENWOOD, 1727-1792
The Greenwood-Lee Family
Ca. 1747, Boston, oil on canvas; 56 x 68 in.
Promised gift to the Museum of Fine Arts

John Greenwood's idea for this ambitious portrait of his family may have come after seeing similar compositions by Smibert of Bishop Berkeley and his entourage or Robert Feke's painting of the Isaac Royal family. A native Bostonian, Greenwood was apprenticed to the artist Thomas Johnston in 1742. Greenwood's shortcomings in painterly quality are offset by his enthusiasm for detail and sharp focus in this canvas done at age twenty. The women, who include his mother, sisters, fiancée, and her sister, are shown as formal, well-dressed ladies with the attributes of eighteenth century feminine pastimes: needlework, fan, and ladies' magazine, *The Spectator*.

Ref.: Museum of Fine Arts, Boston, *American Paintings in the Museum of Fine Arts*, Boston, 1969, vol. 1, p. 125, no. 462.

Decimal," young ladies might be taught Dresden work, Embroidery with Gold and shell-work, tent-stitch, cross-stitch, sprigging, diaper, and all kinds of darning, French quilting, marking, plain work and knitting. Shopkeepers and artisans usually had a ready supply of materials necessary for all types of handiwork, mostly imported from abroad. Simon Smith, needlemaker from London, advertised in 1742 that he was "*removed from the Rainbow and Dove in Marlborough Street, now in Union Street near the Corn fields; continues to make and sell all sorts of white Chapple Needles, and all other sorts round and square.*"[2] Ladies were able to buy the latest patterns drawn on canvas from London, and Mrs. Condy advertised in 1738 that one could buy at her shop near the Old North Meeting House: "*All sorts of beautiful Figures on Canvas, for Tent Stick; the Patterns from London, but drawn by her much cheaper than English drawing; All sorts of Canvas, without drawing; also Silk Shades, Slacks, Floss, Cruells of all Sorts, the best White Chappel Needles, and every thing for all Sorts of Work.*"[3]

The variety of instruction available for "*the Amusement and Benefit of the Ladies*" was certainly diverse and constantly changing with the mode of fashion. In 1740, John Waghorne of Boston advertised that he "*had lately Received a fresh parcel of materials for the new Method of Japaning, which was invented in France.*" Mr. Waghorne was willing to teach ladies at their own homes, or "*to make the Expence less to others, he designs a School at Five Pounds for each Scholar.*"[4] By 1767 the colonists were confronted with the nonimportation of fancy goods from England because of increasingly harsh trade laws. In that year Elizabeth Courtney advertised that she would open a school to teach painting on gauze and catgut and also the making of all sorts of French trimmings, flowers, and feather muffs and tippets, so that "*every Lady may have a power of serving herself of what she is now obliged to send to England for, as the whole process is attended with little or no expense.*"[5]

Women pursued their handiwork with great pride and diligence, embroidering family coats of arms, pocketbooks, quilted petticoats, and handsome waistcoats, or making things for their small children. When Mrs. Copley journeyed to New York in 1771 with her husband, John Singleton Copley, she pursued her needlework while her artist husband worked on his commissions. In July, Copley wrote his half-brother Henry Pelham: "*I will give you a minute detail and of the manner in which Sukey and myself spend our time. But to begin with the most important. Sukey and myself are very well; she is imployed in working on muslin, and my self in the Labours of the pencil. We commonly rise by six oClock in the morng, breakfast at 8, go to our respective Labours till 3, when we dine.*"[6]

2. *Boston News-Letter*, April 15/22, 1742, in George Francis Dow, *The Arts & Crafts in New England 1704-1775* (Topsfield, Mass.: Wayside Press, 1927), p. 273.
3. *Boston News-Letter*, April 27/May 4, 1738, in Dow, *Arts & Crafts*, p. 274.
4. *Boston Gazette*, May 19/26, 1740, in Dow, *Arts & Crafts*, p. 267.
5. *Boston Gazette*, Oct. 19, 1767, in Dow, *Arts & Crafts*, p. 275.
6. *Letters and Papers of J. S. Copley and Henry Pelham, 1739-1776*, Collections, No. 71 (Boston: Massachusetts Historical Society 1914), p. 127.

93

BENJAMIN BLYTH, 1746-1787 ?
Abigail Smith Adams (Mrs. John), 1744-1818
1766, Salem, Massachusetts, pastel on paper;
23 x 17½ in.
Massachusetts Historical Society, Boston

Abigail Adams was a woman of unusual perception and intellect who had little formal education. Throughout her life she was surrounded by men and women of intelligence and importance associated with her husband, who was a lawyer, politician, and statesman. Abigail became well known for her voluminous correspondence with her husband and friends. While John Adams was in Philadelphia from 1774 on, she reported on home-front conditions with a keen insight into the political and military activities and persons of the day. She questioned him about his activities at the Continental Congress with understanding, and she did not hesitate to offer him advice on the country's affairs when she thought it was needed. Her portrait by the Salem artist Benjamin Blyth shows her bold features and strong inner resourcefulness at an early age.

Ref.: Andrew Oliver, *Portraits of John and Abigail Adams,* Cambridge, Mass., Harvard University Press, 1967, pp. 5-13.

94

JOHN SINGLETON COPLEY, 1738-1815
Mercy Otis Warren (Mrs. James), 1728-1814
Ca. 1763, Boston, oil on canvas; 51¼ x 41 in.
Museum of Fine Arts, bequest of Winslow Warren. 31.212

Mercy Otis Warren, close friend and constant correspondent of Abigail Adams, is painted in elegant feminine laces and satin. Her strong face and determined gaze are the only indication in this youthful portrait by Copley of her later talents as poet, writer, political critic, and historian during the Revolution.

Although she had no formal education, she was allowed to sit in on her brother's lessons and browse in the library of her uncle, a local minister. Mercy bore five sons but still found time to write for the Revolutionary cause. Her first satirical play, *The Adulateur,* appeared under a pseuduonym in the *Massachusetts Spy* in 1772, and her writing career continued for some twenty-five years, culminating in the three-volume *History of the Rise, Progress and Termination of the American Revolution* in 1805. Today her work is valued not for its great literary merit but for the author's strong personal opinions and her observations on people and events of her time.

Refs.: Museum of Fine Arts, Boston, *American Paintings in the Museum of Fine Arts, Boston,* Boston, 1969, vol. 1, p. 62, no. 260. Maud M. Hutcheson, "Mercy Warren, 1728-1814," *William and Mary Quarterly,* 3rd series, vol. 10, no. 3 (July 1953), pp. 378-402.

Numerous sewing and handiwork projects were associated with the birth of a child in New England. A well-documented custom that survived until the early years of the nineteenth century call for a pin cushion to be presented to the mother of the newborn. These conventional little gifts were usually stuck with varying size round-headed pins in a design that included the date, initials, or a simple greeting to the baby. In 1771 Anna Green Winslow recorded in her journal the arrival of Josiah Waters into the world: *"Yesterday between meetings my aunt was called to Mrs. Water's & about 8 in the evening Dr. Lloyd brought little master to town (N.B. As a memorandum for myself. My aunt stuck a white sattan pincushion for Mrs. Waters. On one side is a planthorn with flower, on the reverse, just under the border are, on one side stuck these words, Josiah Waters, then follows on the end, Decr 1771, on the next side & end are the words, Welcome little Stranger.)"*[7]

During the eighteenth century women's lives were much taken up with the rearing of their children. Children were seen as small adults. A great deal was expected of them in terms of work and behavior. Their moral and religious training was taken seriously by their parents and elders. In the few family portraits that survive from the early eighteenth century (nos. 105, 107) the familial relationship often appears tender and close.

Infants and children, then as now, had their own playthings and special diversions. A variety of rattles and teething toys and wooden objects to pacify infants were easily made and later discarded. Rattles, whistles, and teething devices were also made of gold or silver and coral, and are among the more precious infant playthings that have survived. Occasionally they appear in the hands of young children in family portraits (no. 107). Some children in America in the early eighteenth century were fortunate enough to have had other silver playthings. Small items were made specially for young children such as the porringer made by Paul Revere I for little David Mason (no. 113). *"Silver Baby-things"* were mentioned in Bethia Shrimpton's will when she died in 1713, suggesting that the objects were preciously guarded through life.[8]

Throughout the eighteenth century advertisements for children's toys appeared. Importers like James Buck and William Price were selling *"English and Dutch Toys,"* and in 1771 the *Boston News-Letter* published this notice: *"To be sold at the Three Sugar-Loaves in Cornhill, . . . several complete Tea-table Sets of Children's cream-colored Toys."*[9]

While it is generally thought that young children were restricted in their merry-making, there were times when they had evenings of revelry and fun among themselves. Anna Green Winslow has left a striking account of a *"very genteel well regulated evening"* that she spent with some other young ladies about her age, ten or twelve years old, where *"the elderly part of the*

7. Alice Morse Earle, ed., *Diary of Anna Green Winslow: A Boston School Girl of 1771* (Cambridge, Mass.: Riverside Press, 1894), p. 12.
8. John D. Kernan, "American Miniature Silver," *Antiques* 80 (December 1961), 567-569.
9. Dow, *Arts & Crafts*, p. 94.

101
Attributed to MERCY SCOLLAY, 1741-? or DEBORAH SCOLLAY, 1736-1794
Embroidered overmantel or chimneypiece
1766, Boston, silk yarns, dated in lower right corner; 21 x 49 in.
Private collection

An abundance of imported prints in Boston during the eighteenth century provided ample source material for needlework embroideries by talented young ladies. Undoubtedly prints supplied the sources for this ambitiously large embroidered overmantel, which seems to be a combination of two distinct scenes. It may also be the product of two different girls, since there is a clear center division in technique as well as theme.

This superb piece of needlework has descended in the family of John Scollay of Boston (1712-1790), and tradition relates that it was worked by one of his daughters, either Mercy or Deborah. The subtle blending of colors, the skillful detailing of both architecture and light, and the delightful bucolic mood indicate a sensitivity and talent that surpassed that of a pure copyist.

95
Card table
1750-1770, Boston, mahogany with pine and maple and embroidered top, made by Mercy Otis Warren; H. 27¼ in., W. 41⅛ in., DEPTH (open) 38½ in.
Collections of the Pilgrim Society, Plymouth, Massachusetts

Mercy Otis Warren was not primarily known or remembered for her skill with the needle, but like most women of her era she probably did her share of embroidery. This card table top must have been one of her finest accomplishments. Occasionally in her correspondence with Abigail Adams, one senses the women's love of "fine linnen, satten and muzlin," as they alternate their interest in education and Molière's works with French cotton, "garlick thread," yards of "mussel" and skeins of sewing silk.

The intensity and brightness of the colors in this needlework top suggest that the table was usually kept closed and against a wall except when used for an afternoon or evening's entertainment of cards. Its simple Queen Anne form relates it to a small group of Boston card tables, among which is one originally owned by Peter Faneuil.

Ref.: Richard H. Randall, Jr., *American Furniture in the Museum of Fine Arts, Boston*, Boston, 1965, pp. 111-113, no. 79 (for a similar table).

102

HANNAH OTIS, 1732-1773
Embroidered picture of the Boston Common
Ca. 1755-1760, Boston, silk, wool, and metallic
yarns on linen; 24 x 53 in.
Private collection

A number of embroidered pictures of the
eighteenth century illustrate motifs similar to
those seen in this one and are usually called "the
fishing lady on the Boston Common." Thomas
Hancock's stone mansion, built in 1737, the
Beacon on the hill to the right, and the duck
pond at the foot of the Common on the left, all
identify the scene accurately. In 1829 Harrison
Gray Otis, then mayor of Boston, described this
picture, which he then owned: "A view of the
Hancock House, and appendages, and of the
Common, and its vicinity, as they were in
1755-60. It was the boarding school lesson of
Hannah Otis, . . . It was considered a chef-
d'oeuvre, and made a great noise at the time.
The science of perspective was not too worthy
of Claude Lorraine, but perhaps not behind that
of some who since then have had the care of the
Common." Needlework of this sort was an
integral part of every young woman's education
and life during the eighteenth and early nineteenth century.

Ref.: Nancy Graves Cabot, "The Fishing Lady and
Boston Common," *Antiques* 40 (July 1941), 28-31.

105

JOHN SMIBERT, 1688-1751
Mary Fitch Oliver (Mrs. Andrew), 1706-1732,
and Andrew Oliver, 1731-1799
1732, Boston, oil on canvas; 50¼ x 40¼ in.
Oliver family

Few American portraits painted before 1750
picture infants in their mother's arms. So
Smibert's picture of Mrs. Andrew Oliver and
her restless young son, Andrew, provides us
with an unusual and charming image of eighteenth century family life. Mrs. Oliver died
shortly after this portrait was made, but her son
lived to maturity. She was the first wife of
Andrew Oliver, the future lieutenant governor
of Massachusetts, and the daughter of a successful upholsterer, Col. Thomas Fitch.

Ref.: Andrew Oliver, *Faces of a Family*, privately
printed, 1960, p. 6, no. 6.

100

Embroidered picture

1756, New England, wool and silk yarns on linen, dated on clock tower: "1756"; 20½ x 14¾ in.

American Antiquarian Society, Worcester, Massachusetts

The wedding scene of this needlework may be that of Hannah Greene and Gardiner Chandler, who were married in 1755 and in whose family the picture descended. An unusual scene for a mid-eighteenth century needlepoint, the picture contains a variety of detail, which can only be ascribed to a specific incident in the life of the embroiderer. Most needlepoint pictures of this type derive more directly from European sources of pastoral landscapes and domestic architecture scattered with shepherds, shepherdesses, and appropriate wildlife.

company were spectators only, they mix'd not in either of . . . the described scenes." Anna wrote: "There was a large company assembled in a handsome, large, upper room in the new end of the house. We had two fiddles, & I had the honor to open the diversion of the evening in a minuet with miss Soley. . . . our treat was nut raisins, Cakes, Wine, punch, hot & cold, all in great plenty. We had a very agreeable evening from 5 to 10 o'clock. For variety we woo'd a widow, hunted the whistle, threaded the needle, & while the company was collecting, we diverted ourselves with playing of pawns, no rudeness Mamma I assure you."[10]

Miss Winslow must have been dressed in some of her very finest garments and accessories, for the image that she left of herself on that night is indeed a splendid one for a girl of her age: "I was dressed in my yellow coat, black bib & apron, black feathers on my head, my past[e] comb, & all my past[e] garnet marquesett & jet pins, together with my silver plume — my loket, rings, black collar round my neck, black mitts & 2 or 3 yards of blue ribbin, (black & blue is high taste) striped tucker and ruffels (not my best) & my silk shoes compleated my dress."[11]

Such diaries and letters as those of Anna Winslow, Abigail Adams, or Mercy Otis Warren provide a rare insight into the lives of eighteenth century women and children. Their human side and interest in each other comes through as they recorded their thoughts on paper. Abigail Adams, in one of her many letters to Mercy Otis Warren, asked her friend, "I am curious to know how you Spend your time? tis very sausy to make this demand upon you, but I know it must be usefully imployd and I am fearful if I do not question you I shall loose some improvement which I might otherways make."[12]

These two women, known today for their intellectual abilities and strongmindedness, are not representative of all eighteenth century women. Their lives, well documented by their remaining letters, diaries, portraits, handiwork, and other material possessions, reveal much about the expectations of colonial women.

10. Earle, *Diary*, p. 17.
11. Ibid., p. 17.
12. *Warren-Adams Letters*, Collections, No. 72 (Boston: Massachusetts Historical Society, 1917), vol. 1, p. 179.

103

JOHN GREENWOOD, 1727-1792
Margaret Fayerweather Bromfield (Mrs. Henry),
1732-1761
Ca. 1749-1750, Boston, oil on canvas;
36 x 25½ in.
Museum of Fine Arts, Emily L. Ainsley Fund.
62.173

Painted in Greenwood's characteristic early
style, Mrs. Bromfield's image is strongly
reminiscent of the Greenwood and Lee family
group made a few years earlier by the artist.
Mrs. Bromfield, daughter of Thomas Fayerweather, a wealthy Boston merchant, married
the successful merchant Henry Bromfield in
1749, so this may have been a wedding portrait.

Refs.: Museum of Fine Arts, Boston, *American
Paintings in the Museum of Fine Arts, Boston,*
Boston, 1969, vol. 1, p. 125, no. 663. [T. N.
Maytham], "Some Recent Accessions," *Boston
Museum Bulletin,* vol. 60, no. 322 (1962), pp.
140-141.

104

Side chair
1750-1760, New York, walnut with walnut
veneer, white pine and maple seat frame, embroidered seat cover; H. 38½ in., W. 22 in.,
DEPTH 18⅜ in.
Museum of Fine Arts, gift of Mrs. Jean Frederic
Wagniere in memory of her mother Henrietta
Slade Warner (Mrs. Henry Eldridge Warner).
68.389

This transitional style side chair with its original
needlework seat cover is one of a set of at least
six chairs that originally belonged to Henry and
Margaret Fayerweather Bromfield. Of New
York origin, it was possibly acquired by the
Bromfields or Captain Fayerweather through
a New York trade connection, since no chairs
this elaborate, with veneered splat and delicately
carved crestrail and knees, were being made in
Boston at the mid-century. The transition from
Queen Anne to Chippendale can be seen in the
combination of the solid splat and curved crestrail of the Queen Anne style with the new fashioned claw and ball feet of the Chippendale
style. The seat frame of one of the chairs is inscribed "Capⁿ Fayerweather," and the original
needlework seat covers have been traditionally
attributed to Margaret Fayerweather Bromfield.

Ref.: Two of these chairs are at the Brooklyn
Museum, two at Historic Deerfield Foundation,
and two in the Museum of Fine Arts, Boston.

90

107

JOHN SINGLETON COPLEY
The Copley Family (grisaille study)
1776, England, oil on canvas; 20¾ x 26¼ in.
Private collection

Perhaps no more charming or loving family group was ever painted by a colonial American artist than this one that John Singleton Copley painted of his own family soon after they arrived in London. This grisaille study was for a much larger canvas, now in the National Gallery of Art, Washington, D.C. The vitality and free brushwork of the sketch are indicative of the beginnings of Copley's mature style, which he was to perfect during his English career.

In search of his artistic destiny and partly because of his mixed feelings about the pending Revolution, Copley left Boston in 1774 never to return to his home. As an artist, he found more abundant patronage in England, where he was elected to the Royal Academy and participated actively in the London art scene. In Boston portraiture had been the only type of painting in demand by the wealthy. But in England Copley turned to making large-scale canvases of heroic scenes of historical and contemporary events, establishing his reputation and insuring his success.

Ref.: Jules David Prown, *John Singleton Copley*, 2 vols., Cambridge, Mass., Harvard University Press, 1966, vol. 2, pp. 262-263, fig. 346.

109

THOMAS EDWARDS, 1701-1755
Whistle and bells with coral
Ca. 1722, Boston, silver with coral end, marked: "TE" in rectangle on side of stem near coral end; engraved with Fayerweather crest and inscribed with initials "IF" on side and under whistle; L. 4½ in.
The Art Institute of Chicago, gift of Mrs. J. Ogden Armour through the Antiquarian Society of Chicago

Early portraits often show children and babies holding silver or gold whistles with bells and coral such as this. Marked American whistles with bells and coral are rare, but occasionally they are found listed in eighteenth century inventories and newspaper advertisements. In 1765 the Boston silversmith Joseph Edwards, Jr., advertised that his shop had been broken into and "3 child's Whistles" stolen along with several other items.

Refs.: Martha Gandy Fales, *Early American Silver for the Cautious Collector*, New York, Funk and Wagnalls, 1970, p. 105, plate 102. Bernice Ball, "Whistles with Coral and Bells," *Antiques* 80 (December 1961), 552-555.

113

PAUL REVERE I, 1702-1754
Porringer
Ca. 1726-1730, Boston, silver, marked: "PR" in shield on upper side of bottom, inscribed "D*M" on handle and "D Mason" on underside of bottom; H. 1½ in., DIAM. (lip) 3⅞ in., L. (handle) 2¼ in.
Private collection

Just as children in the eighteenth century were expected to act like miniature adults, so they were sometimes given pieces of silver such as caudle cups, porringers, or tankards in the form and style of adult possessions. Paul Revere I made this small child's porringer for David Mason (1726-1794) and embellished the handle with the youth's initials.

108

JOSEPH BLACKBURN, active in America 1754-1763
Elizabeth and James Bowdoin III as children
Ca. 1760, Boston, oil on canvas; 36⅞ x 58 in.
Bowdoin College Museum of Art, Brunswick, Maine, bequest of Mrs. Sarah Bowdoin Dearborn

Dressed in full costume as miniature adults, the children of merchant James Bowdoin II, Elizabeth and "Jemmy," exemplify the basic rules for children's behavior such as "Be always Cleanly" and "Let not play Entice thee" that were put forth in the primer texts for behavior in the eighteenth century, such as *The School of Good Manners.*

Joseph Blackburn was one of the most accomplished artists in Boston in 1760, when the young Copley's talents were beginning to mature. Probably trained in London, Blackburn left England for Bermuda in 1752 and by 1755 moved to Boston. For the remainder of the decade he enjoyed substantial patronage from Boston's wealthy merchants until surpassed by the rising genius of Copley. Blackburn subsequently returned to England in 1763.

Ref.: Marvin Sadik, *Colonial and Federal Portraits at Bowdoin College,* Brunswick, Maine, Bowdoin College Museum of Art, 1966, pp. 70-73.

Entertainment

DIARIES written by men, women, and children in pre-Revolutionary Boston reveal that life in the city afforded a wide variety of social and cultural activities, pursued both in the home and about the town. All elements of society had their diversions. As a middle-class mechanic and craftsman, Paul Revere frequented the Green Dragon Tavern. He participated in the grand illuminations and celebrations that marked special anniversaries or state occasions. He attended political meetings and was a member of a Masonic lodge. Charles Apthorp and his family, as members of the wealthy upper classes, entertained lavishly in their home, which was equipped in every way to offer hospitality and comfort. The extravagant luxuries and ostentatious display afforded by merchant wealth provided a living for the craftsmen and tradesmen of Boston. The dining, dancing, tea-drinking, the lectures and musicales, and the pastimes of needlework or gaming of the wealthy all required specially manufactured or imported objects or commodities. A fine silver tea- or coffee pot made by Revere or Jacob Hurd, an English porcelain dinner service, ribbons and lace from France for Mrs. Hancock's party dress, or tea imported from the East Indies via England were all an integral part of the consumer's economy in eighteenth century Boston.

Certainly tea-drinking was one of the most widespread social diversions of the middle and upper classes in eighteenth and early nineteenth century America. Tea was imported in tremendous volume into the colonies; it was such an important commodity that it eventually caused friction in the colonial relationship with England. In 1767 it was taxed as a result of the Townshend Acts. Later, in 1773, the large-scale dumping of cheap tea on the colonial market as a government solution to the bankruptcy of the East India Company resulted in the Boston Tea Party. A majority of the citizens joined in the protest over British control of their favorite beverage: *"a large Number of the Mistresses of Families, some of whom are Ladies of the highest Rank, in this Town, have signed an Agreement against drinking Tea ... they engage not only to abstain from it in their Families (Sickness excepted) but will absolutely refuse it, if it should be offered to them upon any Occasion."*[1]

For the "Ladies of the highest Rank," the wealthy merchant class, tea-drinking was a status ritual in which both the ceremony and the accoutrements were important, including the silver utensils and the table from which tea was served, and the china teacups and saucers from which it was drunk.

Tea was usually taken twice a day by most people. In 1781 the Baron Cromot du Bourg noted during a visit to Boston that the people took *"a great*

1. Alice Morse Earle, *Colonial Dames and Goodwives* (Boston: Houghton Mifflin, 1895), p. 246.

121
JOHN SINGLETON COPLEY, 1738-1815
Dorothy Quincy (Mrs. John Hancock),
1747-1830
Ca. 1772, Boston, oil on canvas; 50 x 39 in.
Museum of Fine Arts. Charles H. Bayley Fund
and partial gift of Anne B. Loring. 1975.13

Copley painted this striking portrait of Dorothy Quincy, daughter of Edmund Quincy the merchant, about four years before her marriage to John Hancock. Soon after her marriage Mrs. Hancock became well known as a hostess in Boston, for she and her husband in every way lived up to the immense fortune he had inherited from his uncle. This portrait was made late in Copley's American career. It is close in pose, dress, pensive mood, and sensitive handling to the luminous portrait he made of her cousin, Mrs. Richard Skinner, in 1772. Brilliant rendering of textures and the quality of light and psychological insight make this image of Dorothy Quincy one of Copley's finest portraits.

Ref.: Jules David Prown, *John Singleton Copley*, 2 vols. Cambridge, Mass., Harvard University Press, 1966, vol. 1, p. 85, fig. 316.

122
Tea table
1740-1765, Boston, mahogany with white pine;
H. 27 in., W. 29 in., DEPTH 19 in.
Mr. and Mrs. Eric M. Wunsch

This handsome mahogany tea table was originally owned by Sarah Bradlee Fulton (1740-1836), sister-in-law of Robert Fulton, inventor of the steamboat. The Fultons (m. 1762) lived at the corner of Hollis and Tremont streets in Boston. The form and excellent proportions of this table combine to make it a superb example among the few Boston tables of its type. The molded tray top, the rarity of original slides with all the underbracing intact, and the symmetry and liveliness of the shaped skirt on all sides make it evident that this table was meant to be used in the center of a room, without any tablecloth or covering.

The growth of tea drinking as a social custom in the eighteenth century occasioned the production and importation of much fine furniture and extravagant equipage. The tea table was the focal point of the whole ceremony.

Ref.: Barry A. Greenlaw, *New England Furniture at Williamsburg,* Charlottesville, the University Press of Virginia, 1974, pp. 148-150, no. 129 (for a similar table).

123

BENJAMIN BURT, 1729-1805
Teapot
Ca. 1765, Boston, silver with wooden handle, marked: "B. BURT" in rectangle on bottom, engraved with Hancock coat of arms on pourer's side; H. 8½ in., DIAM. (base) 3¾ in., DIAM. (rim) 2¾ in.
Mrs. Harlan P. Hanson

Accustomed to being surrounded by luxurious furnishings, John Hancock continued to maintain himself in style after receiving his inheritance upon the death of his uncle, Thomas, in 1764. This finely fashioned teapot bearing the Hancock coat of arms surrounded with garland swags engraved around the shoulder may have been among the first articles Hancock purchased after his uncle's death. In the very latest fashion and form, it was made by the Boston silversmith Benjamin Burt, son of John Burt, who was apprenticed to John Coney, as was Appollos Rivoire, Paul Revere's father. Benjamin Burt and Paul Revere II were contemporaries and equally prominent and talented silversmiths.

Ref.: Kathryn C. Buhler and Graham Hood, *American Silver, Garvan and Other Collections in the Yale University Art Gallery*, New Haven, Conn., 1970, pp. 171-172, no. 220.

deal of tea in the morning" privately, had dinner at two o'clock, and "about five o'clock they take more tea, some wine, Madeira [and] punch."[2] The tea table was the focal point of the ceremony (no. 121). Around the middle of the century it might have had a turret top, a tilt top, or drop leaves or slides that pulled out from the underside to hold candlesticks, teacups, or the pot as it was being filled with hot water from the kettle. The table was made of handsome mahogany, walnut, or maple, or perhaps even pine with an elaborate japanned surface.

On the table was an imposing array of utensils which could have been of pewter, ceramic, or silver: a teapot, cream or milk pot, sugar bowl, slop bowl, tea cannister, sugar tongs, strainer, spoons with spoon tray, and teacups and saucers. Also on the table, or on a nearby separate stand, might have been a hot water kettle and lamp such as the one made by Jacob Hurd about 1740 for the Lowell family (no. 125). During this period the silver tea service was rarely made as a set, though eventually several pieces might be made that were similar to one another. Cups and saucers were usually china, imported from the orient via England; sometimes the entire tea set would be ceramic.

The vogue for drinking tea and owning a variety of equipage was so great by mid-century that in the 1759 inventory of Charles Apthorp tea tables and accompanying objects were found in three rooms. The *"Great Parlour"* contained *"a Tea Table, a sett of Chaina & Tea Chest, a Tin Sugar Chest . . . 1 Tea Stand, 2 Teaboards,"* and *"a Parcell of Chaina, Delph & glass."* In the *"Best Parlour"* were *"2 Mahogany Tables & 1 Japand Tea Table & Voider"* and *"a Parcel of Chaina, Delph & glass Ware."* Apparently the dining room upstairs was also used for tea, since it had *"a Tea Table & sett of Chaina,"* and *"a Tea Kettle & Stand."*[3]

Dining in an elaborate fashion was another favorite pastime in the homes of the elite. The occasion might be a wedding, an important visit, or a graduation from Harvard College such as the party Ralph Inman gave when his son George graduated. It was *"the Genteelest Entertainment I ever saw"* John Rowe, a guest, thought, as he described it in his diary: *"Two hundred & Ten at one Table — amongst the Company The Gov' & Family, The Lieut Governor & Family, The Admirall & Family & all the Remainder, Gentleman & Ladies of Character & Reputation. The whole was conducted with much Ease & Pleasure & all Joyned in making each other Happy — such as Entertainment has not been made in New England before on any occasion."*[4] While this was an unusually large celebration, many lavish dinners were served for up to fifty guests. Enormous quantities of food and beverage — wine, rum, punch, or cider — were served.

2. Rodris Roth, "Tea Drinking in 18th Century America: Its Etiquette and Equipage," *Paper 14: Tea Drinking in 18th Century America*, Bulletin 225: Contributions from the Museum of History and Technology, Smithsonian Institution, p. 66 (n.d.).
3. Suffolk Probate Records, docket 11871.
4. Anne Rowe Cunningham, ed., *Letters and Diary of John Rowe, Boston Merchant* (Boston: W. B. Clarke, 1903), p. 231.

124

WILLIAM PLUMMER, active 1755-1762
Basket
1760, London, silver, maker's marks on outside
center of one of scroll-cut panels; H. (at end)
3¾ in., L. 14⅞ in.
Museum of Fine Arts, Theodora Wilbour Fund
in memory of Charlotte Beebe Wilbour. 66.286

The Hancock family could well afford the best
English silver in 1760 when this ornate cutwork
basket was ordered from London. It probably
graced the tea table or sideboard at many
elegant occasions in the great Hancock mansion
on Beacon Hill. In John Hancock's 1794 inventory it is listed as a bread basket and was left
presumably to his widow. When his wife,
Dorothy Hancock Scott, died in 1830, she willed
to her niece "my large silver cake basket" and
requested "it be used at the weddings of my
nieces and nephews as it has been heretofore."

125

JACOB HURD, 1702/3-1758
Tea kettle on stand
1730-1740, Boston, silver, marked: "I HURD" in
cartouche on bottom at center point and
"Hurd" in ellipse on cover near vent hole, en-
graved on pourer's side with coat of arms of
Lowell quartering Leversedge; H. 14⅜ in.,
DIAM. 7½ in.
Museum of Fine Arts, gift of Esther Lowell
Abbott in memory of her mother, Esther Lowell
Cunningham, granddaughter of James Russell
Lowell. 1971.347a, b

Rivaling any English teakettle on stand for per-
fection of form, this one by Jacob Hurd demonstrates the fact that provincial craftsmen in
Boston were equal in skill to, and sometimes
surpassed, their London competitors. A rare
form in colonial silver, and the work of one of
Boston's foremost silversmiths as well as a contemporary of the Reveres, it is the only silver to
bear the eighteenth century arms of Lowell
quartering Leversedge.

Ref.: Buhler, *American Silver in the Museum of
Fine Arts,* vol. 2, p. 642, no. 543.

127

PAUL REVERE I, 1702-1754
Covered milk pot
1730-1750, Boston, silver, marked: "PR" in
shield with line above and below at left of
handle and over center point on bottom; H.
4⅝ in., DIAM. (base) 2⅛ in., DIAM. (lip) 1⅞ in.
Museum of Fine Arts, bequest of Frederick W.
Bradlee. 28.45

Superbly simple in form, this covered milk pot
has the quiet grace of line and understated
ornament also found on the best of Queen
Anne style furniture. Paul Revere I undoubtedly
absorbed from his master, John Coney, his sense
of the Queen Anne style of simple beauty and
dignified restraint that Coney introduced in his
silver as early as 1718.

Ref.: Buhler, *American Silver in the Museum of
Fine Arts,* vol. 1, p. 186, no. 150.

129

JOHN SINGLETON COPLEY, 1738-1815
Nicholas Boylston, 1716-1771
Ca. 1767, Boston, oil on canvas; 50¼ x 40¼ in.
Museum of Fine Arts, bequest of David P.
Kimball. 23.504

Nicholas Boylston was the son of one of the
wealthiest merchants in Massachusetts, yet he
accumulated a sizeable fortune on his own as
well. Elegant surroundings and lavish entertain-
ments were part of his daily routine, and in this
portrait Copley has appropriately portrayed
him in a richly flowing damask banyan, or
dressing gown, and turban. When John Adams
dined at the Boylstons he recorded: *"An elegant
Dinner indeed! Went over the House to view
the Furniture, which alone cost a thousand
Pounds sterling. A seat it is for a noble Man, a
Prince. The Turkey Carpets, the painted Hangings, the Marble Tables, the rich Beds with
crimson Damask Curtins and Counterpins, the
beautiful Chimny Clock, the Spacious Garden,
are the most magnificent of any Thing I have
ever seen."*

This portrait is a replica of one now at Harvard.
Copley also painted Nicholas' brother, Thomas,
about the same time. When Nicholas Boylston
died in 1771 he left Harvard a large sum of
money to endow a chair of rhetoric and oratory.
His generosity prompted the Fellows of Harvard
College to commission Copley to make a full-
length portrait of Boylston, which was taken
directly from the first version of 1767.

Refs: L. H. Butterfield, ed., *Diary and Autobiography of John Adams,* Cambridge, Mass., Harvard
University Press, 1961, vol. 1, pp. 294-295. Museum
of Fine Arts, Boston, *American Paintings in the
Museum of Fine Arts,* Boston, 1969, vol. 1, p. 68,
no. 275. Jules David Prown, *John Singleton Copley,*
Cambridge, Mass., Harvard University Press, 1966,
vol. 1, pp. 54-55, fig. 184.

130

Corner chair

1760-1790, probably Boston, mahogany with birch and pine; H. 31⅞ in., W. 18⅛ in., DEPTH 18⅛ in.

Mr. and Mrs. Lewis T. Steadman

This corner chair, along with six side chairs, comprises a set that descended in the Richardson family of Bolton, Massachusetts. Probably made in Boston, this fine chair has typical Boston characteristics. The raked-back talons on the claw and ball foot, and sharply carved and clearly defined leafage on the cabriole leg, and the familiar splat seen in several Copley portraits, point to a Boston origin. Along with its corresponding side chairs, this chair exemplifies the high quality and achievements of Boston's chairmakers in the face of competition and importation from abroad.

Ref.: Art Institute of Chicago, *American Art of the Colonies and Early Republic,* Chicago, 1971, p. 36, no. 37.

132

Easy chair

Ca. 1750-1790, Boston area, mahogany with eastern white pine and red maple; H. 47½ in., W. 36 in., DEPTH 28 in.

The Metropolitan Museum of Art, purchase, the Friends of the American Wing Fund, 1967

The costliness of textiles in the eighteenth century contributed to the expense of a handsome upholstered chair such as this one once owned by the Bromfield family of Boston. The refined carving on the knees strongly relates it to the school of Boston carving. Frequently located in bedrooms and upstairs chambers, easy chairs were used for the comfort of every household member, but especially the aged and infirm.

Ref.: Morrison H. Heckscher, "Form and Frame: New Thoughts on the American Easy Chair," *Antiques,* 100, no. 6 (December, 1971), 886-893.

103

After a large meal had been savored, the remainder of the evening might be spent in card-playing, backgammon, chess, or perhaps singing and dancing. A number of musical instruments were owned privately, most of them imported (no. 135). The inventories of Charles Apthorp (1759) and John Hancock (1794) indicate that each had a spinet. Wind and string instruments were also heard both in the home and in public concert. Music books were usually imported, with some being printed in Boston by mid-century. Paul Revere is known to have engraved copperplates for three notable books of music: *A Collection of the Best Psalm Tunes* (1764) and *Sixteen Anthems* (1766), published by Josiah Flagg, and *The New-England Psalm Singer* (1770) by William Billings[5] (no. 136).

Music and dancing required instruction. Advertisements by such men as John Waghorne, Josiah Carter, John Rice, and Peter Pelham, Copley's stepfather, appeared in newspapers throughout the century. In 1753 Rice offered to teach a variety of instruments, including the spinet, harpsichord, violin, and German flute. Peter Pelham announced in 1732 a monthly *"Entertainment of Musick and Dancing, (call'd by the fashionable name of an Assembly)."*[6] He also held concerts at his studio, as he announced in December 1731: *"There will be performed a Concert of Music on sundry Instruments at Mr. Pelham's great Room, being the House of the late Doctor Noyes near the Sun Tavern."*[7] Other concerts followed this one, some in Faneuil Hall and some in King's Chapel. Gilbert Deblois and his brother, the organist at King's Chapel, constructed a shop with a concert hall above it in 1754. On at least two different occasions John Rowe spent an entertaining evening at Concert Hall: once *"there was a Concert Dance"* and another time there was *"a fine Ball, excellent Musick & a good large Plumb Cake."*[8]

Concerts were also held at taverns, where a variety of activities went on besides the *"drinking drams of flip, carousing and swearing."*[9] All levels of society mixed at taverns and at great public events and festivals such as a public auction, a political meeting, or even the viewing of an exotic wild animal. Public curiosities were endless, with waxwork displays, fireworks, or even public hangings of criminals often attracting a large crowd. Perhaps the most important function served by taverns in the era just before the Revolution was as a meeting place for secret political groups and clubs. The Green Dragon Tavern on Union Street was so well known as a meeting place for the Sons of Liberty that Daniel Webster later called it the headquarters of the Revolution. Paul Revere, John Hancock, Sam Adams, and dozens of others met regularly to plot the course of protest. The Green Dragon was purchased in 1764 by the Masonic Lodge of Saint Andrew. Other lodges

5. Clarence S. Brigham, *Paul Revere's Engravings,* rev. ed. (New York: Atheneum, 1969), pp. 36-38, 86-93.
6. George Francis Dow, *The Arts & Crafts in New England 1704-1775* (Topsfield, Mass.: Wayside Press, 1927), p. 10.
7. *Boston News Letter,* Dec. 16-23, 1731, in William Arms Fisher, *Notes on Music in Old Boston* (Boston: Oliver Ditson, 1918), p. 15.
8. *Letters and Diary of John Rowe,* pp. 211 and 188.
9. John Hull Brown, *Early American Beverages* (New York: Bonanza Books, 1966), p. 19.

134
Gawen Brown, 1719-1801
Tall clock
1755-1775, Boston, mahogany with white pine;
H. 91¼ in., W. 22⅝ in., DEPTH 10¾ in.
Private collection

The monumental and architectural proportions of this tall clock and case make it one of the most handsome and ambitious clocks produced in pre-Revolutionary Boston. Gawen Brown, its maker, came from England and was working in Boston by 1749. Certainly his elaborate brass dials and faces were imported from England, and frequently Brown advertised other imported items for sale. In 1768 he made an enormous clock that was exhibited at the town meeting as "a superb stately Town-Clock" with "two great wheels near 90 pound weight of cast brass." This clock was offered to South Church July 23, 1768. Brown's second wife was Elizabeth Byles, a daughter of Rev. Mather Byles. Their only child was Mather Brown, the painter, who studied with Benjamin West in London and spent his life in England.

owned taverns in Boston, indicating that the relationship between fraternal conviviality, secret organizations, and the growth of revolutionary spirit and activity centered around the tavern.

In 1753, to promote local linen manufacture, a spinning and weaving exhibition was held on the Common. The purpose was two-fold: to encourage the employment of the poor and to help make the colonials less dependent on imported cloth, which was at times difficult and expensive to obtain. The *Boston Gazette* reported that *"several thousand spectators assembled on this Occasion."* They gaped at the spinners and weavers and enjoyed music all afternoon, after a sermon in the morning, and *"near 300 Spinners, some of them children of 7 or 8 years old and several of them Daughters of the best Families among us, with their Wheels at Work, sitting orderly in three Rows, made a handsome Appearance on the Common."*[10]

State occasions were also cause for celebration and public gatherings. Fireworks and illuminations at night were an exciting way to attract attention to events such as the appointment of William Shirley as governor of Massachusetts in 1741. *"There was several fine Fire-Works displayed from the Top of the Town-House and other Places"* reported the *Boston Gazette* in its August 10, 1741, issue. Sometimes, as on this occasion, accidents happened: *"unluckily one of the Serpents fell into the Town House Lanthorn where all the Fire-Works lay, and set them all off at once, which made a pretty Diversion; several Gentlemen were in the Lanthorn, and some of them were a little scorcht, but no other Damage done."*[11]

When news of the repeal of the Stamp Act was received in 1766 there was joyous celebration, and *"in the Evening the whole Town was beautifully illuminated."*[12] An obelisk made of oiled paper and illuminated from within was erected on the Common. This structure was more temporary than planned, however, for after the fireworks went off, it was consumed by fire. The only visual record of its short existence is Paul Revere's engraving (no. 152).

During the years of the war, while such public spectacles with political overtones probably took precedence, there was no dearth of merry-making on the part of Bostonians. Artillery drills and elections had always been the cause for drinking and eating and so continued to be whenever possible during the war. The arrival of the French fleet in 1778 introduced a new and foreign element to Boston society. Abigail Adams reported on her dinner on board ship, with Count Charles d'Estaing, the Commanding Officer of the fleet: *"We went, according to the invitation, and were sumptuously entertained, with every delicacy that this country produces, and the addition of every foreign article that could render our feast splendid . . . The temperance of these gentlemen, joined to many other virtues . . . are sufficient to make*

10. *Boston Gazette*, Aug. 14, 1753, in George Francis Dow, *The Arts & Crafts in New England 1704-1775* (Topsfield, Mass.: Wayside Press, 1927), pp. 281-282.
11. *Boston Gazette*, Aug. 10-17, 1741, in George Francis Dow, *Everyday Life in the Massachusetts Bay Colony* (Topsfield, Mass.: Wayside Press, 1935), pp. 116-117.

*Europeans, and Americans too, blush at their own degeneracy of manners
... Most that I have seen appear to be gentlemen of family and education."*[12] Entertainment and socializing among all levels of society seemed
to continue and flourish in a variety of ways, in spite of the hardships of war.

12. Charles Francis Adams, *Familiar Letters of John Adams and His Wife Abigail Adams, during
the Revolution* (Boston: Houghton Mifflin, 1875), p. 342.

135
JOHN HARRIS, active in Boston from 1768
Spinet
1769, Boston, mahogany with maple and pine,
labeled above keyboard: "John Harris, Boston,
New England fecit"; H. 32½ in., w. (rear edge)
73 in.
Mrs. Walter B. Robb

The survival of this finely veneered and inlaid
spinet, which rests on a turned Queen Anne
style frame, is testimony to the importance of
music in the home during the eighteenth century. Instruments were usually imported; this
spinet is believed to be the first made in America. The announcement of its manufacture was
first made on September 18, 1769, in the *Boston
Gazette*: "*It is with pleasure we inform the
Public That a few days since was shipped for
Newport, a very curious Spinnet, being the first*

*ever made in America, the performance of the
ingenious Mr. John Harris, of Boston (Son of
the late Mr. Joseph Harris, of London, Harpsichord and Spinnet Maker), and in every respect does Honour to that Artist, who now
carries on Business at his House, a few Doors
Northward of Dr. Clark's, North end of
Boston."*

John Harris came to Boston from London in
November 1768. When he arrived in Boston he
immediately advertised that he lived "at Mr.
Gavin Brown's Watch-maker, North-side of
King Street."

Refs.: Edith Gaines, "The Robb Collection of
American Furniture, Part II," *Antiques* 93, no. 4,
(April 1968), pp. 484-490. Ralph E. Carpenter, Jr.,
*The Arts and Crafts of Newport, Rhode Island,
1640-1820*, Newport, Preservation Society of New-
port County, 1954, p. 78, fig. 50.

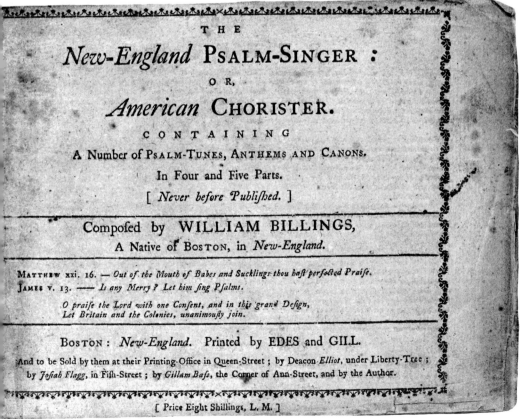

THE

New-England PSALM-SINGER :

OR,

American CHORISTER.

CONTAINING

A Number of PSALM-TUNES, ANTHEMS AND CANONS.

In Four and Five Parts.

[*Never before Published.*]

Composed by WILLIAM BILLINGS,

A Native of BOSTON, in *New-England.*

MATTHEW xxi. 16. — *Out of the Mouth of Babes and Sucklings thou haſt perfected Praiſe.*
JAMES v. 13. —— *Is any Merry? Let him ſing Pſalms.*

O praiſe the Lord with one Conſent, and in this grand Deſign,
Let Britain and the Colonies, unanimouſly join.

BOSTON: *New-England.* Printed by EDES and GILL.

And to be Sold by them at their Printing-Office in Queen-Street ; by Deacon *Elliot,* under Liberty-Tree ;
by *Joſiah Flagg,* in Fiſh-Street ; by *Gillam Baſs,* the Corner of Ann-Street, and by the Author.

[Price Eight Shillings, L. M.]

136
WILLIAM BILLINGS, 1746-1800
PAUL REVERE II, 1735-1818
The New-England Psalm Singer
1770, Boston, line engraving, signed under
picture on frontispiece: "P Revere Sculp";
6¼ x 8½ in.
Mrs. G. Gordon Olsen

Paul Revere engraved this frontispiece and the
entire 116 pages of music for William Billings'
New-England Psalm Singer in 1770, his largest
single project as an engraver. Billings, a tanner
by trade, was a self-taught musician, choir-
master, and composer. As one of the earliest and
most prolific of the New England musicians, he
had a great influence on eighteenth century
music in this country.

Ref.: Clarence S. Brigham, *Paul Revere's Engravings,* New York, Atheneum, 1969, p. 65.

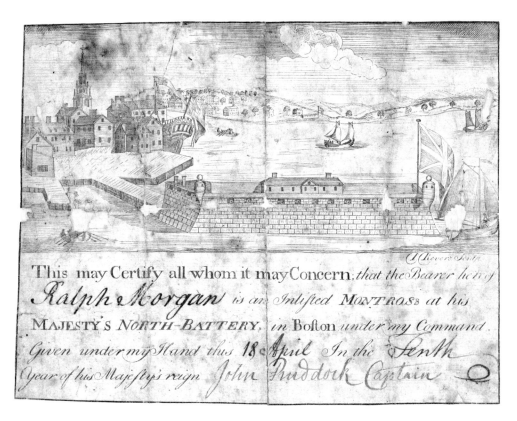

146

THOMAS JOHNSTON, ca. 1708-1767
South Battery certificate
Before 1765, Boston, line engraving, signed under picture of South Battery: "T. Johnston, Sculp!"; 7¾ x 10¾ in.
American Antiquarian Society, Worcester, Massachusetts

Certificates such as these were given to the men who served as "montrosses," or artillerymen at the fortresses. The North and South batteries were Boston's main seaward defenses in the years before and immediately after the Revolution. The date of this certificate is uncertain, but between 1758 and 1767, Johnston engraved blank commissions for the Massachusetts province, and he had already made plates for a number of maps and military plans before this, so he obviously had a military clientele.

Johnston's skill as an engraver was demonstrated in a variety of ways: on maps, views, bookplates, currency, music sheets, and trade cards. On his own trade card he advertised himself as being skilled in japanning, varnishing, drawing, gilding, and painting and also selling such varied items as looking-glasses, tea tables, writing desks, and clock cases. He was a man of wide talents in the eighteenth century tradition.

Ref.: Sinclair Hitchings, "Thomas Johnston," in *Boston Prints and Printmakers, 1670-1775*, Boston, Colonial Society of Massachusetts, 1973, pp. 83-132.

147

PAUL REVERE II, 1735-1818
North Battery certificate
Ca. 1762, Boston, line engraving, signed lower right: "P Revere Sculp"; 5⅞ x 8¼ in.
American Antiquarian Society, Worcester, Massachusetts

Revere's print of the North Battery was probably inspired by Johnston's of the South Battery, and made about the same time. It is Revere's earliest known copperplate engraving. By comparison with the South Battery certificate, it is clear that Thomas Johnston was at this time a more accomplished and experienced engraver and illustrator than Revere. Revere's print clearly shows the North End of Boston. The steeple of Christ Church (Old North) towers above the neighborhood, and Charlestown is seen across the river.

Ref.: Clarence S. Brigham, *Paul Revere's Engravings*, New York, Atheneum, 1969, pp. 13-14.

IV Revolutionary Boston

BOSTONIANS WERE LEADERS among Colonials in political thought and action during the pre-Revolutionary era. They reacted first and most violently to any real or imagined infringement of their rights by the British. During the fifteen years prior to 1775 the ideological lines on each side hardened at an accelerated pace. The more Britain asserted her military, legislative, and economic powers of empire, the more Bostonians, and Colonials in general, resented it and searched for an independent course. "Liberty" and "tyranny" became words common to everyone's vocabulary.

Merchants, artisans, craftsmen, scholars, and divines joined in the protest against British rule. The course of events reached the point of no return when the first armed conflict broke out at Lexington and Concord on April 19, 1775. *"O! What a glorious morning is this!"*[1] Sam Adams is said to have exclaimed when he heard the news. He had worked unceasingly for this day, constantly harassing local authority in word and deed for ten years. He was not alone in his endeavors; many in Boston joined him. For those who did not join the patriot side, life became intolerable. They left Boston, many on March 17, 1776, when General Howe evacuated the British troops from the city. The troops never returned and neither did many of those Bostonians who remained loyal to the crown.

The ravages of war endured only a short period in Boston, from April 1775 to March 1776, and for those who stayed and fought life was difficult but rewarding. The war was an inevitable path to independence for Colonials who for the most part thought of themselves as British with violated rights. Four generations of settlement and an increasingly varied population, as well as three thousand miles of ocean, separated the Colonials from the mother country. Economic and institutional ties existed but were maintained in a loose and careless manner. This policy of "salutary neglect" ceased when the British government went deeply in debt over the French and Indian War, which ended in 1763. To recoup losses of the war fought on colonial territory, the British Parliament levied new taxes and trade tariffs on the Colonies, and more importantly they endeavored to enforce them.

Boston merchants were the first to protest England's right to legislate taxes on the Colonies. During the French and Indian War (1756-1763), they had done a brisk—and illegal—trade with France, the enemy. The enormous fortunes of the Apthorps, Hancocks, Faneuils, and others were made at this time, partially from lucrative supply contracts for British forces, and mostly as a result of illegal trade. They profited from both sides in the conflict.

---

1. Esther Forbes, *Paul Revere and the World He Lived In* (Boston: Houghton Mifflin, 1969), p. 269.

154
CHRISTIAN REMICK, 1726-1773
*A Perspective View of the Blockade of
Boston Harbour*
Ca. 1768, Boston, watercolor, signed in shield
upper right: "Christian Remich"; 16⅛ x
64⅛ in.
Massachusetts Historical Society, Boston

Soon after October 1, 1768, when the British
troops landed in Boston, Christian Remick produced six similar watercolors of the event.
Several of the views are dedicated to specific
patrons, including John Hancock, who probably
commissioned the work. The landing of the
troops and blockade of Boston had serious con-
sequences for the crown and the colonies.
Bostonians did not accept British occupation
easily. Tension mounted, and tempers finally
exploded on March 5, 1770, in an armed
skirmish, the Boston Massacre.

Christian Remick was a self-taught painter who
was first a mariner and ship's captain between
1747 and 1769. He turned to painting professionally in 1769, when he advertised "Speci-
mens of his Performances, particularly an
accurate View of the Blockade of Boston . . .
may be seen at the Golden Ball and Bunch of
Grapes Taverns, or at Mr. Thomas Bradford's,
North End, Boston." Remick drew a variety of
views, painted coats of arms, and colored numerous prints. Apparently, though, his work
did not provide an adequate income, for he died
in the almshouse on March 10, 1773.

Refs.: Clarence S. Brigham, *Paul Revere's Engrav-
ings,* New York, Atheneum, 1969, pp. 80. Henry W.
Cunningham, *Christian Remick,* Boston, Club of
Odd Volumes, 1904.

Infuriated British leaders demanded stricter enforcement of prevailing laws against smuggling. Throughout the year 1760 illegal cargoes that entered Boston Harbor were impounded, many with the aid of writs of assistance, or general search warrants, issued by the superior court.

The merchants, threatened and aggravated by such action, found opportunity to protest when the news of the king's death reached Boston in December 1760, rendering all writs issued in his name invalid and requiring their renewal within six months under the new king, George III. In February 1761, sixty-three Massachusetts Bay merchants, led by Boston lawyers James Otis, Jr., and Oxenbridge Thacher, requested a hearing in superior court to determine the constitutionality of the writs. Otis set the tone of Colonial thought in his argument, although he lost his case against Thomas Hutchinson, chief justice and lieutenant governor. *"Otis was a flame of fire,"* recorded John Adams (no. 151), who was among hundreds who became involved in the cause as they heard Otis argue the case. His plea that a man's constitutional right to his life, his liberty, and his property was being violated by the tyranny of power in the indiscriminant use of the writs was heard with awe and understanding by his followers and with fear and foreboding by the winning side. The mood was such that local officials, including Governor Bernard, no longer dared use the writs and enforcement of all trade laws gradually relaxed.[2] Hutchinson (no. 160), a loyal public servant in defending his government's policies, gradually turned into something of a tragic figure. This battle over the Writs of Assistance was the first of many controversies between him and his fellow colonists, which finally forced him into exile in 1774.

Hutchinson was the victim of angry Bostonians on the night of August 26, 1765, when a violent mob attacked his house, ransacking it and destroying his possessions. This reaction to the passage of the Stamp Act in 1765 demonstrated that Bostonians were well prepared to take issue with British law. While formal protest surfaced throughout the Colonies, culminating in the Stamp Act Congress in New York in October, it was in Boston that violence first erupted. Bostonians set a new standard of behavior by their actions, one that they were to follow in ensuing years. Bernard, Hutchinson, and Andrew Oliver, the appointed stamp collector who had been hanged in effigy on August 14, fled to Castle William in Boston Harbor (no. 191) to escape the mob that had been instigated by the Loyal Nine, under the leadership of Samuel Adams (no. 172).

The Sons of Liberty, as the Loyal Nine came to be known, were the heart of Revolutionary organization and thinking in Boston. Members came from all sectors of society: Paul Revere, mechanic, joined with John Hancock and Sam Adams, merchants, Dr. Joseph Warren, orator and scholar, and Benjamin Edes and Moses Gill, printers, and others, in sustained dissent. Together they forged an effective system of open rebellion. They made speeches, published polemical essays and newspaper articles; they form-

---

2. Lillian C. Miller, et al., *In the Minds and Hearts of the People* (Greenwich, Conn.: New York Graphic Society, 1974), p. 39.

The BLOODY MASSACRE perpetrated in King—ı—Street BOSTON on March 5th 1770 by a party of the 29th REGt

Engrav'd Printed & Sold by PAUL REVERE BOSTON

UnhappyBoston! see thy Sons deplore,
Thy hallow'd Walks besmear'd with guiltless Gore:
While faithless P—n and his savage Bands,
With murd'rous Rancour stretch their bloody Hands;
Like fierce Barbarians grinning o'er their Prey,
Approve the Carnage and enjoy the Day.

If scalding drops fromRage from AnguishWrung,
If speechless Sorrows lab'ring for a Tongue,
Or if a weeping World can ought appease
The plaintive Ghosts of Victims such as these;
The Patriot's copious Tears for each are shed,
A glorious Tribute which embalms the Dead.

But know, Fate summons to that awful Goal,
WhereJUSTICE strips the Murd'rer of his Soul.
Should venalC—ts the scandal of the Land,
Snatch the relentless Villain from her Hand.
Keen Execrations on this Plate inscrib'd,
Shall reach a JUDGE who never can be brib'd.

The unhappy Sufferers were Messrs. SamL GRAY SamL MAVERICK, JAMS CALDWELL, CRISPUS ATTUCKS & PATK CARR
Killed. Six wounded; two of them (CHRISTR MONK & JOHN CLARK) Mortally

Colourd by ChristR Remich

165
The Bloody Massacre perpetrated in King Street
PAUL REVERE II, 1735-1818
1770, Boston, line engraving, colored by
Christian Remick (1726-1773), signed lower
right: "Engrav'd Printed & Sold by PAUL
REVERE BOSTON"; signed bottom right:
"Col⁴ by Christ⁵ Remick"; 9⅝ x 8⅝ in.
Museum of Fine Arts, gift of Watson Grant
Cutter. 67.1165

This engraving of the Boston Massacre is Revere's best-known print. Copied and reproduced
countless times throughout the eighteenth, nineteenth, and twentieth centuries, it was originally
issued twenty-three days after the first open
encounter between the British and the Bostonians, March 5, 1770. The print is historically
inaccurate. Revere knew the facts, but he
represented them in a politically inflammatory
manner. The British soldiers did not as in this
view, line up and directly open fire on the
Bostonians. In fact, the trial held six months
after the Massacre proved that the soldiers were
deliberately provoked by an angry mob and that
only two of them had actually fired. With the
help of this print, the event quickly became
ingrained in the public memory as an important
symbol of British tyranny.

Revere is known to have plagiarized this scene
from a young engraver, Henry Pelham, Copley's
half-brother. Pelham angrily wrote Revere on
March 29, 1770, calling his deed "one of the
most dishonorable Actions you could well be
guilty of."

Refs.: Clarence S. Brigham, *Paul Revere's Engravings*, New York, Atheneum, 1969, pp. 52-78. Metropolitan Museum of Art, *American Paintings &
Historical Prints from the Middendorf Collection*,
New York, 1967, pp. 88-91.

ulated the ideology of protest. They corresponded with other groups in
near and distant colonies, and they actively incited insurrection. The literary
and visual evidence of their energy that remains today is rich with the
iconography of protest, the ideals of liberty, and a growing sense of themselves as Americans.

Two cartoons issued in 1765, Paul Revere's *View of the Year 1765*
(no. 149) and John Singleton Copley's *The Deplorable State of the Nation*
(no. 150), indicate the complexity of the events that took place in that year
on both sides of the ocean.[3] Both cartoons were adapted from English
sources also published in 1765. The symbolism, which seems obscure and
complex to the modern mind accustomed to instantaneous visual impact,
can be easily understood if the cast of characters and individual events are
known. The cartoon made a point that few Bostonians or other Colonials
of the period missed.[4] One symbol among the many that appear in these
cartoons, the Liberty Tree, is fairly easily understood today. The large elm
tree stood at the corner of Essex and Newbury (now Washington) streets,
near the Common and the Mall. After the hanging in effigy of Andrew
Oliver on August 14, 1765, it was named the Liberty Tree, and a com-
memorative brass plaque was fastened to it.[5] From that point onward it
became a focal point of Revolutionary action and a strong symbol of
Revolutionary thought. Copley has included the plaque, *"The Tree of
Liberty Aug 14 1765,"* in his print, as well as a small piece of rope caught
in the branches. At the foot of the tree is the dying figure of America, with a
liberty cap on her head, a snake in her side. She is refusing *"the horrid box"*
that a royal presence in the form of a hovering woman offers her, saying,
"Take it Daughter it is only ye S[tam]p A[c]t." The box is labeled *"Pan-
dora's Box."* In Revere's engraving the hanging in effigy of Grenville and
Huske from the Liberty Tree on November 1, 1765, when the Stamp Act
took effect, is memorialized.

From this time onward the art and the political activity of Paul Revere
were a part of almost every protest, celebration, or Revolutionary action in
Boston. As a Mason and a member of the Sons of Liberty and the North End
Caucus, all powerful political organizations whose membership overlapped
one another, Revere was aware of every event of importance. When the
news of the Stamp Act repeal reached Boston on May 16, 1766, Bostonians
were much relieved and excited. Revere's print of the obelisk (no. 152) that
was erected on the Common to celebrate the event on May 19 was ready
that very day.

Parliament did not cease its efforts to tax the Colonists after the repeal of
the Stamp Act. In 1767 Charles Townshend, chancellor of the exchequer,

3. Edmund S. and Helen M. Morgan, *The Stamp Act Crisis: Prologue to Revolution* (New York:
   Collier Books, 1962) has a good description of events in Boston and elsewhere that are too
   complicated to go into here. According to them, "probably no American did more than Samuel
   Adams to bring on the revolutionary crisis" (p. 368).
4. E. P. Richardson, "Stamp Act Cartoons in the Colonies," *Pennsylvania Magazine of History and
   Biography* 96 (July 1972), 275-297.
5. Morgan, *The Stamp Act Crisis*, p. 173.

149

PAUL REVERE II, 1735-1818
A View of the Year 1765
Ca. 1765, Boston, line engraving, signed lower right: "Engrav'd Printed & Sold by P*Revere• Boston"; 6 x 7⅝ in.
American Antiquarian Society, Worcester, Massachusetts

This engraving protesting the Stamp Act was inspired by two sources, an English cartoon published in London in 1763 entitled *View of the Present Crisis,* and mob actions in Boston. On November 1, 1765, the Stamp Act took effect in the Colonies, and George Grenville and John Huske, supporters of the act in Parliament, were hung in effigy from the Liberty Tree, shown at the right. This event was deliberate and orderly in comparison to earlier mob action on August 14, when Andrew Oliver, the appointed stamp collector, and the Earl of Bute were hung in effigy, and the mob ransacked Oliver's house and wharf.

Ref.: Clarence S. Brigham, *Paul Revere's Engravings,* New York, Atheneum, 1969, pp. 22-25.

150

JOHN SINGLETON COPLEY, 1738-1815
The Deplorable State of America
1765, Boston, etching, inscribed in the hand of Pierre Du Simitiere (ca. 1736-1784): "The Original Print done in Boston by Jº S. Copley."; 10¼ x 14⅞ in.
The Library Company of Philadelphia, Philadelphia

This print is the only known impression of an etching by John Singleton Copley. It was found among the papers of Pierre Du Simitiere, an avid eighteenth century collector of documents pertaining to the Revolution. As a model for this print, Copley used an English cartoon called *The Deplorable State of America, or Sc——h Government,* which protested the Stamp Act. Political cartoons were a vivid form of protest in the eighteenth century. The figure of America, shown almost dead beneath the Tree of Liberty, dramatically emphasized what the Colonists felt would result from enforcement of the Stamp Act in 1765.

Ref.: E. P. Richardson, "Stamp Act Cartoons in the Colonies," *Pennsylvania Magazine of History and Biography* 96 (July 1972), 275-297.

151

BENJAMIN BLYTH, 1746-1787?
John Adams, 1735-1826
1766, Salem, Massachusetts, pastel on paper,
23 x 17½ in.
Massachusetts Historical Society, Boston

John Adams became involved in political issues
and events early in his law career when he heard
the Writs of Assistance case pleaded by James
Otis in 1761. Adams was a man of moderate
views who took a rational, legalistic attitude
toward the conflicts between the crown and the
colonies. He was nonetheless concerned about
the tyrannies of British rule. In his diary he
recorded that "the Year 1765 has been the most
remarkable Year of my Life. That enormous
Engine, fabricated by the british Parliament, for
battering down all the Rights and Liberties of
America, I mean the Stamp Act, has raised and
spread, thro the whole Continent, a Spirit that
will be recorded to our Honour, with all future
Generations."

Adams was one of three lawyers who accepted
the unpopular case of defending the British
soldiers who engaged in the Boston Massacre of
1770. Much to his credit, it was proved that the
soldiers had not been ordered to fire. Only two
of the many soldiers at the Massacre were
responsible for the deaths of five Bostonians.
Adams' political and diplomatic career grew in
importance to the emerging nation as he served
in the first and second Continental Congress, as
the first Minister to England after the Revolution, and as President of the United States
in 1797.

Ref.: L. H. Butterfield, ed., et al., *The Diary and
Autobiography of John Adams,* Cambridge, Mass.,
Harvard University Press, 1961, vol. 1, p. 263.

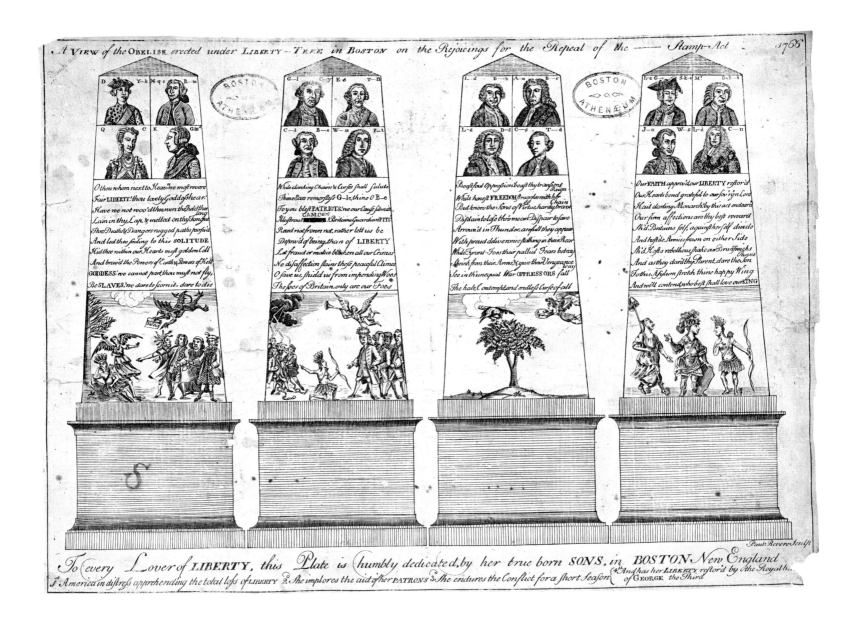

152
PAUL REVERE II, 1735-1818
A View of the Obelisk
1766, Boston, line engraving, signed lower right:
"Paul Revere Sculp"; 9½ x 13½ in.
The Boston Athenaeum

Three days after news of the repeal of the Stamp
Act was received in Boston, the townspeople
joyously celebrated. John Rowe, wealthy merchant and Whig sympathizer, recorded in his
diary for May 19 that "in the evening there was
very Grand Illuminations all over the Town. In
the Common there was an Obelisk very
beautifully Decorated & very grand fireworks
were displayed."

This print of the obelisk is one of Revere's
rarest and most original engravings. The twelve
portraits encircling the top of the obelisk are
Englishmen considered friends of the colonies,
including John Wilkes and William Pitt. The
story of the Stamp Act and its repeal is explained
beneath the portraits where the Indian represents the American colonies. Made of oiled
paper and lit from within by 280 lights, it was
"to be placed under the Tree of Liberty, as a
standing monument of this glorious Aera."
However, "by accident [it] took Fire about One
o'clock, and was consumed." Because Revere
had his print ready for sale on the day the celebration took place, it seems probable that he had
a hand in designing and erecting the obelisk.

Refs.: Clarence S. Brigham, *Paul Revere's Engravings,* New York, Atheneum, 1969, pp. 25-31. Anne
Rowe Cunningham, ed., *Letters and Diary of John
Rowe, Boston Merchant,* Boston, W. B. Clarke,
1903, p. 95.

proposed new duties on imported lead, printer's paper, and tea, the revenue
from which would pay royally appointed officials in the Colonies. In order
to collect these and other taxes a new board of customs commissioners was
appointed for America. Again Boston's merchants were in the vanguard of
protest activity. John Rowe, merchant, was the principal originator of a
nonimportation agreement that spread throughout the Colonies with some
success in 1768 and 1769.[6] John Hancock (no. 173) deliberately provoked
an incident on June 11, 1768, when his ship *Liberty* brought in an illegal
cargo of wine.

Sam Adams, as clerk of the House, proposed a letter of protest against
the acts to be sent to all Colonial assemblies. The Circular Letter, approved
February 11, 1768, and forwarded for consideration by the other Colonies,
was ordered to be revoked, and ignored by Lord Hillsborough, Britain's new
secretary of state.[7] In an act of political daring, and in response to the
Liberty incident, ninety-two members of the Massachusetts House voted on
June 30, 1768, not to rescind the letter. To commemorate the event, fifteen
members of the Sons of Liberty commissioned their fellow member, Paul
Revere, to make a silver punch bowl. The bowl (no. 155), an object of
simple beauty but complex symbolism, has since become an icon of American political liberty.

On October 1, 1768, the British responded to Massachusetts Bay
Colony's actions by sending troops to occupy Boston (no. 154). The troops
had an uneasy time; with no place to live they were finally ordered to be
quartered in public buildings. Their presence was bitterly resented, and after
a year and a half of occupation an angry local mob provoked some of them
to gunfire on March 5, 1770. Revere's print, *The Bloody Massacre perpetrated in King Street . . .* (no. 165) could be thought of as a journalistic
editorial report of current events. Ready for sale soon after the action had
taken place, it served to further the Colonial cause by inaccurately representing the scene. In 1770 Revere also issued his version of the 1768 landing
of the troops (no. 158) capitalizing on anti-British sentiment. As he has
represented it, the troops are the only people to be seen; no Bostonians are
pictured, so that the troops appear to be invading Boston, rather than merely
landing. The large ships of war surround the town, and long boats, crowded
with soldiers, ply back and forth from the ships to the wharf.

Protest began anew in 1773 after a relatively quiet time in Boston following the Massacre. The only activity of importance had been the start of a
Committee of Correspondence in 1772 in response to the knowledge that the
governor, Thomas Hutchinson, and other high officials were now paid
directly by royal funds. They were no longer under the control of the
colony's legislature. With governmental power slipping from their reach,
another economic crisis with the passage of the Tea Act in 1773 inflamed the
spirits of all Bostonians—radical or moderate. The Tea Act involved a basic
commodity and thus affected the entire population. Revere's cartoon *The*

6. Miller et al., *Minds and Hearts,* pp. 101-106.
7. Ibid., pp. 103-105.

156

PAUL REVERE II, 1735-1818
Liberty bowl

1768, Boston, silver, marked: "REVERE" in rectangle slanted at right of center point on bottom, inscribed in script below the rim: "Caleb Hopkins, Nath¹ Barber, John White, Willᵐ Mackay, Danˡ Malcolm, Benjⁿ Goodwin, John Welsh, Fortescue Vernon, Danˡ Parker, John Marston, Ichabod Jones, John Homer, Willᵐ Bowes, Peter Boyer, Benjᵃ Cobb." Engraved on one side with circle with a scroll and foliated frame topped by a Liberty Cap flanked by flags inscribed respectively: "Magna/Charta" and "Bill of/Rights," inside the circle is inscribed: "Nº 45./Wilkes & Liberty" over a torn page labeled "Generall/Warrants"; inscribed on the other side: "To the Memory of the glorious NINETY-TWO: Members/of the Honᵇˡ House of Representatives of the Massachusetts-Bay,/who, undaunted by the insolent Menaces of Villains in Power,/from a Strict Regard to Conscience, and the LIBERTIES/of their Constituents, on the 30th of June 1768,/Voted NOT TO RESCIND."; H. 5½ in. (uneven), DIAM. (base)

5¾ in. (uneven), DIAM. (lip) 11 in. (uneven)
Museum of Fine Arts, gift by subscription and Francis Bartlett Fund. 49.45

Perhaps no single piece of American silver is as well known as this punch bowl made by Revere in 1768. The Liberty Bowl, as it is more widely known, was made in honor of ninety-two members of the Massachusetts House of Representatives who refused to rescind a circular letter they had sent to the other Colonies protesting the Townshend Acts. When this bowl was first used, John Rowe noted in his diary for August 1, 1768: "Spent afternoon at the General Merchants Meeting at Fanewill Hall at which place there were present sixty-two—sixty of which signed an agreement I have on File not to Import any Goods. Spent the evening at Mʳ Barber's Insurance Office & the Silver Bowl was this evening for the first time introduced, Nº45. Weighs 45 ounces & holds 45 gills . . ." The bowl stands as a memorial to those men who defied the direct order of the king's Secretary of Colonial Affairs in order to follow the dictates of their conscience. In the years before the

Revolution, the phrase "the Glorious Ninety-Two" became a call to patriotism.

The simple, elegant form of the bowl demonstrates Revere's skill as a silver craftsman. Its shape has since become archetypal in American silver manufacturing, with facsimiles made every year as trophies and gifts. The Liberty Bowl itself has continued to arouse the imagination and patriotism of Americans. In 1949 it was acquired by the Museum of Fine Arts, partially through a public subscription advertised in a newspaper campaign. A letter was also circulated to the Boston Public School system, asking for donations from school children to "enshrine the Paul Revere Liberty Bowl in Boston at the Museum of Fine Arts where it will remain on exhibition as a symbol of our early struggle for freedom." At that time it was called the nation's "third most cherished historical treasure" after the Declaration of Independence and the Constitution.

Refs.: Buhler, *American Silver in the Museum of Fine Arts,* vol. 2, pp. 408-409, no. 356. Anne Rowe Cunningham, ed., *Letters and Diary of John Rowe, Boston Merchant,* Boston, W. B. Clarke, 1903, p. 171.

To the Memory of the glorious NINETY-TWO: Members of the Hon.ble House of Representatives of the Massachusetts-Bay, who, undaunted by the insolent Menaces of Villains in Power, from a strict Regard to Conscience, and the LIBERTIES of their Constituents, on the 30th of June 1768.

Voted) NOT TO RESCIND.

157

Attributed to JOHN BACON, 1740-1799
Figure of John Wilkes, 1727-1797
Ca. 1765, Derby, England, soft-paste porcelain,
H. 12⅜ in.
Museum of Fine Arts, bequest of Mrs. Martin
Brimmer. 06.2439

This small polychrome Derby figurine celebrates the Englishman John Wilkes, long a member of the opposition in Britain. His hand rests on the Bill of Rights, while the cherub below holds a Liberty Cap. At Wilkes' feet is a volume of the writings of John Locke. All of these were symbols of Wilkes' opposition to arbitrary government. Wilkes was imprisoned in London in 1763 for criticizing the king in his magazine, *The North Briton*. After being released from prison, he was elected to Parliament but was denied his seat. Colonists felt that the persecution of Wilkes paralleled the abridgement of their rights as Englishmen. The references on the Liberty Bowl to "No. 45" (the issue of Wilkes' magazine in which he criticized the king), and "Wilkes and Liberty," clearly show how Colonists related the abuse of Wilkes to their own cause. The bowl itself was appropriately made from about 45 ounces of silver, another evidence of the high regard in which the American radicals held Wilkes.

Ref.: Pauline Maier, "John Wilkes and American Disillusionment with Britain," *William and Mary Quarterly* 3rd ser., 20 (1963), 373-395.

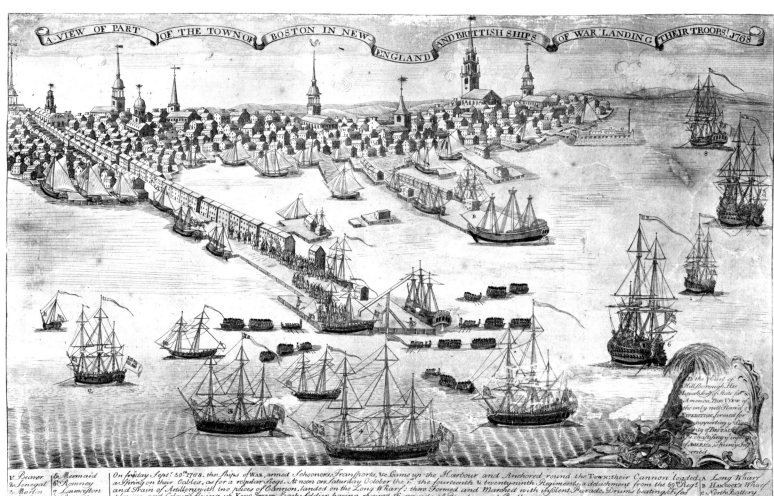

A VIEW OF PART OF THE TOWN OF BOSTON IN NEW ENGLAND AND BRITTISH SHIPS OF WAR LANDING THEIR TROOPS! 1768

1. Beaver
2. Senegal
3. Martin
4. Glasgow
5. Mermaid
6. Romney
7. Launceston
8. Bonetta

On friday Sept.r 30th 1768, the Ships of War, armed Schooners, Transports, &c. Came up the Harbour and Anchored round the Town: their Cannon loaded. a Spring on their Cables, as for a regular Siege. At noon on Saturday October the 1.st the fourteenth & twentyninth Regiments, a detachment from the 59.th Regt. and Train of Artillery, with two pieces of Cannon, landed on the Long Wharf: there Formed and Marched with insolent Parade, Drums beating, Fifes playing, and Colours flying, up KING STREET. Each Soldier having received 16 rounds of Powder and Ball.

A. Long Wharf
B. Hancock's Wharf
C. North Battery

ENGRAVED PRINTED, & SOLD by PAUL REVERE, BOSTON.

To the Earl of Hillsborough, His Majest.y Sec.y of State for America, This View of the only well Plan'd EXPEDITION, formed for supporting y.e dignity of BRITAIN & chastising y.e insolence of AMERICA, is humbly Insc.d

120

155
PAUL REVERE II, 1735-1818
A View of the Town of Boston in New England and Brittish Ships of War Landing their Troops!
1770, Boston, line engraving, signed lower right: "ENGRAVED, PRINTED & SOLD by PAUL REVERE BOSTON"; 8⅝ x 15⅜ in.
The Boston Athenaeum

One of Christian Remick's six watercolor views of the landing of the troops probably gave Paul Revere II the graphic representation necessary for this engraving. The ships and the soldiers landing in the longboats in Revere's print and in Remick's watercolors are similar. While Revere was influenced by and may have collaborated with Remick, his view is clearly different from any by Remick. It shows the whole town of Boston with a perspective and detail reminiscent of the Burgis view of 1743 (no. 23). Revere has thus skillfully combined two sources in this print, which he dedicated to "the Earl of Hillsborough, His Majests. Secy. of State for America." While offering a semblance of humility in the dedication, Revere at the same time described the British soldiers' parade up the Long Wharf as "insolent," a word that was not lost on Bostonians.

Ref.: Clarence S. Brigham, *Paul Revere's Engravings,* New York, Atheneum, 1969, pp. 79-85.

Able Doctor or America Swallowing the Bitter Draught (no. 170) vividly reflects how Americans and British felt and acted after the "Tea Party." The "Tea Party," which took place in Boston Harbor on December 16, 1773, was the last outbreak of large-scale mob violence in Boston before April 19, 1775. England's reaction was to close the port of Boston until reparations had been made for damages. Boston's pace-setting action in dumping the resented cargo of tea into the harbor signaled groups in other ports, and several "Tea Parties" took place elsewhere in the Colonies. Plans for this event, and many others, had probably been made at the Green Dragon Tavern (no. 167) in the North End not far from the dock area. It was the physical center of patriotic organization.

In addition to the Boston Port Bill, which was clearly punitive, other bills were proposed and passed by Parliament in 1774. An act for *"Regulating the Government of Massachusetts Bay"* gave greater power to the governor of the colony and thus to the crown. He could appoint most high officials, including the upper house of the legislature, the Council, prohibit town meetings, and exercise a veto over the Council. Juries were to be appointed by the sheriff. The political power and legal rights of the people of Massachusetts were effectively curtailed. Two other of the "Coercive Acts" provided for the quartering of troops in private homes and for the trial in London of any royal official who commited a capital offense in the line of duty.[8]

General Thomas Gage was appointed governor with an express mandate to keep political activity at a minimum and ease the tense situation. From this time onward Revolutionary activities increasingly moved outside the town of Boston to the surrounding countryside, and those loyal to the crown moved into Boston to obtain the protection of Gage and his troops. That Revolutionary energies were forced underground is evident in Paul Revere's description in 1798 of his place in the situation: *"In the Fall of 1774 and Winter of 1775 I was one of upwards of thirty, chiefly mechanics, who formed our selves in to a Committee for the purpose of watching the Movements of the British Soldiers, and gaining every intelegence of the movements of the Tories. We held our meetings at the Green Dragon Tavern. We were so carefull that our meetings should be kept Secret; that every time we met, every person swore upon the Bible, that they would not discover any of our transactions, But to Messrs.* HANCOCK, ADAMS, *Doctors* WARREN, CHURCH, *and one or two more."*[9] In the spring of 1775 Massachusetts was declared to be in a state of rebellion. The stage was set for action by April 19.

Paul Revere's participation in the battles of Lexington and Concord was only as citizen-patriot, not as artist-craftsman, or soldier. He was in the center of the action; unlike Amos Doolittle, who recorded the battles in print (nos. 176-177), he was unable to go home to his engraver's copperplate and draw the scenes of which he had been an eyewitness. After April 19

8. Ibid., pp. 177-178.
9. *Paul Revere's Three Accounts of his Famous Ride,* introduction by Edmund S. Morgan (Boston: Massachusetts Historical Society, 1968), letter to Jeremy Belknap.

160

EDWARD TRUMAN, active 1741
Thomas Hutchinson, 1711-1780
1741, London, oil on canvas, signed lower left:
"Edward Truman 1741"; 27¼ x 22¾ in.
Massachusetts Historical Society, Boston

Hutchinson was in London when this portrait
was painted. He had been a representative to the
Massachusetts House of Representatives for the
previous four years and served again in that
position until 1749, when he became a coun-
cillor. Prior to the Revolution, he became
governor of the colony, a position he never
sought. Before the controversy began between
the Colonies and Britain, he was a well-
respected public servant of Massachusetts Bay,
but his conservative views on the relationship
of the Colonies to the English crown marked
him as a traitor when citizens of Massachusetts
Bay began to assert their rights. This forced his
unhappy exile to London in 1774.

Little is known of Edward Truman, the painter
of this portrait. He was an English painter and
is known to have painted one other portrait.
The painting of Hutchinson suffered at the
hands of the mob that ransacked Hutchinson's
house during the Stamp Act riots; subsequent
restoration partially obscures Truman's original
work.

162

JOHN SINGLETON COPLEY, 1738-1815
Thomas Flucker, 1719-1783
Ca. 1770-1771, Boston, oil on canvas, 28⅞ x
24 in.
Bowdoin College Museum of Art, bequest of
Mrs. Lucy Flucker Knox Thatcher

Thomas Flucker was one of the many Loyalists
who left Boston for England in the turbulent
years immediately preceding the Revolution. Of
French Huguenot descent, he was related to
both the Bowdoins and the Waldos through his
two marriages. From the position of justice of
the peace in 1756, he eventually became the last
secretary of state of the colony. He left for
London with General Gage in September 1775,
and his wife followed on March 17, 1776.

This is one of Copley's most intense and striking
Kit-Kat size portraits. He has revealed the
strength and determination of Flucker, a man
faced with the reality of separating himself from
his family and a secure way of life. His daughter,
Lucy, married the patriot Henry Knox in March
1774. She remained in Boston while her parents
spent the remainder of their lives in England,
receiving annual stipends from the British
government as Loyalist refugees.

Ref.: Marvin S. Sadik, *Colonial and Federal Portraits at Bowdoin College,* Brunswick, Maine,
Bowdoin College Museum of Art, 1966, pp. 79-85.

Boston was in command of the British; the patriots and the provincial government were forced to flee to Watertown.

Paul Revere's only record of his activity on April 18 and 19 remains in two written depositions, probably made in 1775 at the request of the provincial congress, and in a letter to Jeremy Belknap, corresponding secretary of the Massachusetts Historical Society of 1798.[10] His midnight ride has become as much a part of American popular historical culture as his print of the Boston Massacre or the silver Liberty Bowl. The artist-craftsman was also a man of action in the American tradition. Called by Dr. Joseph Warren to ride to Lexington to warn Sam Adams and John Hancock, as well as the surrounding countryside, of the impending arrival of the British troops, Revere proceeded at a rapid pace through Charlestown, along the Mystic Road to Lexington. He described his route and his ride in detail in his depositions, but it was not until 1798 that he remembered to include a description of his lantern signal system. Stopped at several points by British soldiers, he was *often insulted by the officers calling [him] damned Rebel &c. &c.* When he was captured, a British officer said to him: " *'We are now going towards your friends and if you attempt to run, or we are insulted, we will blow your Brains out.' I told him he might do as he pleased,*" Revere replied.[11] Revere, along with Hancock and Adams, was able to escape safely.

Along with many of his fellow patriots, Revere lived in Watertown during the British seige of Boston in 1775-1776. The Provincial government was established there and directed civil and military affairs for the state as best it could. During this time Revere printed the paper currency for the government, which, although almost worthless in purchasing power, was an absolute necessity for the new regime. The only battle fought during the British occupation was in Charlestown at Breed's and at Bunker Hill on June 17, 1775, soon after Lexington and Concord (nos. 179-181). The British won, but at great cost. They lost half of their force against the ill-trained but heroic Provincial militia. The death of Dr. Joseph Warren, as well as the performance of the Americans, who managed to inflict heavy casualties in spite of being outnumbered and outmaneuvered by the British soldiers, made this early battle in the war memorable as an example of patriotism and heroic action.

The British, now firmly ensconced in Boston, transformed the city, as Henry Pelham reported while he surveyed for his map in 1775-1776 (no. 188). The population dwindled to 6,000 citizens, with approximately 13,000 troops occupying the city. During the winter every possible tree and fence was hacked down and many wooden houses were torn down for use as firewood. Even the Liberty Tree was cut down on January 2, 1776 — reportedly it made fourteen cords of wood.[12] The best mansions of the town

172
JOHN SINGLETON COPLEY, 1738-1815
Samuel Adams, 1722-1803
Ca. 1770-1772, Boston, oil on canvas, 50 x 40½ in.
Museum of Fine Arts, deposited by the City of Boston

Copley's portrait of Sam Adams is one of his most powerfully expressive characterizations of a tense moment and a forceful personality. There is a primitive directness in Adams' facial expression and thrusting hand gesture, as he points to the papers of state. Copley painted him as he faced Chief Justice Thomas Hutchinson in a dramatic confrontation over the Boston Massacre case in 1770.

Samuel Adams' political career began in 1764-65 with the opposition to the Sugar Acts and the Stamp Acts. A principal organizer of the "Loyal Nine" and Sons of Liberty, he was a central figure in stirring up mob violence in the protests of 1765. From this time until the actual separation of the Colonies from Great Britain in 1775-76, Adams was the Bostonian most responsible for perpetuating Colonial resistance in terms of ideology and action.

A natural leader of men and a person with a questionable financial reputation, his greatest talent lay in his ability to fire the imaginations of all classes of citizens. Adams wrote incessantly for newspapers between 1765 and 1775, developing his arguments on the relationship of the Colonies and the mother country to a fine point, rarely neglecting to mention the tyrannies of British rule. He had the political advantage of being a member of the General Court during the entire Revolutionary period. In his position as clerk of the House, he was able to express his incendiary opinions on official documents and to direct forceful opposition against local government officials and many British measures.

Pointing to the Massachusetts Charter as support of Colonial rights against the crown in this dramatic portrait, Adams is pictured at the peak of his career as a volatile political organizer. Although he later served as governor of Massachusetts after the Revolution, his political talents and influence waned and his reputation rested mainly on his earlier Revolutionary activities.

Ref.: Museum of Fine Arts, Boston, *American Paintings in the Museum of Fine Arts,* Boston, 1969, vol. 1, p. 74, no. 286, fig. 69.

10. All versions are reproduced in facsimile and transcription in *Paul Revere's Three Accounts of his Famous Ride* (Boston: Massachusetts Historical Society, 1968).
11. Ibid.
12. Justin Winsor, ed., *The Memorial History of Boston* (Boston: Ticknor, 1881), vol. 3, p. 159.

GREEN DRAGON TAVERN

Where we met to Plan the Consignment of few Shiploads of Tea.
Dec 16 1773

John Johnson
7 Water Street
Boston Mass.
1773

167

JOHN JOHNSTON, 1753-1818
Green Dragon Tavern
1773, Boston, pen and ink with watercolor
wash, signed bottom center: "John Johnson";
8⅛ x 12¼ in.
American Antiquarian Society, Worcester,
Massachusetts

Taverns were traditionally the meeting places
for social and political groups and were an
integral part of neighborhood life. This tavern
in the North End of Boston, the Green Dragon,
was purchased in 1764 by Revere's own
Masonic lodge, the Lodge of Saint Andrew, and
was used as a regular meeting place. The Sons
of Liberty, several of whom were also members
of the Lodge of Saint Andrew, also met at the
Green Dragon. It was here, according to the
inscription at the bottom of the drawing, that
the Boston Tea Party was planned in 1773. Paul
Revere, who lived in the North End, participated in the Tea Party and was a member of the
Sons of Liberty and the Masons, undoubtedly
visited the tavern often.

Few watercolor views survive of eighteenth century Boston. This small sketch has been saved
probably because of the importance of the
Green Dragon Tavern during the Revolution.
John Johnston, son of Thomas Johnston, the
early eighteenth century Boston artist and engraver, is better known for his portrait painting.

Ref.: Sinclair Hitchings, "Thomas Johnston,"
Boston Prints and Printmakers, 1670-1775, Boston,
Colonial Society of Massachusetts, 1973, pp.
121-122.

Nº X Engraved for Royal American Magazine. Vol. I.

The able Doctor, or America Swallowing the Bitter Draught.

170

PAUL REVERE II, 1735-1818
*The Able Doctor, or America Swallowing the
Bitter Draught*
1774, Boston, line engraving, signed lower right:
"P Revere Sculp"; 7 x 4⅞ in.
Massachusetts Historical Society, Boston

The June 1774 issue of the *Royal American
Magazine,* published by Isaiah Thomas, contained this political cartoon, which Revere
copied from the *London Magazine* of April
1774. The cartoon symbolically recalls the
Boston Tea Party of the previous December,
which had been incited by the large-scale dumping of cheap tea on the colonial market in an
effort to relieve the financial problems of the
East India Company. Here America, in the form
of a woman, is being forced to drink tea, "the
Bitter Draught," by a member of parliament.
In defiance she spits the tea back into his face.
In the man's coat pocket is a copy of the Boston
Port Bill that closed Boston and ordered all
ships to land in Salem, Massachusetts, until the
East India Company and the revenue officers
involved had been compensated for the damages
wreaked by the mob on the night of the
Tea Party.

Ref.: Clarence S. Brigham, *Paul Revere's Engravings,* New York, Atheneum, 1969, pp. 117-118.

173

JOHN SINGLETON COPLEY, 1738-1815
John Hancock, 1737-1793
1765, Boston, oil on canvas, signed and dated lower left: "J.S. Copley pinx 1765"; 49½ x 40½ in.
Museum of Fine Arts, deposited by the City of Boston

Soon after John Hancock inherited an immense fortune from his uncle, Thomas Hancock, he commissioned this portrait by Copley. His rise to wealth and status as the richest young man in Massachusetts is indicated in the richness of his clothing with its gold buttons and braid, and the massive account book upon which he rests his left hand. Copley has clearly pictured a man who, unlike his uncle, was neither mentally nor physically imposing. Prone to headaches and illness, Hancock was an indecisive man who was swayed easily by the stronger personalities of men about him.

Had this portrait been made five years later, Hancock might have been surrounded by a different set of attributes, for by this time he had become an ardent patriot and a supporter of colonial resistance to the British trade regulations. He continued to be known for his extravagantly high style of living, but his money also bought him popular support during politically and economically troubled times. Hancock, as a merchant whose large profits depended on the freedom to trade outside British regulation and the avoidance of customs duties, was naturally opposed to the strict trade laws formulated by Parliamentary acts beginning in the early 1760's. In 1768 Hancock's ship *Liberty* was seized by royal customs inspectors for illegally importing wine. John Adams defended Hancock on this occasion. Hancock's subsequent exoneration and his defiance of royal authority by inciting mob retaliation landed him in the radical camp of Boston politics. He was described "as closely attached to the hindermost Part of Mr. Adams [Samuel] as the Rattles are affixed to the Tail of a Rattle Snake" by Chief Justice Oliver in 1769.

After this initial activity, Hancock wavered between the radical and moderate patriot cause, serving as representative to the First and Second Continental Congresses and as the first governor of Massachusetts under the new Con-stitution from 1780 to 1785. Hancock, while a popular figure, was not a political leader nor did he have the business acumen of his uncle. A good part of his fortune disintegrated because of his bad management and his inattention to his business.

Refs.: Museum of Fine Arts, Boston, *American Paintings in the Museum of Fine Arts, Boston*, Boston, 1969, vol. 1, pp. 63-64, no. 264. *Sibley's Harvard Graduates; biographical sketches of those who attended Harvard College . . .*, Boston, Massachusetts Historical Society, 1873-19—, vol. 13, pp. 416-446.

were occupied by the commanding officers: General Clinton took over John Hancock's house on Beacon Hill, Burgoyne was in the Bowdoin house, and when General Howe arrived he lived in the Province House, former mansion of the governors of Massachusetts Bay Colony.[13] The soldiers of lesser rank fended for themselves as best they could; some in barracks, some in deserted houses, others in homes of loyalists. Churches were pulled down, and Old South Church was made into a riding school. Faneuil Hall, the former Town Hall, was used as a theater.[14]

General George Washington, who had been made commander in chief of the Continental forces in June, was encamped across the river in Cambridge. Ironically he occupied the elegant Vassall house, which had been deserted by the Loyalist John Vassall, as he fled to Boston and later to England. Washington began to gather and organize his forces, such as they were, and made plans to free Boston. With the news of the fall of Fort Ticonderoga in New York, it was decided to bring the cannon to Boston and place them on Dorchester Heights, the commanding peninsula to the south of Boston. From this advantage the Continental forces could perhaps retake the town. Henry Knox was in charge of dragging the cannon south, and they were in place by the beginning of March 1776. Preliminary skirmishes took place, but before a large-scale battle could erupt General Howe evacuated the British troops and all those Loyalists who wished to leave, on March 17, 1776. Both sides were short of supplies and ammunition by the end of the winter, and a smallpox epidemic raged in Boston. General Washington (no. 186) won his first victory of the war without a battle. Bostonians repossessed their city and started life anew.

While the war was fought for another seven years, the British never reappeared in Boston. Periodically there were rumors that they were coming and temporary panic resulted. The forts were maintained — Paul Revere was commander of Castle William, now Fort Independence, in Boston Harbor — and hardships of a wartime economy were endured. Many Bostonians served in the Continental Army, and the leaders of the rebellion served as governors of the new country in Philadelphia. Sam Adams, John Hancock, John Adams, James Otis, and others whose ideas and power had been instrumental in bringing about the Colonies' separation from the British Empire now helped guide the new nation.

174
JOHN SINGLETON COPLEY, 1738-1815
Joseph Warren, 1741-1775
Ca. 1772-1774, Boston, oil on canvas, 50 x 40 in. Museum of Fine Arts, gift of Buckminster Brown, M.D., through Church M. Matthews, Jr., trustee. 95.1366

Copley revealed the qualities of the ideal eighteenth century man when he painted Dr. Joseph Warren, scholar and patriot. Rich, softly modeled tones, relaxed pose, and an easy, generous expression on his face seem to make visible the personality of Warren, who was respected and admired by all who knew him. A close friend and associate of Paul Revere, Dr. Joseph Warren was known as "Chief" among Boston's radicals before the Revolution. He was leader in the North End Caucus, the Masons, and the Sons of Liberty. He died at the Battle of Bunker Hill in 1775.

Warren graduated from Harvard in 1759 and later studied medicine. When Copley painted this portrait, Warren was deeply involved in political events to the neglect of his medical practice. He is nonetheless shown here with his elbow resting on some anatomical drawings, as a tribute to his medical skills. He wrote frequent articles against British tyranny for the newspapers and became well known as an impassioned orator for the colonists' cause. His association with Samuel Adams, James Otis, John Hancock, and Paul Revere was close, and the five men were organizers, instigators, or participants in almost every argument or skirmish during the era that immediately preceded the armed conflict of the Revolution.

Ref.: Museum of Fine Arts, Boston, *American Paintings in the Museum of Fine Arts, Boston*, Boston, 1969, vol. 1, p. 77, no. 292.

13. Ibid., p. 155.
14. Ibid., pp. 159-161.

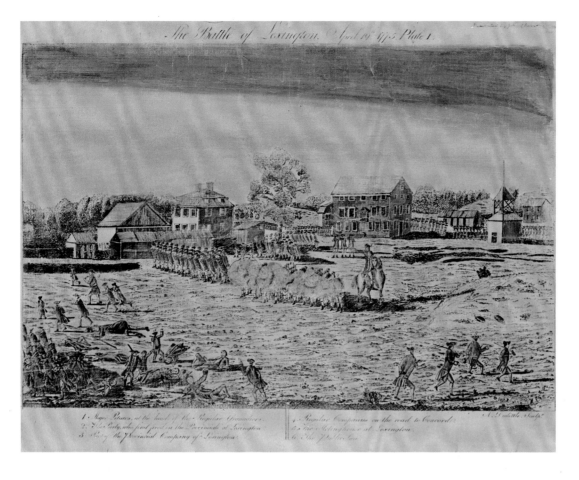

The Battle of Lexington, April 19 1775. Plate 1.

1. Major Pitcairn at the head of the Regular Grenadiers.
2. The Party who first fired on the Provincials at Lexington.
3. Part of the Provincial Company of Lexington.
4. Regular Companies on the road to Concord.
5. The Meetinghouse at Lexington.
6. The Publick Inn.

A. Doolittle Sculp.

Plate III. The Engagement at the North Bridge in Concord.

1. The Detachment of the Regulars who fired first on the Provincials at the Bridge.
2. The Provincials headed by Colonel Robinson & Major Buttrick at The Bridge.

A. Doolittle.

175

AMOS DOOLITTLE, 1754-1832
The Battle of Lexington, April 19th, 1775
1775, New Haven, Connecticut, hand-colored line engraving, signed lower right: "A. Doolittle Sculpt"; 13 x 17½ in.
The Connecticut Historical Society, Hartford

The first battles of the Revolution at Lexington and Concord became a call to arms for the Colonials, whose growing resentment of British military occupation was finally able to surface in armed conflict. The news of the battles of April 19, 1775, spread quickly throughout the Colonies. Militia companies from surrounding areas, including the Connecticut governor's Second Company of Guards, came immediately to the aid of the Massachusetts regiments. The Connecticut Guards under the command of Benedict Arnold arrived in Cambridge by April 29, staying three or four weeks before returning home. Among their ranks was Amos Doolittle, a New Haven engraver. At some point during this month he journeyed out to Lexington and Concord, where he made sketches and took notes on the battle action. Upon his return to New Haven, he made four views of the battles and the towns of Lexington and Concord, which he prepared for sale by December 13, 1775. His prints, which are historically and topographically accurate, were the first American prints of a Revolutionary battle scene and as such must have caused a popular sensation and sold widely.

Doolittle has taken some artistic license in his rendering of the Battle of Lexington, in that the British troops fought in a far more disorderly way than they appear to be doing here. Like Revere before him in his print of the Boston Massacre in 1770, Doolittle capitalized on patriotic sentiment by emphasizing the tyranny of the British with their superior forces lined up in regimental fashion firing on the irregularly trained and gathered Americans. In reality, the British were surprised and unprepared to meet the colonial forces.

Ref.: Ian M. G. Quimby, "The Doolittle Engravings of the Battle of Lexington and Concord," *Winterthur Portfolio 4*, Charlottesville, University of Virginia Press, 1968, pp. 83-108.

177

AMOS DOOLITTLE, 1754-1832
The Engagement at the North Bridge in Concord
1775, New Haven, Connecticut, hand-colored line engraving, signed lower right: "A. Doolittle Sculpt"; 13 x 17½ in.
The Connecticut Historical Society, Hartford

The battles of Lexington and Concord came about as a result of General Gage's orders to destroy provincial military supplies that were

stored in Concord. Gage started preparing for his mission on April 15 in secret, but his objectives and operations were soon open knowledge to the patriots. Paul Revere, William Dawes, Joseph Warren, and other Sons of Liberty prepared their own plans to warn the countryside of the impending action. It was also rumored that John Hancock and Sam Adams, who were visiting in Lexington, were to be arrested, so the patriots were interested in rescuing their own comrades, as well as stopping a military operation. It was at this time that Revere devised his warning system with lanterns, one if the troops came by land over the Boston Neck, two if the troops came by sea across the Charles River.

The British expedition forces got off to a slow start across the Charles River, the sea route, and all along the road they encountered rumors about the local militia waiting for them in Lexington. Revere and Dawes made their rides during the night, and sent the alarm through the countryside. After the skirmish at Lexington, in which the British far outnumbered the

Americans, the British troops set out for the goal of their mission, the military stores at Colonel Barrett's farm in Concord. Crossing the North Bridge on the Concord River, the British were met by a large band of Americans, guarding the bridge. Shots were again fired, resulting in several dead and wounded on each side. This time the British, who were outnumbered, fled back to the town of Concord, and then retreated to Boston, thus ending the incidents that were to permanently change the crown-colonial relationship.

Ref.: Ian M. G. Quimby, "The Doolittle Engravings of the Battle of Lexington and Concord," *Winterthur Portfolio 4*, Charlottesville, University of Virginia Press, 1968, pp. 83-108.

181

JOHN TRUMBULL, 1756-1843
The Battle of Bunker Hill
Ca. 1786-1820, London, oil on canvas, 20 x 29¾ in.
Private collection

When Abigail Adams saw the first version of this battle sketch in London in 1786 her "blood shivered" and she "felt a faintness at [her] heart." She recognized Trumbull as "the first painter who has undertaken to immortalize by his pencil those great actions, that gave birth to our nation. By this means he will not only secure his own fame, but transmit to posterity characters and actions which will command the admiration of future ages."

The heroic death of the patriot Dr. Joseph Warren at the Battle of Bunker Hill was an event that immediately captured the imagination of Americans. The tragedy of this moment was understood and enlarged upon by Trumbull, who recreated the death of Warren in almost theatrical terms. The actual participants in the battle—Putnam, Prescott, Howe, Clinton, and others—are identifiable in the confusion and turbulence of battle surrounding them. Warren's fallen body lies in the center of the scene, dramatically lighted, as his comrades keep back

(continued overleaf)

the British soldiers. Warren, fighting in the ranks during this battle, was to have assumed command of the Provincial forces, so his battlefield death was all the more tragic.

Trumbull painted eight Revolutionary War events in a highly romantic manner, of which *The Battle of Bunker Hill* was the first. He further developed the tradition of historical painting initiated by Benjamin West with his painting *The Death of General Wolfe* in 1771.

Trumbull's ultimate intention was to install large versions of his paintings in the United States Capitol. He was successful in securing a contract for four pictures in 1818: *The Declaration of Independence, The Surrender of the British to the American Forces at Saratoga, The Surrender of the British to the American Forces at Yorktown,* and *The Resignation of General Washington at Annapolis.* He finished the commission in 1828 at the age of seventy-two.

The Battle of Bunker Hill, the only event Trumbull actually witnessed, was later engraved in Stuttgart, Germany. The print edition did not appear until 1797, twenty-two years after the battle, and was not a financial success, in spite of Abigail Adams' prediction. Trumbull was known, however, in his own lifetime as the new republic's "patriot-artist."

Refs.: Theodore Sizer, ed., *The Autobiography of Colonel John Trumbull Patriot-Artist 1756-1843,* New Haven, Conn.: Yale University Press, 1953. Theodore Sizer, *The Works of Colonel John Trumbull,* New Haven, Conn.: Yale University Press, 1950, p. 72.

179

RICHARD WILLIAMS
Plan of the Heights of Charles Town and Works taken from the Rebels on the 17th June 1775
1775, Boston, pen and ink, signed lower right: "Rd Williams Lt R:W:Fuziliers"; 10¾ x 17½ in.
Mrs. Ellery Sedgwick

This British military plan of the fortifications and battle at Breed's Hill in Charlestown clearly demonstrates the superior position of the British during the battle. They were firmly encamped on a narrow point of land (at the left in the drawing), thus preventing the Colonial forces (to the right in the "Rebel's Redout" in the picture) from escaping. Tactical maps and plans were made in great numbers during the Revolution. Men with engineering and drafting skills such as Lieutenant Williams were no doubt in great demand on both sides of the conflict.

180

BERNARD ROMANS, ca. 1720-1843
An Exact View of The Late Battle at Charlestown June 17th, 1775
1775, Philadelphia, line engraving, signed lower right: "B:Romans in AEre incidit";
11⅛ x 16⅛ in.
Massachusetts Historical Society, Boston

The battle that took place June 17, 1775, in Charlestown, popularly known as the Battle of Bunker Hill, actually occurred on Breed's Hill. In Romans' "exact view," the Americans under General Putnam are seen to the right, surrounded by the British in a superior military position. Charlestown, Boston, and the British frigate *Somerset* are all in flames. The British won the battle, but they suffered such heavy losses that the battle was hardly a triumph.

Bernard Romans was a versatile and skilled man. An engineer, surveyor, and botanist, he worked on the fortifications at West Point, New York, following his stay in Boston in the spring of 1775. This engraving was published in Philadelphia in December 1775. It was one of several by patriotic artists that capitalized on early interest in battle scenes.

Refs.: George C. Groce and David H. Wallace, *The New-York Historical Society's Dictionary of Artists in America, 1564-1860,* New Haven, Conn., Yale University Press, 1957, p. 546. Helen Comstock, "Spot News in American Historical Prints 1755-1800," *Antiques* 80 (November 1961), 446-449.

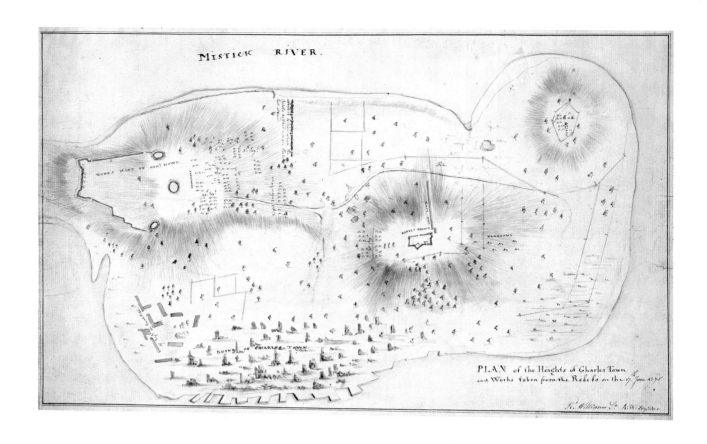

MISTICK RIVER.

WORKS MADE BY GENL. HOWE

RUINS OF CHARLES TOWN

PLAN of the Heights of Charles Town
and Works taken from the Rebels on the 17th June 1775

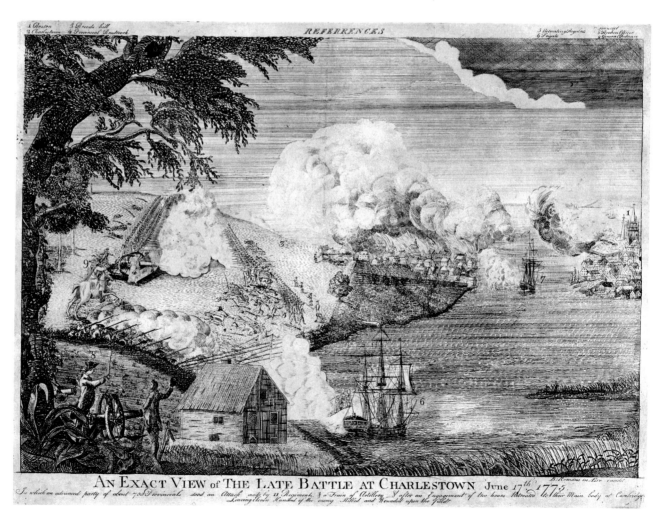

AN EXACT VIEW of THE LATE BATTLE AT CHARLESTOWN June 17th 1775
In which an advanced party of about 700 Provincials stood an Attack made by 11 Regiments, & a Train of Artillery, & after an Engagement of two hours Retreated to their Main body at Cambridge,
Leaving Eleven Hundred of the enemy Killed and Wounded upon the Field.

183

JOHN SINGLETON COPLEY, 1738-1815
Colonel John Montresor, 1736-1799
Ca. 1771, New York, oil on canvas, 30 x 25 in.
The Detroit Institute of Arts, Detroit, Gibbs-
Williams Fund

In this powerful portrait of John Montresor, Chief British Civil Engineer for North America, Copley demonstrated his ability to combine realism and strong psychological insight with brilliant coloristic effect. Montresor, shown holding a book of field engineering, spent most of his life in the Colonies, primarily in New York. He was sent to Detroit during the Pontiac Uprising in 1763. After this he returned to the East Coast, where he helped put down the Stamp Act riots in New York and Albany. Montresor planned the British defenses for Boston in 1775, his last Colonial assignment.

As a British officer and engineer, Montresor was trained as a draughtsman, mapmaker, and quick-sketch artist, since these were the skills he frequently used when planning defenses. Several sketches and maps he executed survive today, as do some maps engraved in London from his plans.

Ref.: Detroit, Detroit Historical Museum, *Pontiac Uprising (1763-1963): A Catalog of the Bicentennial Exhibit, January 25-June 9, 1963*, no. 37.

188

HENRY PELHAM, 1749-1806
A Plan of Boston in New England
1777, London, line engraving, signed in ink, lower right: "Henry Pelham"; 41½ x 29 in.
The Trustees of the Boston Public Library

As a Loyalist, Henry Pelham had access to British military maps and plans, as well as a pass that enabled him to visit British and American fortifications in and around Boston. His topographical map was the finest and most accurate produced to that date. Pelham was appalled at the changes in the Boston countryside he saw as he was making his survey. "Not a Hillock 6 feet High but What is entrench'd, not a pass where a man could go but what is defended by Cannon; fences pulled down, houses removed, Woods grubed up, Fields cut into trenches and molded into Ramparts," he reported to his step-brother, John Singleton Copley, who had left Boston for England. Pelham made his survey during the worst wartime period in Boston, between the battles of Bunker Hill and Dorchester Heights.

Ref.: John W. Reps, "Boston by Bostonians: The Printed Plans and Views of the Colonial City by its Artists, Cartographers, Engravers, and Publishers," *Boston Prints and Printmakers, 1670-1775*, Boston, Colonial Society of Massachusetts, 1973, pp. 3-56.

138

Campagne du Vice-amiral C.te d'Estaing
en Amérique, Commandant une Escadre de
12 Vaisseaux et de 4 frégattes, sortie de Toulon
le 13 avril 1778.
n° XII

BOSTON capitale des Etats-Unis de l'Amérique Septentrionale
Vûe de la Rade nommée Kings Road

186

GILBERT STUART, 1755-1828
Washington at Dorchester Heights
1806, Boston, oil on panel, 107½ x 71¼ in.
Museum of Fine Arts, deposited by the City of
Boston

By the time Gilbert Stuart painted this romantic,
monumental portrait, George Washington had
been dead for seven years and the battle of
Dorchester Heights had been over for thirty
years. Commissioned by Samuel Parkman to
hang in the newly enlarged Faneuil Hall, the
portrait is an appropriately heroic rendition of
Washington, the statesman and soldier who was
called the "Father of his Country" in his own
lifetime. Gilbert Stuart painted many portraits
of Washington. He was paid $600 for this paint-
ing. The head is modeled after the "Athenaeum"
portrait painted by Stuart in 1796, when Washington sat for him in Philadelphia.

Refs.: Mantle Fielding, *Gilbert Stuart's Portraits of
Washington,* Philadelphia, privately printed, 1923.
Museum of Fine Arts, Boston, *American Paintings
in the Museum of Fine Arts, Boston,* Boston, 1969,
vol. 1, p. 247, no. 915.

190

PIERRE OZANNE, 1737-1813
Boston, Capital of the United States
1778, Boston, pen and ink; 11⅝ x 24⅛ in.
The Metropolitan Museum of Art, New York,
gift of William H. Huntington, 1883

Pierre Ozanne, a marine artist and engineer from
Brest, France, accompanied Count d'Estaing as
official artist and engineer for the French fleet.
His watercolor view shows a peaceful Boston,
recovered from the battles of 1775-1776. The
landmarks of Fort Hill, on the left, the dominant
church spires and the Long Wharf, on the right,
had changed little since the early part of the
century.

The French fleet under d'Estaing fought the
British and cruised in American waters briefly
during 1778-1779. Superior to both the British
and American navies, the French navy made
waters safe for American privateers, who
devastated the British merchant marine. The
French did not enter into any major battles.
Count d'Estaing put into Boston briefly for
repairs before going south to the West Indies,
where his fleet remained for the next three years.

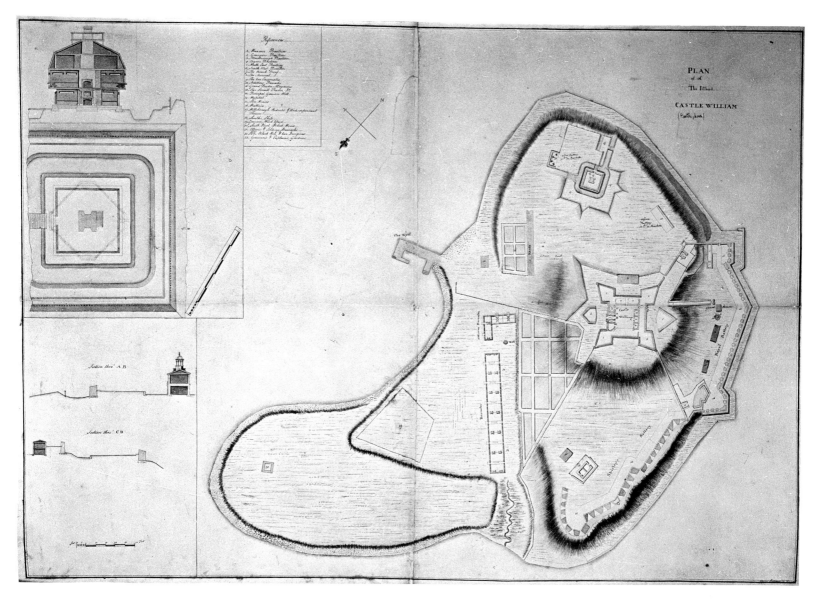

189

JOSEPH BOZE, 1744-1826
The Marquis de Lafayette, 1757-1834
1785-1789, Paris, oil on canvas, 36 x 28½ in.
Massachusetts Historical Society, Boston

Lafayette came to the United States as a young man determined to join the Colonial forces in their struggle against the English. By a special resolution of the Continental Congress he was commissioned a major general in the Continental Army in 1777, serving without pay. He was a close associate of George Washington and was something of a romantic hero from the time he first left France. His popularity grew after the Revolution, as he fought again for the cause of liberty during the French Revolution. He also served America in diplomatic missions and during this period was a close friend of Thomas Jefferson, who was Ambassador to France from 1785 to 1789.

Joseph Boze painted Lafayette's portrait for Thomas Jefferson in the 1780's while Jefferson was in France. He is portrayed in full military uniform, complete with the medal of the Society of the Cincinnati he had been awarded in 1784 for his service under Washington's leadership. Lafayette made a triumphal year's tour of America in 1824 at the invitation of President Monroe. He visited many cities, including Boston, and received a hero's welcome everywhere he went.

Refs.: Massachusetts Historical Society, *Portraits of Men,* Boston: Massachusetts Historical Society, 1955, no. 16. Detroit Institute of Arts, *The French in America 1520-1880,* Detroit, 1951, p. 95, illustrated p. 10, no. 233.

191

HENRY DEBERNIERE
Plan of The Island Castle William
Ca. 1775, Boston, pen and ink with color wash,
signed lower right: "Henry Deberniere
Fecit——"; 28½ x 41½ in.
Private collection

Castle William was the outermost fortified island at the mouth of Boston harbor and as such played several roles during the Revolution. Ensign Deberniere, a member of the British 10th Regiment, was stationed in Boston. He must have made this finely detailed plan prior to the British evacuation in 1776.

During the Stamp Act crisis the Castle served as a refuge for Governor Bernard, Lt. Governor Hutchinson, and other British officials who fled as the mobs wrecked their houses and roamed the streets. The actual papers stamped with the tax symbol that people would have been forced to buy had the act been enforced were also hidden away in the safety of the Castle.

After the Colonials took over the Castle it was renamed Fort Independence. Paul Revere, now Lieutenant Colonel, was put in command of the island several times between 1777 and 1779. He was responsible for its maintenance and operation before leaving on the ill-fated Penobscot Expedition with his regiment.

Procession.

BOSTON, OCT. 19, 1789.

AS this town is shortly to be honoured with a visit from THE PRESIDENT of the United States: In order that we may pay our respects to him, in a manner whereby every inhabitant may see so illustrious and amiable a character, and to prevent the disorder and danger which must ensue from a great assembly of people without order, a Committee appointed by a respectable number of inhabitants, met for the purpose, recommend to their Fellow-Citizens to arrange themselves in the following order, in a

PROCESSION.

IT is also recommended, that the person who shall be chosen as head of each order of Artizans, Tradesmen, Manufacturers, &c. shall be known by displaying a WHITE FLAG, with some device thereon expressive of their several callings—and to be numbered as in the arrangement that follows, which is alphabetically disposed, in order to give general satisfaction.---- The Artizans, &c. to display such insignia of their craft, as they can conveniently carry in their hands. That uniformity may not be wanting, it is desired that the several Flag-staffs be SEVEN feet long, and the Flags a YARD SQUARE.

ORDER OF PROCESSION.

MUSICK.

The Selectmen,
Overseers of the Poor,
Town Treasurer,
Town Clerk,
Magistrates,
Consuls of France and Holland,
The Officers of his Most Christian Majesty's Squadron,
The Rev. Clergy,
Physicians,
Lawyers,
Merchants and Traders,
Marine Society,
Masters of vessels,
Revenue Officers,
Strangers, who may wish to attend.

Bakers,	No. 1.
Blacksmiths, &c.	No. 2.
Block-makers,	No. 3.
Boat-builders,	No. 4.
Cabinet and Chair-makers,	No. 5.
Card-makers,	No. 6.
Carvers,	No. 7.
Chaise and Coach-makers,	No. 8.
Clock and Watch-makers,	No. 9.
Coopers,	No. 10.
Coppersmiths, Braziers and Founders,	No. 11.
Cordwainers, &c.	No. 12.
Distillers,	No. 13.
Duck Manufacturers,	No. 14.
Engravers,	No. 15.
Glaziers and Plumbers,	No. 16.
Goldsmiths and Jewellers,	No. 17.
Hair-Dressers,	No. 18.
Hatters and Furriers,	No. 19.
House Carpenters,	No. 20.
Leather Dressers, and Leather-Breeches Makers,	No. 21.
Limners and Portrait Painters,	No. 22.
Masons,	No. 23.
Mast-makers,	No. 24.
Mathematical Instrument-makers,	No. 25.
Millers,	No. 26.
Painters,	No. 27.
Paper Stainers,	No. 28.
Pewterers,	No. 29.
Printers, Book-binders and Stationers,	No. 30.
Riggers,	No. 31.
Rope-makers,	No. 32.
Saddlers,	No. 33.
Sail-makers,	No. 34.
Shipwrights, to include Caulkers, Ship-Joiners, Head-builders and Sawyers,	No. 35.
Sugar-boilers,	No. 36.
Tallow-Chandlers, &c.	No. 37.
Tanners,	No. 38.
Taylors,	No. 39.
Tin-plate Workers,	No. 40.
Tobacconists,	No. 41.
Truckmen,	No. 42.
Turners,	No. 43.
Upholsterers,	No. 44.
Wharfingers,	No. 45.
Wheelwrights,	No. 46.
Seamen,	

N. B.—In the above arrangement, some trades are omitted—from the idea, that they would incorporate themselves with the branches mentioned, to which they are generally attached. For instance—it is supposed, that under the head of *Blacksmiths*, the Armourers, Cutlers, Whitesmiths and other workers in iron, would be included; and the same with respect to other trades.

EACH division of the above arrangement is requested to meet on such parade as it may agree on, and march into the Mall—No. 1 of the Artizans, &c. forming at the South-end thereof. The Marshals will then direct in what manner the Procession will move to meet the President on his arrival in town. When the front of the Procession arrives at the extremity of the town, it will halt, and the whole will then be directed to open the column—one half of each rank moving to the right, and the other half to the left—and then face inwards, so as to form an avenue through which the President is to pass, to the galleries to be erected at the State-House.

IT is requested that the several School-masters conduct their Scholars to the neighbourhood of the State-House, and form them in such order as the Marshals shall direct.

THE Marine Society is desired to appoint some persons to arrange and accompany the seamen.

V

Federal Boston

215

SAMUEL HILL, active 1789-1803
View of the Triumphal Arch and Colonnade
1790, Boston, line engraving, signed lower
right: "Engraved by S. Hill"; 5 x 7⅜ in.
Massachusetts Historical Society, Boston

The triumphal arch shown in this engraving
was erected in what is now Washington Street
at the west end of the State House. It was made
to honor George Washington's visit to Boston
in October 1789. The design was by Charles
Bulfinch and was among his earliest public commissions. According to a report in a New York
newspaper the rusticated arch was eighteen feet
high, with a center arch fourteen feet wide, and
one on each side seven feet wide. On the frieze
above the arches were thirteen stars on a blue
ground, and a white dentile cornice surmounted
the frieze. A balustrade of interlaced work
crowned the entire width with a central oval
tablet inscribed "TO THE MAN WHO UNITED ALL
HEARTS" on one side and "TO COLUMBIA'S
FAVORITE SON" on the other. Over the central
arch, a rich canopy, 20 feet high, displayed an
American eagle perched above; "the whole
forming a spectacle, which while it captivated
the eye of the beholder, added much to the
testimonials of the respect of the day." To the
right of the whole arch was a panel decorated
with a trophy, composed of the arms of the
United States, of the Commonwealth of Massachusetts, and the French allies. This panel
was crowned with a laurel wreath surrounding
the inscription "Boston relieved March 17,
1776." A colonnade built at the west end of the
State House was designed by Thomas Dawes. It
was composed of six columns, fifteen feet high,
"and a ballustrade hung in front with Persian
carpets, on which were wrought thirteen roses."

Refs.: Lincoln Rothschild, "A Triumphal Arch by
Charles Bulfinch," *Old Time New England* 29
(1939), 161-162. "Historic Processions in Boston,
1789-1824," *Bostonian Society Publications* 5
(1908), 65-119.

ON A COLD SATURDAY, October 24, 1789, George Washington (no. 216)
arrived in Boston on his triumphal tour of New England as the first President
of the United States. His tour was an effort to bring the nation together
under its new federal form of government under the Constitution. Everywhere he went Washington was greeted as a hero, and Boston was no exception. A splendid reception awaited him in spite of Governor John Hancock's
unwillingness to meet the President without the assurance that he would
lead the procession as governor of the state. The parade started without
Hancock; Washington was at the head, mounted on an elegant white horse
given to him by King Charles IV of Spain and attended by his secretaries,
Major Jackson and Mr. Lear. The procession, carefully ordered in terms of
the status of its participants, entered Boston from Roxbury via the neck and
headed directly for the State House at the end of the Mall. The artillery in
Roxbury, Dorchester, and Fort Independence in the harbor fired honorary
salutes. Bells were rung, and the population of the whole town and environs
turned out for the celebration.[1]

At the State House, Washington passed through a magnificent triumphal arch (no. 215) designed by the architect Charles Bulfinch for the occasion. The President reviewed the parade from a colonnade built for this
purpose at the west end of the State House by Thomas Dawes, a builder and
early collaborator with Bulfinch. The ceremonies of this first day's visit of
state ended in the evening with fireworks in several parts of the town. Even
French ships at anchor in the harbor added to the festivities with fireworks.

The Boston that President Washington came to in 1789 was a far different place from the last time he had seen it, in 1776, as a ravaged wartime
town, with population and normal commercial activity greatly diminished.
By 1790 its population had returned to normal levels, and the traditional
means of livelihood connected with the sea, trade, privateering, fishing, and
shipbuilding had strengthened the economic life of the town. New areas of
trade developed as Boston followed New York in opening up her own direct
trade with China. In 1787 a small group of enterprising merchants recognized the merit of using the fur trade of the Northwest coast of America as a
means of entering and maintaining trade with China. In August 1790 the
ship *Columbia* (no. 240) returned to Boston from China having initiated
trade that brought exotic and precious new luxuries to Boston's fashionable
society (nos. 243 and 245).

1. "Historic Processions in Boston," *Publications of the Bostonian Society* 5 (1908), 65-119.
   Harold Kirker and James Kirker, *Bulfinch's Boston* (New York: Oxford University Press,
   1964), p. 100.

View of the triumphal ARCH and COLONNADE, erected in BOSTON, in honor of the president of the UNITED STATES. Oc. 24. 1789

Gaps in the social and economic structure of the town created by the departing Loyalists were quickly filled by newcomers from the surrounding countryside. Merchants who had been patriot leaders during the war and were social and political leaders in their own areas seized a ripe opportunity and moved to Boston. Many were from the rocky coast on the north shore of Boston in Essex County. Known as the Essex Junto, this new Boston elite was made up of the Higginson, Cabot, Pickering, Parson, Jackson, and Lowell families. They challenged the old order in Boston and eventually dominated the economic and social scene as they gained wealth and power in the economy based on large-scale manufacturing, which evolved after the War of 1812.[2] By 1822 when Boston was incorporated as a city under a new charter, her citizens faced the new era with a confidence gained through great physical growth, the settling of political disputes, and an acceptance of the new order.

Boston in the 1790's remained a somewhat rural town. Thomas Pemberton observed in 1794 that *"the town is capable of great increase, as many large spaces of land still remain vacant."* According to the 1790 census, Boston had 18,038 residents, only about 2,000 more than fifty years earlier, in 1743, when 16,382 people were listed.[3] Philadelphia and New York were almost twice as large at the end of the Colonial period; clearly there was the

---

2. Ibid., pp. 20-21.

3. Walter Muir Whitehill, *Boston: A topographical History* 2nd ed. (Cambridge, Mass.: Harvard University Press, 1968), p. 47.

216
CHRISTIAN GULLAGER, 1759-1826
George Washington, 1732-1799
1789, Portsmouth, New Hampshire, oil on
canvas; 29 x 24 in.
Massachusetts Historical Society, Boston

While George Washington was in Boston in
1789, John Johnston and Christian Gullager,
reportedly "the two best portrait painters of this
metropolis," were asked to paint his portrait.
Only Gullager is known to have completed an
image of "that illustrious character." The portrait that he produced after a two-hour sitting
by the general in Portsmouth was "considered a
superb painting and likeness and at that time the
only correct one in America." The picture
gallery of Mr. Gullager was visited by thousands
who wanted to see the portrait. Gullager also
executed a plaster of Paris bust of Washington
during the winter of 1789-90. His work, illustrative of the national mania to honor Washington,
also shows an increasing sense of national
awareness among American artists. The *Massachusetts Centinel* praised his efforts on
March 27, 1790: "While our country is favored
with the presence of such denizens as Mr. G.
there will be little occasion for the continuation
of the absurd and degrading practice of sending
to Europe for our statues and monuments."

Ref.: Louisa Dresser, "Christian Gullager, An
Introduction to His Life and Some Representative
Examples of His Work," *Art in America* 37 (July
1949), 105-179.

219

BENJAMIN BURT, 1729-1805
Tankard

1786, Boston, silver, marked: "BENJAMIN BURT" in cartouche on body at each side of handle, inscribed "R[D]E" on handle, engraved with view of the Charles River Bridge on side opposite pourer, on pourer's side inscribed: "Presented to/Richard Devens, Esq[r]·/by the Proprietors of/CHARLES RIVER BRIDGE,/in Testimony of their entire Approbation/of his faithful Services,/as a special Director of that Work./begun A.D. 1785,/and perfected/A.D. 1786."; H. 9⅛ in., DIAM. (base) 5¼ in., DIAM. (lip) 4¼ in. Museum of Fine Arts, the M. and M. Karolik Collection of Eighteenth Century American Arts. 36.459

The 1780's brought numerous technological advances to Boston. In 1786 the first bridge across the Charles River was built by a group of private speculators and proprietors. This toll bridge replaced the Charlestown and Boston Ferry. Built on 75 piers of oak timber, it was 1,470 feet long and 42 feet wide. The draw was 30 feet wide, and there was also a 6-foot passage on either side of the bridge for pedestrians. Forty lamps illuminated it at night. When the bridge was finally completed after thirteen months of construction, it was opened on June 17, 1786, with much festivity and celebration. A great procession moved from the State House across the bridge, while thirteen cannon were discharged from Copp's Hill. In Charlestown, 800 persons enjoyed an elegant dinner, complete with toasts and music.

The proprietors of the bridge showed their appreciation to the directors of the construction by presenting them with gifts of silver. This large tankard, weighing 31 ounces, was presented to Richard Devens for "his faithful Services." Engraved on one side is a view of the bridge and on the other is an appropriate inscription. Twentieth century inscriptions have been added below the midband. The same inscription and view of the bridge was engraved on a teapot made by Zachariah Brigden and presented to David Wood, another director.

Refs.: Buhler, *American Silver in the Museum of Fine Arts*, vol. 1, pp. 348-349, no. 307; pp. 377-378, no. 331. "Historic Processions in Boston, 1789-1824," *Bostonian Society Publications* 5 (1908), 69.

potential for development in Boston, one that increased as technology advanced. The center of the town was still the North End, crowded around the wharves and port. Business and residences were intermingled on the narrow streets, and the square around the State House (no. 217) was a busy social center. In part the stagnation of Boston's development was due to her geographical location on a peninsula with only one road connecting her to the rest of the state. In 1786 the first bridge was built over the Charles River (no. 219), linking Boston with Charlestown. As an economic venture and a feat of engineering skill the toll bridge was a great success, and in 1792 a second corporation was formed to construct a bridge between Boston and Cambridge. Boston was now much more effectively a part of the life and economy of the surrounding towns.[4]

The area surrounding the Common remained much as it had been when Thomas Hancock constructed his country mansion there in 1737. The Common was still a cow pasture, and the land to the north and south of it was sparsely settled and continued to be owned in relatively large tracts. In 1787, a fire destroyed about one hundred buildings in the area south of the Common, including the Hollis Street Church. The rebuilding of this church was the first commission for Charles Bulfinch (no. 220), the town's first professional architect and as such destined to shape its growth and appearance for the next twenty years.

Bulfinch (1763-1844) had many ties to Boston. He was descended from two prominent pre-Revolutionary families. His father and grandfather were both physicians who received their medical training in Europe and practiced in Boston. His maternal grandfather was Charles Apthorp (no. 44), one of Boston's wealthiest merchants. Charles Bulfinch graduated from Harvard in 1781 and took a position in the counting house of Joseph Barrell, where he was evidently not well occupied: *"My time passed very idly and I was at leisure to cultivate a taste for Architecture, which was encouraged by attending to Mr. Barrel's improvement of his estate and (the improvements) on our dwelling house & the houses of some friends, all of which had become exceedingly dilapidated during the war."*[5]

Bulfinch traveled in Europe between 1785 and 1787, touring England, France, and Italy, studying the architecture of the past and absorbing the current trends in taste. When he returned to Boston he was well prepared to follow a gentleman's leisure pursuit of architecture. Bankruptcy and financial disaster over his first large-scale speculative venture, the Tontine Crescent, in 1795-1796, put an end to his economic status as a gentleman.[6] From that time on, architecture became his profession, and he pursued it with aesthetic, if not economic, success.

In 1799 Bulfinch was elected chairman of the board of selectmen and chief of police, positions that carried a small salary. He remained in these

4. Ibid., p. 51.
5. Ellen Susan Bulfinch, ed., *The Life and Letters of Charles Bulfinch* (New York: B. Franklin, 1973), pp. 40-41.
6. Harold Kirker, *The Architecture of Charles Bulfinch* (Cambridge, Mass.: Harvard University Press, 1969), pp. 78-85, pls. 35, 36.

220
MATHER BROWN, 1761-1831
Charles Bulfinch, 1763-1844
1786, London, oil on canvas; 30 x 25 in.
Harvard University Portrait Collection

Charles Bulfinch introduced into Boston the
neoclassical style in architecture. Over a span of
almost three decades he designed numerous
buildings. While in London in 1786, he had this
portrait painted by Mather Brown, son of the
Boston clockmaker Gawen Brown and grandson
of the Loyalist minister Mather Byles. On
September 17, 1786, he wrote to his mother
from London: "It is esteemed a good likeness;
but I think it a very dull, unmeaning face; but
we must not blame the painter for that, as it was
not his duty to create, but to copy. It is the work
of Mr. Brown; you will find it very rough, but
that is the modish style of painting, introduced
by Sir Joshua Reynolds."

Refs.: Harold Kirker, *The Architecture of Charles
Bulfinch,* Cambridge, Mass., Harvard University
Press, 1969, pp. 1-16. Harold Kirker and James
Kirker, *Bulfinch's Boston,* New York, Oxford
University Press, 1964.

221
JOHN L. BOQUETA DE WOISERI, active in the
U.S. 1797-1815
View of Boston
Ca. 1810, Boston, line engraving with water-
color; 22¼ x 34½ in. (sight)
Boston Public Library

Bulfinch's Massachusetts State House, built between 1795 and 1797, dominates this panorama
of Boston executed by Boqueta de Woiseri
around 1810. This watercolor is an unusual
view looking toward Boston from across the
Charles River. This watercolor shows many of
the large mansions and other buildings designed
by Bulfinch and erected between 1790 and
1810. At the far left is the Charles River Bridge,
built in 1786. Little is known about the life of
Boqueta de Woiseri. In the *Philadelphia General
Advertiser* of February 21, 1804, he advertised
two engravings and referred to himself as "designer, drawer, geographer, and engineer." He is
known to have executed views of Boston,
Philadelphia, New York, Baltimore, Richmond,
Charleston, and New Orleans.

Refs.: Perry Rathbone, ed., *Mississippi Panorama,*
St. Louis, City Art Museum, 1949, pp. 67-68. Isaac
N. Stokes, *American Historical Prints,* New York,
New York Public Library, 1933, p. 53.

227

GEORGE BRIGHT, active 1750-1805
Armchair
1797, Boston, mahogany with original brass, iron, and wood casters; H. 34 in., W. 22 in., DEPTH 24 in.
The Society for the Preservation of New England Antiquities, Boston

The new State House as designed by Bulfinch was almost completed by the end of 1797. It was elegantly appointed, in part, with thirty chairs made by Boston's "neatest workman in town," George Bright. Bright's bill, dated December 1797, enumerated the following charges:

30 mahogany chairs	$240.00
oyling the seats of 13 windows a.15	1.95
oyling 100 seats in Representative room and table feet	2.70
repairing box case in Sec Office	2.00
	$246.65

Several identical mahogany chairs have descended in the families of Massachusetts senators and representatives and are believed to be the original Bright chairs. This chair once belonged to Senator Joseph Bradlee. Its barrel-backed or bergère form, derived from French precedents, was uncommon in the United States. In 1797 these chairs expressed the height of fashion. They were an elegant complement to the tastefully executed State House interior.

George Bright was from a family of cabinet-makers and upholsterers that spanned three generations in Boston. He was working as early as 1763 and soon became an influential leader among his fellow craftsmen. In the Federal Procession of Mechanics and Artisans in 1788 and the Washington Procession in 1789 he led the group of Boston cabinetmakers.

Refs.: Richard Randall, "George Bright, Cabinet-maker," *Art Quarterly* 27 (1964), 135-149. Charles F. Montgomery, *American Furniture: The Federal Period, 1788-1825*, New York, Viking Press for the Winterthur Museum, 1966, pp. 177-178, pl. 134.

offices until 1817, when he left Boston for Washington to become architect of the national capitol. The combination in Bulfinch of civil servant and master architect produced unrivaled public buildings — hospitals, almshouses, jails, and churches — in an era when institutionalization was becoming increasingly common in American life.

Bulfinch's most noteworthy public building was the Massachusetts State House, built between 1795 and 1797 on the northern corner of the Common. As early as 1787 Bulfinch submitted *"a plan for a new State-House."* In 1795 a plan was accepted. The new State House was built on land purchased from the estate of John Hancock in 1795, and when it was finally completed it cost over four times the originally appropriated sum of £8,000. On January 18, 1798, the *Columbian Centinel* gave a fully detailed description of the building, concluding that *"Too much praise cannot be bestowed upon the Agents who have directed the construction of this superb edifice, for their economy, liberality, and patriotism. — The materials are mostly of the produce of our country, and the composition ornaments were made and moulded on the spot."*[7] A sense of local and national pride was evident. The new State House gave the Common and Beacon Hill fresh potential for residential development and thus meant more commissions for Charles Bulfinch. Park Street, Colonnade Row on Tremont Street, Franklin Place (the Tontine Crescent) just south of the Common, and individual houses on Beacon Hill were designed by Bulfinch on speculation and for individual clients. It is in his designs for houses that the fine qualities of the neoclassical style are best seen.

The development of the neoclassical style in England, Europe, and America owed much to the rediscovery of the ancient ruins of Herculaneum and Pompeii in 1768 and to the publication of Stuart and Revett's *Antiquities of Athens* in 1762 and Robert Adams's *Ruins of the Palace of the Emperor Diocletian at Spalatro in Dalmatia* (London, 1764). These handsome volumes containing measured drawings of classical ruins were widely known and studied by everyone interested in architecture and design, and Charles Bulfinch undoubtedly had access to them while he was a student at Harvard.[8] By the time he arrived in England on his tour in 1786 the classical revival was well established under the leadership of Robert and James Adam. In the design of numerous grand country seats for the English gentry, some of which Bulfinch may have seen, the Adam brothers attended to every detail. Classical motifs of every possible type were carefully combined in the decoration of a room, on the ceiling, walls, and mantles, as well as on the furniture and textiles that became integral parts of the interior decoration. New divisions of living spaces appeared with rooms of specialized uses and different shapes. The delicacy and intimacy of neoclassical decoration were best realized in domestic buildings; the grandest exterior classical proportions in colonnades and porticos were reserved for public buildings.

Men who had a great love and knowledge of architecture, who had

7. Ibid., p. 106, pls. 43-48.
8. Ibid., pp. 1-16.

traveled extensively in Europe and England, such as Bulfinch and Thomas Jefferson, and immigrants trained as architects, such as Benjamin Latrobe, also introduced the style to America. The neoclassical style was adopted with enthusiasm; in fact, it became a national style, and it flourished in varying forms and degrees well into the 1840's and 1850's. It was particularly appropriate for Americans, who thought of themselves as the founders of the only true democratic republic since the days of ancient Athens.

As developed in Boston by Charles Bulfinch, the style was conservative. Based on English models, it was given to understatement on the exterior and simple delicate grace on the interior. While the brick mansions Bulfinch designed for Bostonians such as Harrison Gray Otis were grand and elegant by local standards, they were chastely conservative compared with mansions in the same style in Virginia, Philadelphia, and other American cities.

The three houses that Bulfinch designed for Otis provide an interesting opportunity to study the architect's and the patron's developing taste, and to show the drift of the stylish residential area from the West End toward the newly developed Common. All three houses stand today, at 141 Cambridge Street (1796-1797), 85 Mount Vernon Street (1800-1802), and 45 Beacon Street (1805-1808).[9] The first house (no. 230) is simple, with a carefully proportioned facade delineated by granite stringcourses and windows of graduated size. The central Palladian window on the second floor is reminiscent of an earlier architectural style in America inspired by Georgian English architecture. The second Otis house, larger than the first, has a similar flat brick facade symmetrically relieved by four arched bays over the ground floor windows and four Corinthian pilasters that are supported by the stringcourse at the division of the first and second stories. The last house, facing the by now fashionable Common, is the grandest of the three. Here Harrison Gray Otis lived out his days in splendor. The facade, as simple as the first two, is well proportioned by the arrangement of its windows. Its only neoclassical decorative elements appear at the windows and in the portico at the door. The floor plan is far more elaborate than those of the other two houses and exhibits the new elements of grand circular staircases, oval rooms, and rooms with specialized use: first drawing room, second drawing room, dining room, library-office, and an endless array of attached service quarters.

The wooden houses that Bulfinch designed for James Swan and Perez Morton in the suburban area of Dorchester and Roxbury about 1796 displayed elegant neoclassical features that made them lavish country retreats. Elliptical salons, grand staircases, and beautiful plaster work in the Adam style combining many classical motifs demonstrated well the new taste of Bostonians.[10] Otis, Swan, and Morton were but three of Bulfinch's many clients who demanded elegance in the latest style.

The social lives of these people were often as extravagant as their houses.

217
JAMES B. MARSTON, active ca. 1800-1817
The Old State House and State Street
Ca. 1801, Boston, oil on canvas; 37½ x 52⅛ in.
Massachusetts Historical Society, Boston

By 1801 Boston was a very different city than it had been before the Revolution. This painting shows the west side of State Street looking toward what by then was the "Old State House." It recalls the same general view that Revere offered in his Boston Massacre print of 1770. But within the span of thirty-one years the facades and fashions had dramatically changed. On the right is the brick facade of the old Apthorp house, shown after a face-lifting by Apthorp's own grandson, Charles Bulfinch. The hustle and bustle of daily activity remains much the same, but men now wear new-fashioned French trousers and shorter cut-away coats, while women are seen in the lighter and less cumbersome Empire-style dress.

Ref.: Paul S. Harris, "Gilbert Stuart and a Portrait of Mrs. Sarah Apthorp Morton," in *Winterthur Portfolio One,* Charlottesville, Va., University Press of Virginia, 1964, pp. 207-209.

9. Ibid., pp. 118-124, 158-160, 221-229, respectively.
10. Ibid., 128-140.

154

228

GILBERT STUART, 1755-1828
Harrison Gray Otis, 1765-1848
1809, Boston, oil on mahogany panel;
32 x 26 in.
The Society for the Preservation of New
England Antiquities, Boston
(On view June 1-September 1)

Harrison Gray Otis was one of Charles Bulfinch's most enthusiastic clients. Otis selected
Bulfinch on three occasions to design exceptional houses, all of which stand today. Otis
was also one of the initiators of a private
syndicate, the Mount Vernon Proprietors, that
resulted in the residential development of
Beacon Hill and numerous commissions for
Bulfinch.

Otis was described by his great-grandson,
Samuel Eliot Morison, as a man "endowed . . .
with a winning personality, a keen intellect, the
Otis gift of oratory, and numerous influential
relatives." Between 1799 and 1801 Otis served
as a representative in the United States Congress
in Philadelphia, and later he was elected three
times mayor of Boston, serving from 1829 to
1831. In 1816 John Adams wrote of Otis: "In
the course of nearly thirty years that I have
known him, and throughout the range of ex-
perience that I have had in that time, it has not
fallen to my lot to meet a man more skilled in
the useful art of entertaining his friends than
Otis."

Refs.: Samuel Eliot Morison, "A Brief Account of
Harrison Gray Otis," *Old Time New England* 8
(March 1917), 3-6. Samuel Eliot Morison, *Harrison
Gray Otis: The Urbane Federalist 1765-1848*,
Boston, Houghton Mifflin, 1969.

230

CHARLES BULFINCH, 1763-1844
*Front Elevation of the Harrison Gray Otis
House*
1795-1796, Boston, pen and ink with water-
color; 6⅛ x 5⅝ in. (uneven)
Massachusetts Historical Society, Boston

The first of three houses designed by Charles
Bulfinch for Harrison Gray Otis was constructed on the corner of Cambridge and Lynde
streets, Boston, in 1795-1796. Built on land
acquired from Otis's father-in-law, this mansion
housed the Otis family only briefly, for in 1801
it was sold to Thomas Osborn.

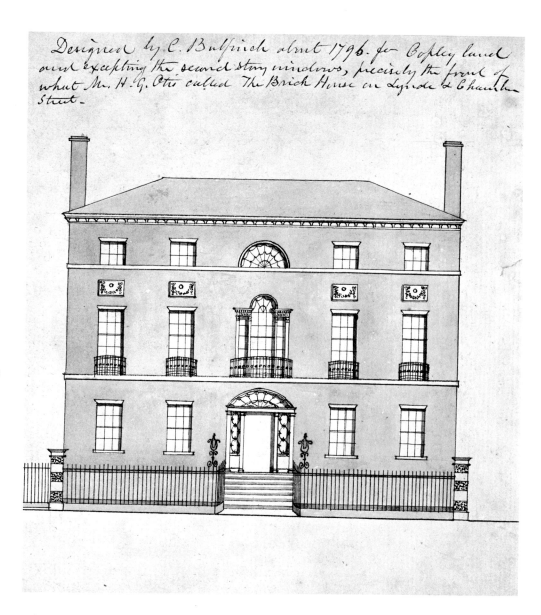

A handwritten notation above this elevation
confirms Bulfinch as the designer. Similar in
detail to the William Bingham house of 1786 in
Philadelphia, the Otis mansion reflects the bal-
anced proportions and fine detail that Bulfinch
developed and that became the style of Federal
Boston. The house has been handsomely restored and furnished by the Society for the
Preservation of New England Antiquities. It
serves today as headquarters for that society.

Ref.: Harold Kirker, *The Architecture of Charles
Bulfinch*, Cambridge, Mass., Harvard University
Press, 1969, pp. 118-124.

During the post-Revolutionary period there was general anxiety about what the new order of things would be. Would the Revolution change the way people behaved and their relationships to each other? How would "liberty" affect the citizens of Boston? Mercy Otis Warren commented in a letter to John Adams in 1778 that *"a state of war has ever been deemed unfriendly to virtue; but such a total change of manners in so short a period, I believe, was never known in the history of man."*[11] Concern remained, for later in 1785, Sam Adams wrote to John Adams also that people were *"imitating the Britons in every idle amusement and expensive foppery which is in their power to invent for the destruction of a young country."*[12] New customs and new personalities were emerging in this democratic society. Although some would not have advocated a complete return to the pre-Revolutionary order, they still wished to retain control of society against more liberal forces. The French Revolution, with its excesses of violence in overthrowing the old order between 1789 and 1800, and American participation in the War of 1812 only aggravated the worries of the conservatives in Boston.

Harrison Gray Otis (no. 228), who graduated from Harvard in 1783, was heir to two political traditions. His maternal grandfather, Harrison Gray, was the last royal treasurer of Massachusetts Bay Colony and a prominent Loyalist. His father, Samuel Otis, was the brother of two ardent patriots, James Otis and Mercy Otis Warren. The politics of the new nation were central to the cultural life of Boston after the Revolution, and Otis in his own career as a politician and lawyer reflected his background. A strong leader of the conservative Federalist party and a loyal public servant in several capacities, at the same time he feared and abhorred the democratic mob. His beliefs were those of the conservative elite. In his private life also Otis reflected his conservatism and his love of luxurious ways. He entertained on a lavish scale in great style. Each of his three houses designed by Bulfinch was increasingly grand. Number 45 Beacon Street was the last large mansion designed by Bulfinch before the depression caused by Jefferson's embargo set in prior to the war. Otis continued living according to his own high standards, effectively coexisting with the new order of things, though largely disregarding it.

An example of the conservative nature of Bostonians of the time appears in the opposition to the Sans Souci Club. When Sarah Morton (no. 231) and Hepzibah Swan started the club in 1785, a debate ensued in the newspapers for two or three months over its meaning and contribution to Boston life. Was this tea assembly that encouraged dancing, drinking, and gambling *"a very harmless meeting, decent even to dullness,"* a *"laudable"* institution? Or was it an *"invention for ruin,"* as its first critic, *"Observer,"* purportedly Sam Adams, maintained? The *"Observer"* claimed that *"new dissipations are introduced to lull and enervate those minds already too much softened, poisoned and contaminated by idle pleasures, and foolish gratifications. We*

11. Charles Warren, "Samuel Adams and the Sans Souci Club in 1785," *Proceedings of the Massachusetts Historical Society* 60 (1926-1927), 319.
12. Ibid., p. 315.

231
JOSEPH CALLENDER, 1751-1821
Medal
1795, Boston, gold, engraved recto with relief picture of the Boston Theatre, underneath which is inscribed: "This MEDAL/entitles/ CHARLES BULFINCH, Esqr/to a Seat in the BOSTON THEATRE/during Life;/Benefit Nights excepted," inscribed verso: "Presented/by the PROPRIETORS/of the BOSTON THEATRE/To CHARLES BULFINCH, Esqr/For his unremitted and liberal Attention/in the Plan and Execution of/That Building;/The elegance of which is the/best Evidence of his/Taste and Talents"; DIAM. 2½ in.
Private collection

In 1792 a law prohibiting the performance of stage plays in Boston was repealed. Plans were promptly made for the construction of the city's first theater. With Harrison Gray Otis and Perez Morton as supporters, the Federal Street Theatre was designed by Charles Bulfinch in 1793-1794. It was built at the corner of Federal and Franklin streets. This remarkable gold medal was commissioned by the proprietors of the theater from Joseph Callender in 1795. It was presented to Charles Bulfinch as a token of appreciation for his impressive design and for his assistance in overthrowing the 1750 prohibition. The Theater was destroyed by fire in 1798 but was subsequently rebuilt.

Refs.: Richard Stoddard, "A Reconstruction of Charles Bulfinch's First Federal Street Theatre, Boston," in *Winterthur Portfolio Six,* Charlottesville, University Press of Virginia, 1970, pp. 185-208. Buhler, *American Silver in the Museum of Fine Arts,* vol. 2, pp. 457-458, no. 406.

are exchanging prudence, virtue and economy, for those glaring spectres luxury, prodigality and profligacy. We are prostituting all our glory as a people, for new modes of pleasure . . . totally detrimental to the well being of society." The club became the subject of a farce entitled *"Sans Souci, alias, Free and Easy: — On an Evening's Peep in a Polite Circle, An entirely new entertainment in three Acts."* and it also became embroiled in politics.[13]

Partisan politics entered the theater as well. Following the repeal of the 1750 law banning theatrical productions in Boston a theater was designed by Charles Bulfinch and finished by 1794. The Federal Street Theatre (no. 232) was a handsome and lavishly appointed structure as it was described in 1794 by Thomas Pemberton: *"The Theater in Federal street, is a lofty and spacious edifice, substantially built of brick, with stone fascias, imposts, &c. . . . The front and rear are decorated with Corinthian columns and pilasters."* The interior was as elegant as the exterior: *"The back walls are painted a light blue, and the front of the boxes, the columns &c. are of straw and lilach in color: the mouldings, balustrades, and fretwork are gilded: a crimson silk drapery suspended from the second boxes, and twelve elegant brass chandeliers of five lights each, complete the decoration."* Stage plays were not the only amusement the theater afforded: *"At the east end of the building, a noble and elegant dancing room is contrived. This is . . . richly ornamented with Corinthian columns and pilasters, and a ceiling en bereau, elegantly finished with stucco in compartments. The furniture of glasses, chandeliers, and girandoles are very handsome, and promise much satisfaction to the lovers of innocent and cheerful amusement."*[14]

The plays at the new theater soon reflected the Federalist politics of its chief backers, Harrison Gray Otis and Perez Morton. This prompted the building in 1796 of a second theater, the Haymarket, which was controlled by men of more "republican" politics. They were assured that anti-French and anti-Jacobin jokes would not be slipped into the scripts of their plays. The Haymarket was erected on Common Street opposite the Mall. It had a capacity of about 2,000 people, almost twice that of the Federal Street Theater.[15]

There were other less controversial cultural opportunities in Boston at the end of the eighteenth century. The Massachusetts Historical Society and the Boston Library Society both found their first home in the central pavilion of Bulfinch's Tontine Crescent. The Boston Athenaeum, founded in 1806, was a formal result of the Monthly Anthology, a literary club, and its library served as one of the few intellectual retreats in the town.[16] There was even the Columbian Museum, organized by a Mr. Bowen in 1801, which exhibited a variety of curiosities including *"Fifty Large Figures of Wax-work."*

13. Ibid., pp. 326, 322, 332.
14. Thomas Pemberton, "Topographical and Historical Description of Boston," *Collections of the Massachusetts Historical Society* 3 (1794), pp. 241-304.
15. Richard Stoddard, "The Haymarket Theatre, Boston," *Educational Theater Journal* 27, no. 1 (March 1975), n.p.
16. Harold Kirker and James Kirker, *Bulfinch's Boston* (New York: Oxford University Press, 1964), pp. 214-217.

158

GILBERT STUART, 1755-1828
Sarah Wentworth Apthorp Morton (Mrs.
Perez), 1759-1846
1802, Philadelphia, oil on canvas; 29¼ x 24 in.
Museum of Fine Arts, Juliana Cheney Edwards
Collection. Bequest of Hannah Marcy Edwards
in memory of her mother. 36.681

As heiress to the social status and great wealth
of two of Boston's mercantile families, the beautiful Sarah Wentworth Apthorp Morton became
an influential leader of the new Federal society.
Granddaughter of Charles Apthorp and cousin
to Charles Bulfinch, in 1781 she married Perez
Morton, a brilliant young lawyer who had already begun to win acclaim. By the mid-1780's
Mrs. Morton and Mrs. James Swan distinguished themselves as social leaders of the new
elite with the formation of the Sans Souci Club,
or Tea Assembly.

Mrs. Morton won fame and recognition for her
poetry. The critic Thomas Paine dubbed her the
"American Sappho." Two of her best-known
works were the 1790 narrative *Ouabi, or the
Virtues of Nature, an Indian Tale* and the 1797
verse account of the American Revolution,
*Beacon Hill, a Local Poem, Historical and
Descriptive.* In 1797 the Mortons moved into a
new house on the Roxbury-Dorchester line, designed by Charles Bulfinch and close by the
residence of Colonel and Mrs. James Swan. By
1808 the Mortons were residing in another new
house, nearby the earlier one.

This sensitive portrait of Mrs. Morton is one of
three painted of her by Gilbert Stuart between
1801 and 1802. Stuart was working in Philadelphia when all of these portraits were made, for
it was not until 1805 that he settled permanently
in Boston. Mrs. Morton was on a trip to Philadelphia and Washington when this, the second
of the three portraits was done. The Henry
Francis du Pont Winterthur Museum owns the
first portrait. The third, an unusual and intrigu-
ing unfinished painting is in the Worcester Art
Museum.

Refs.: Charles Warren, "Sam Adams and the Sans
Souci Club in 1785," *Proceedings of the Massachu-
setts Historical Society* 60 (1926-1927), 318-344.
Paul S. Harris, "Gilbert Stuart and a Portrait of
Mrs. Sarah Apthorp Morton," in *Winterthur
Portfolio One*, Charlottesville, University Press of
Virginia, 1964, pp. 198-220. *American Paintings in
the Museum of Fine Arts, Boston*, Boston, Museum
of Fine Arts, 1969, vol. 1, pp. 245-246, no. 910.
Walter Muir Whitehill, "Perez Morton's Daughter
Revisits Boston in 1825," *Proceedings of the Mas-
sachusetts Historical Society* 82 (1970), 21-47.

One of these was a figure of *"John Adams, President of the United States,
elegantly situated in the centre of the Museum Hall, surrounded by two
beautiful Wax figures, representing Peace . . . And Plenty . . . The President
is dressed in an elegant suit, and the likeness is universally allowed to be
very perfect. — All as large as life."*

One of the greatest attractions at the museum seemed to be the exhibition of *"100 Elegant Paintings."* The list was diverse to say the least, and it
included such subjects as Medea and Jason; the Surrender of Calais to
Edward III; Mary, Queen of Scots; Miss Smith of Baltimore; Bacchus,
Ceres, and Cupid; an Egyptian fortune-teller; John Wilkes; six elegant
views of different parts of the East Indies, drawn from nature, by the
Chinese painters; and His Excellency John Hancock, late governor of Massachusetts, painted by Copley. The museum also had a large collection of
natural and artificial curiosities. The building was reported to be 108 feet by
30 feet, with the principal hall being 90 feet long and 28 feet wide, and the
whole was *"universally allowed to be one of the most entertaining places of
Amusement in the United States."* The interior of the museum was *"elegantly finished and decorated with five superb glass chandeliers, and is
illuminated with upwards of 30 Patent Lamps."* It was open every day and
three evening a week *"with music on a large Concert Organ."*[17]

The cultural interests and opportunities of Boston were becoming more
diverse as the nineteenth century began. Many upper class Bostonians were
preoccupied with their politics and their adjustment to the new nation, but
it did not prevent them from enjoying a life of luxury and ease. The luxurious houses in the neoclassical style called for new modes of interior design,
furniture, and other decorative arts. Derived mainly from English precedents, as was the architecture of Charles Bulfinch, the neoclassical style in
the decorative arts was influenced by imported pieces, by emigrating craftsmen, and by design books brought to this country. Technological innova-
tions, particularly in manufacturing processes such as sheet-rolling of silver,
also contributed to the development of a full-blown neoclassical style. The
style was delicate and linear in proportion, with an emphasis on surface
pattern and ornament. In furniture this was expressed by the use of veneers
and inlays or colorful painted decorations; silver was engraved with a
variety of Greek motifs. Often an actual Greek form was adapted such as
the urn, a most popular one, especially in silver (nos. 302, 304).

By the 1790's the demand was great for elegant furniture to complement
the designs of the new mansions, and Boston's artisans and craftsmen were
eager and able to meet the challenge. Men such as Paul Revere, George
Bright, Benjamin Frothingham, and Stephen Badlam started working in the
new style when the economy of postwar Boston revived. Exactly when the
first pieces of neoclassical furniture were produced in Boston is unknown,
but the correspondence between David Spear and his fiancée Marcy Higgins
in January 1784 suggests that there was a certain novelty attached to it:

17. "Columbian Museum," Broadside printed by D. Bowen, 1801, Massachusetts Historical
 Society Collections.

234
GILBERT STUART, 1755-1828
Colonel James Swan, ca. 1750-1831
Ca. 1793-1798, New York or Philadelphia; oil
on canvas; 28¾ x 23½ in.
Museum of Fine Arts, bequest of Elizabeth
Howard Bartol. 27.538

James Swan came to Boston from Scotland as a
child and served an apprenticeship with a
mercantile firm. During this period, his political
sentiments quickened with his membership in
the Sons of Liberty and active participation in
the Revolution. In 1776 Colonel Swan married
Hepzibah Clarke, daughter of a wealthy merchant and ship owner whose inheritance allowed her husband to enter trade and land
investment. In spite of a promising start, Swan
found himself in debt by 1787, and set off for
France. During the French Revolution, Swan
built up a lucrative trade by importing essential
goods to France and exporting fine furnishings
confiscated from the nobility by the new republic. Most of these items found new owners
in New York, Philadelphia, and Baltimore,
where political sentiment was more favorable
to the revolutionary French than it was in
Boston. Some French pieces did furnish Mrs.
Swan's country estate in Dorchester, designed
by Charles Bulfinch in 1796. In 1808, Colonel
Swan became a voluntary resident of a
Parisian debtors' prison for his refusal to meet a
creditor's demand that he considered unjust. He
was released during the July Revolution of
1830, and lived just long enough to enjoy a
reunion with his old friend, General Lafayette,
before succumbing to a stroke at the age of 81.

Refs.: James Kirker, "Bulfinch's Houses for Mrs.
Swan," *Antiques* 86 (October 1964), 442-444.
*American Paintings in the Museum of Fine Arts,
Boston,* Boston, Museum of Fine Arts, 1969, vol. 1,
p. 243, no. 906.

235, 236
Attributed to PIERRE GOUTHIERE, 1732-1814
Pair of andirons
Ca. 1785-1800, France, ormolu (gilt bronze);
H. 19 in., W. 17⅞ in.
Museum of Fine Arts, Swan Collection. Bequest
of Miss Elizabeth Howard Bartol. 27.521

During the 1790's French taste was popular in
America, and there survive today several groups
of French furniture and furnishings used in this
country during that period. These ormolu, or
gilt bronze, andirons were among the objects
that James Swan sent from France between 1795
and 1798 for his house in Roxbury. Of superb
quality and ornate design, they are representative of his excellent taste. Among the other items
he acquired were several pieces of upholstered
furniture, a carved and gilt fire screen, and a
magnificent carved and gilt bed, now in the
collections of the Museum of Fine Arts. Smaller
but no less lavish items included silver salts
made by Marc Etienne Janety of Paris and a pair
of imposing French porcelain urns made at the
manufactory at Sèvres.

Refs.: Donald Torrey Pitcher, "Colonel James Swan
and His French Furniture," *Antiques* 37, no. 2
(February 1940), 69-71. Howard C. Rice, "Notes on
the 'Swan Furniture,'" *Bulletin of the Museum of
Fine Arts* 38, no. 227 (June 1940), 43-48.

"*Mr. Bright, who is an old Friend and Acquaintance of my Father's is to
make all the mahogany Furniture . . . and I doubt not but that we shall have
very good furniture from him — the chairs are different from any you ever
saw but they are very pretty, of the newest Taste.*"[18] The craftsmen of pre-
Revolutionary Boston were joined by men who arrived from England such
as John Jackson Jarves and John and Thomas Seymour, or from the Isle of
Jersey, such as David Poignand in the late 1780's and early 1790's. By the
turn of the century furniture-making was established in large shops of
craftsmen. Craftsmen had also become businessmen in the modern sense.

Today John Seymour and his son, Thomas, are among the best-known
post-Revolutionary Boston cabinetmakers largely because of three known
labeled pieces of furniture and a number of other pieces that can be attributed to them on the basis of similar form and ornament (nos. 281-284, 286).
The furniture made by and attributed to the Seymours exemplifies the finest
production in the neoclassical style in Boston. The Seymours came to Boston
in 1794, and in 1796 John Seymour was listed in the Boston Directory as a
cabinetmaker on Creek Street. When a public auction of the contents of the
house of Dr. J. Flagg was advertised in 1798, furniture "*of the workmanship
of Mr. Seymour*" was listed in the sale.[19]

The Seymours, who came to Boston as skilled cabinetmakers, brought
the taste for the neoclassical style and forms to America with them. In addition to a first-hand knowledge of the style, Thomas Seymour owned
Thomas Sheraton's *Cabinet-Makers and Upholsterer's Drawing Book*
(London, 1791-1793). Sheraton's book, the first of several publications by
him, along with George Hepplewhite's *Cabinet-maker and Upholsterer's
Guide* (London, 1788), was fundamental in disseminating neoclassical de-

18. Robert Bartlett Haas, "The Forgotten Courtship of David and Marcy Spear, 1785-1787,"
 Old Time New England 52 (Winter 1962), 61-74.
19. Mabel M. Swan, "John Seymour & Son, Cabinetmakers," *Antiques* 32 (October 1937),
 176-180.

238
GILBERT STUART, 1755-1828
Bishop Jean-Louis Lefebvre de Cheverus,
1768-1836
1823, Boston, oil on canvas; 36¼ x 28½ in.
Museum of Fine Arts, bequest of Mrs. Charlotte
Gore Greenough Hervoches du Quilliou. 21.9

In this striking portrait, Gilbert Stuart has recorded the wise and kindly Bishop Cheverus.
Born in Mayenne, France, Cheverus was ordained in Paris December 18, 1790, in the last
public ordination in Paris before the Revolution. He fled to England in 1792 and finally
arrived in Boston in 1796, prepared to work
with a former friend and teacher, Father
François Antoine Matignon. In 1797 Cheverus
went to Maine as a missionary to the Indians,
but he returned to Boston by 1799 to aid with
the building of a new church for the Catholics
of Boston. In 1810 Cheverus was consecrated
Bishop of Boston. As his health was failing in
1822, the king of France summoned Cheverus to
return as Bishop of Montauban. So well-loved
was the bishop that 226 non-Catholic citizens
of Boston sent a petition to the French government begging that he be left in Boston. The king
would not accede to the request, and in September 1823 Cheverus left for France.

Refs.: Walter M. Whitehill, *A Memorial to Bishop
Cheverus: with a Catalogue of the Books Given by
Him to the Boston Athenaeum,* Boston, Boston
Athenaeum, 1951. *American Paintings in the
Museum of Fine Arts, Boston,* Boston, Museum of
Fine Arts, 1969, p. 257, no. 943.

239
MATTHIEU DE MACHY, active 1770-1789
Coffee urn
1789, Paris, silver, maker's marks on front of
plinth, top of warmer, and bottom of urn, in-
scribed on front over spigot: "To CHARLES
BULFINCH/Esqʳ/Presented by the Catholics/OF
BOSTON/Janʸ 1.1806"; H. 16⅛ in.
Museum of Fine Arts, gift of Miss Ellen Susan
Bulfinch. 16.223

The Catholics of Boston were extremely grateful to Charles Bulfinch for his help and generosity in the planning and building of Holy
Cross Church, their first proper sanctuary,
built between 1800 and 1803. In January 1806
they presented him with this silver coffee urn
made in Paris by Mathieu de Machy about
1789. It was presumably owned in Boston by a
member of the church before its presentation to
Bulfinch.

Bulfinch helped the church obtain land at the
southern end of the Tontine Crescent, then
owned by the proprietors of the Federal Street
Theater. Since Bulfinch was a member of that
corporation he was able to secure the land for
them at "the moderate price of 2500 Dols."
Then he made plans without charge and super-
vised every step of the building. He also assisted
in promoting the subscription taken to provide
funds for the building, with more than one-fifth
of the $17,000 being donated by the Protestants
of Boston. John Adams headed the list with a
gift of $100. When the building was completed
in 1803, William Bentley noted in his diary on
October 7 that it was "neat but without a pro-
fusion of ornament; the altar not highly but
handsomely decorated."

Refs.: Harold Kirker, *The Architecture of Charles
Bulfinch,* Cambridge, Mass., Harvard University
Press, 1969, pp. 161-164. Robert Lord, John E.
Sexton, and Edward T. Harrington, *History of the
Archdiocese of Boston,* New York, 1944, vol. 1,
p. 556.

163

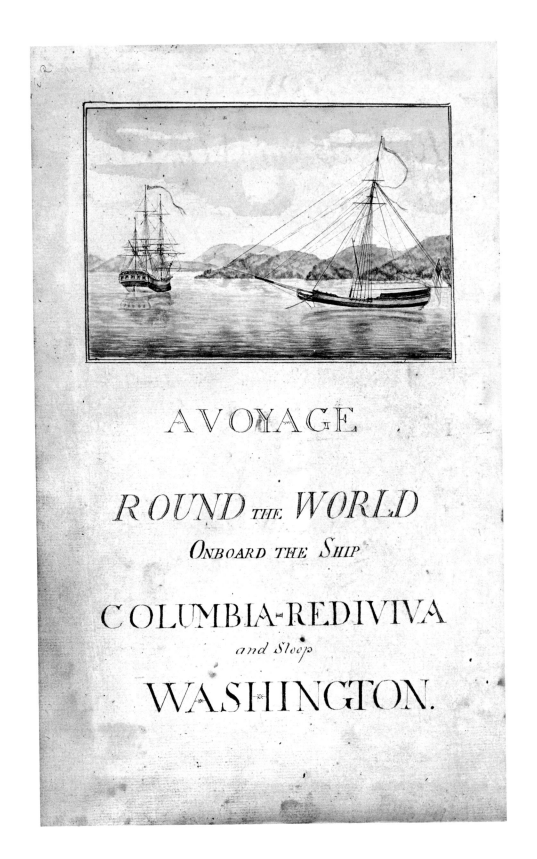

A VOYAGE

ROUND THE WORLD

ONBOARD THE SHIP

COLUMBIA=REDIVIVA

and Sloop

WASHINGTON.

240

ROBERT HASWELL, 1768-ca. 1801
A Voyage Round the World Onboard the Ship Columbia-Rediviva and Sloop Washington
1787-1790, Boston, Oregon, Pacific Ocean, manuscript logbook; 12⅞ x 8⅛ in.
Massachusetts Historical Society, Boston

The *Empress of China,* the first American vessel to depart for Canton, returned to New York in May 1785, initiating five decades of extensive American trade with China. The Boston merchant Joseph Barrell and five associates, including Charles Bulfinch, realizing the lucrative potential, outfitted two ships, the *Columbia-Rediviva* and its tender sloop *Washington.* On September 30, 1787, the vessels sailed from Boston Harbor.

This log kept by Robert Haswell, third mate on the *Columbia,* is the only record of that pioneer voyage. Having traded Northwest skins in China, the *Columbia* returned to Boston on August 9, 1790, the first vessel to carry the Stars and Stripes around the world. In a subsequent venture initiated by Barrell, Captain Robert Gray of Boston explored the mouth of the Columbia River (1792). These early ventures in the Northwest Coast started Boston's long success in the China trade.

Refs.: *Collecting for Clio,* Boston, Massachusetts Historical Society, 1969, pp. 40-41. Frederic W. Howay, ed., *"Voyages of the 'Columbia' to the Northwest Coast, 1787-1790, and 1790-1793,"* Collections, 79. Boston, Massachusetts Historical Society, 1941.

243

Punch bowl

1790, China, hard-paste porcelain, inscribed: "Boston. N. 75/These are to Certify that CAP^T JAMES MAGEE/was by a Majority of Votes regularly admitted a Member/of the BOSTON MARINE SOCIETY at a Meeting held the/5th day of Novem^rb 1782. Given under my hand and the/Seal of the Society this 9th day of Feby Annoque Domini/ ^1789 SAM^L BLAGGE Sec^y Mungo Mackay President," and under this: "Presented to the/BOSTON MARINE SOCIETY/by James Magee"; H. 5⅞ in., DIAM. (rim) 14⅜ in. Boston Marine Society

Some of the finest Chinese export porcelain that has survived from the late eighteenth century was specially ordered by merchants or ship captains engaged in the China trade. This punch bowl and cider jug (no. 244), painted in black and gold with marine scenes and a facsimile of James Magee's Boston Marine Society membership certificate, were ordered by Captain Magee and presented to the Marine Society in 1790. Joseph Callender had engraved the certificate early in 1789, and the punch bowl and jug were received just sixteen months later.

James Magee (1750-1801), "a convivial noble-hearted Irishman" from Boston, served as the captain of the ship *Astrea,* which belonged to the Salem merchant, Elias Hasket Derby. In 1789 Magee sailed to Canton with a miscella-neous cargo supplied by Derby and several private adventurers. Magee and another Bostonian, Thomas Handasyd Perkins, took madeira, port, loaf sugar, Geneva, brandy, snuff, and tobacco as their merchandise. They returned the following year with Hyson and Bohea tea, chinaware, silk, floor mats, pictures, lacquerware tea boxes, and other goods. Most likely Magee obtained this porcelain punch bowl and pitcher on this early voyage to Canton.

Refs.: Samuel Eliot Morison, *The Maritime History of Massachusetts, 1783-1860,* Boston, Houghton Mifflin, 1924, p. 48. H. A. Crosby Forbes and Carl L. Crossman, "Boston: A Key to Chinese Export Porcelain for the American Market, 1786-1870," Milton, Mass., Museum of the American China Trade, 1972.

signs and forms in America and must have been owned by many prominent architects and cabinetmakers. Thomas Seymour's copy is the only one known today with an American cabinetmaker's signature on the title page. Both Sheraton and Hepplewhite introduced a variety of new forms of furniture, which often ingeniously combined several functions in one piece. Writing tables, drawing tables, dressing tables, bed steps with commode, washstands with bidets, dressing glasses with writing stands, and particularly ladies' work tables (no. 258), were some of the new forms that became popular in America. The designs in the book were carefully presented in measured drawings and included a proliferation of decorative detail (in classical motif), sometimes enlarged and measured for ready accurate copying onto a piece of furniture.

The Seymours' business grew rapidly, for in December 1804 they advertised that they were about to open a *"Commission furniture warehouse."* In 1805 Thomas Seymour listed his *"furniture warehouse, Common Street"* in the city directory. Other furniture warehouses offered him competition, but he continued expanding his enterprise by selling fabrics and wallpapers, meeting all the interior decoration needs of his patrons. Thomas Seymour undoubtedly had a large number of cabinetmakers working for him as well as others bringing him pieces of finished furniture to sell on commission. A looking-glass with the brand of "s. BADLAM" on it as well as the label of Seymour's cabinet warehouse is evidence of the cooperation among craftsmen in the Boston area.

When Stephen Badlam died in 1815 Thomas Seymour was listed as a debtor to his estate for $1,300, probably for Badlam's furniture that he had sold in his Boston warehouse (no. 266). Badlam had a large cabinetmaking shop in Dorchester Lower Mills, where there were also chocolate and paper mills, the Vose's cabinet shop, and the Crehore family's shop, where they made musical instruments and later playing cards. Badlam must have employed many skilled craftsmen, for the inventory of his shop in 1815 indicated that it contained the following equipment and stock: *"8 large moulding planes & irons, 98 fancy moulding planes and irons, 1 frame saw, 13 hand screws, lot chisels, sundry tools, 9 bench planes, 10 squares & bevels, 4 benches, 2 grind stones, 72 files, 27 chisels & gages, 23 pine saws, 12 plane irons, lot of cabinet furniture and looking glass frames . . ."*[20] Many pieces of furniture that bear Badlam's branded name also are stamped with other initials, probably those of his journeymen or apprentices.

There were other centers of growing industrial activity and cabinetmaking shops aside from Boston and Dorchester. In Roxbury John Doggett made looking-glasses and carved and gilded frames and decorative parts of furniture (no. 279). His account books document the extraordinary interrelationships of local craftsmen, small shop owners, and patrons. Some members of the Willard family of clockmakers also worked in Roxbury, as well as in Boston (nos. 276-278), and were among Doggett's customers.

245
Covered tureen
1790-1800, China, hard-paste porcelain inscribed: "JA" in script monogram; H. 6⅜ in., L. 5¾ in.
Museum of Fine Arts, gift of the Winfield Foundation. 51.1153 a, b

Much of the Chinese porcelain imported by American ships consisted of large services for the table. Prosperous merchants frequently ordered services with their initials or coat of arms surrounded by a border that varied from the very simple to extremely elaborate. Several sample plates are known to have been owned by supercargoes or captains to facilitate the selection and ordering of specific border patterns. Services for breakfast, dinner, dessert, tea, or coffee were all available. It was not unusual for 300 or more pieces to comprise a dinner service.

While the porcelain that the Chinese exported was not nearly as fine as what they made for their own market, this diminutive covered tureen represents the best quality bought by affluent Americans. Originally owned by the Amory family and bearing the initials "JA," this handsome tureen was ordered by either John Amory (no. 64) or his son John Amory, Jr.

20. Mabel M. Swan, "Boston's Carvers and Joiners, Part II," *Antiques* 53 (April 1948), 281.

251
Samuel F. B. Morse, 1791-1871
The Morse Family
1811, Charlestown, Massachusetts, watercolor;
12 x 15 in.
Smithsonian Institution, National Museum of
History and Technology, Washington, D.C.

After the Revolution Americans began to think
of themselves as separate from the rest of the
English-speaking world. One result of this
attitude was the publication of American text-
books. The Reverend Jedidiah Morse, a Congregational minister in Charlestown, who has
been called the "father of American geography,"
was the first to conceive of and publish a
geography text specifically treating American
geography. He published *Geography Made Easy*
in 1784. This text went through at least twenty-
five editions, and in 1789 he published a larger
work, *The American Geography*, which had
seven American editions.

This charmingly detailed watercolor, drawn by
Morse's son Samuel when he was twenty years
old, pictures the entire family gathered together
for a lesson in geography. Surprisingly, while
the Morses seem to have a very fashionable
carpet or painted cloth on their floor, their furniture appears to be old and out of fashion for
the date, 1811. Even the architecture of the room
is in the Georgian style of the Revolutionary era.

Charlestown was also a cabinetmaking center where Jacob Forster (no. 268)
and Benjamin Frothingham, Jr. (no. 273) lived and worked. Frothingham,
who had moved there about 1754, was the leading cabinetmaker after the
Revolution. Little is known today of Forster, but the following would suggest that he was a man of some importance in his trade. In 1803 this notice
appeared in the *Columbian Centinel: "To Cabinet Makers — The Masters
of Shops in Boston and vicinity are invited to meet at the Green Dragon
Tavern on July 4 at 5 P.M. on business of great importance . . . J. Forster,
Clerk of Boston Association of Cabinet Makers."*[21]

Virtually nothing is known today about this early nineteenth century
association of cabinetmakers. Clearly the previously casual economic and
social relationship of craftsmen was becoming more formalized. In 1795
Paul Revere was chairman at a series of meetings of *"master mechanics of
Boston"* held at the Green Dragon Tavern. The result of these meetings was
the formation of the Massachusetts Charitable Mechanics Association, of
which Revere was chosen the first president. Forster's cabinetmakers' association in 1803 was yet another step in institutionalizing the needs of one
economic group. Large-scale capitalization and manufacturing of furniture
and other goods lay only a generation away from these craftsmen.

21. Mabel M. Swan, "Furniture Makers of Charlestown," *Antiques* 45 (October 1944), 205.

254

GERRIT SCHIPPER, 1775-ca. 1830
Isaiah Thomas, 1749-1831
1804, Boston or Worcester, pastel on paper;
7¾ x 5¾ in.
American Antiquarian Society, Worcester,
Massachusetts

This delicately drawn pastel portrait bust shows
the leading printer-publisher-bookseller in
Massachusetts, Isaiah Thomas, at a point in his
life when he had achieved considerable means.
A contemporary of Revere's and fellow artisan
and Mason, Revere and Thomas are known to
have worked together. Revere engraved two
bookplates for Thomas and cut illustrations for
The Royal American Magazine when Thomas
first began issuing it. On April 16, 1775, Thomas
escaped from Boston, taking his press with him.
He relocated in Worcester, where he continued
to publish his newspaper, *The Massachusetts
Spy*. After the Revolution, Thomas became the
leading publisher in this country. He employed
over 150 people, operated seven presses, and
owned a paper mill and bindery. He published
over four hundred titles, of which at least a
hundred were children's books. After 1802 he
devoted his energies to scholarship and in 1810
published his two-volume *History of Printing in
America*. In 1812 Thomas was one of the
founders of the American Antiquarian Society,
and his superb library formed the nucleus of
what is today one of the most valuable resources
of American prints and publications.

From June to August in 1804 the Dutch-born
miniaturist and crayon portrait artist, Gerrit
Schipper, worked in Salem and Worcester.
During that period he made this sensitive rendering of a man full of great spirit, knowledge,
and ambition.

Ref.: *A Society's Chief Joys,* Worcester, Mass.,
American Antiquarian Society, 1969, pp. 7-8.

247

JOHN MASON FURNESS, 1763-1809
John Vinall, 1736-1823
Ca. 1785, Boston, oil on canvas; 50 x 40⅝ in.
The Brooklyn Museum, Dick S. Ramsay Fund

John Vinall was a noted Boston schoolmaster and the author of the arithmetic text *The Preceptor's Assistant* (1792). He was painted with a case of drawing instruments at his elbow and a large globe beside the table. As early as 1756 Vinall advertised in the *Gazette* that he taught "Writing, Vulgar and Decimal Arithmetick, etc. . . ., etc. . . ., at Eight Shillings per Quarter." That same year he also conducted an evening school at the South Writing School. By 1776 he had left Boston and was conducting an evening school in Newburyport. In the late 1790's he was back in Boston living on Beacon Street opposite the Common.

Little information has survived about the life and production of the Colonial artist John Mason Furness. It is known that he married Ann

Hurd, sister of the engraver and silversmith Nathaniel Hurd. In 1777 Hurd bequeathed his tools to Furness, and apparently Furness engraved some bookplates and certificates.

Ref.: "Face of America: The History of Portraiture in the United States," November 14, 1957-January 26, 1958, Brooklyn Museum, cat. no. 30, fig. 8.

257

JOHN RITTO PENNIMAN, 1783-1837, painter
Work box
Ca. 1800, Boston, satinwood with bird's-eye maple veneer and mahogany bottom, satin lining, shell painting on top signed: "J.R.P.";
H. 3½ in., W. 8 in., L. 10⅝ in.
Private collection

This brilliantly veneered ladies' work box is one of a small number of professionally painted and signed pieces of furniture of the Federal period. Disguised in the leafage directly beneath the

conch shell are the initials "J.R.P.," for John Ritto Penniman, a Boston painter and ornamental decorator. The painting on the top of the box is directly related to the shell painting, also by Penniman, on the top of a commode made in 1809 by Thomas Seymour for Mrs. Elizabeth Derby, the widow of Elias Hasket Derby of Salem. It is possible this box also came from the cabinet shop of Thomas Seymour.

Work boxes of this small size were popular after the Revolution. They were a new form developed in the Federal period, in part to supply the needs of female academies and seminaries, where sewing was a part of their school curriculum. Young ladies often painted and decorated such boxes themselves.

Refs.: Mabel Swan, "John Ritto Penniman," *Antiques* 39 (May 1941), 246-248. Edwin J. Hipkiss, *Eighteenth-Century American Arts, The M. and M. Karolik Collection,* Cambridge, Mass., Harvard University Press for the Museum of Fine Arts, Boston, 1941, p. 76, no. 42.

258
Work table
1790-1805, Boston, satinwood with rosewood and mahogany; H. 29¼ in., w. 21¼ in., DEPTH 17 in.
Richard S. duPont

Just as work boxes were a form introduced during the Federal period, the same was true of ladies' work tables. This masterfully turned and lavishly veneered table represents the epitome of craftsmanship and design at the beginning of the nineteenth century. This work table has a history of ownership in the family of John Franklin, brother of Benjamin. Visual movement over the surfaces of this table is achieved by the interplay of contrasting veneers and varied turnings. Such variety of form and ornamentation also extends to the number of functions that the table might have served. Most importantly, it is of light construction and delicate proportion and is easily moved from place to place. Finished on all four sides, it is obviously meant to be seen freestanding. The position of the feet also indicates that this table was to be admired from every vantage point. The upper drawer pulls out to reveal an adjustable writing slide and several compartments on the right side. To the right of the drawers on the side is a brass knob that pulls out a frame or slide customarily fitted with either a fixed or loose silk bag in which a woman could place all her sewing or needlework. Frequently a lock on the side of the table secured the bag and kept curious little hands from the temptation of exploring mother's sewing.

Refs.: Vernon Stoneman, *John and Thomas Seymour, Cabinetmakers of Boston, 1794-1816,* Boston, Special Publications, 1959, p. 240, no. 153; supplement, 1965, pp. 77-78, no. 52. Mrs. Russell Hastings, "Some Franklin Memorabilia Emerge in Los Angeles, Part III . . .," *Antiques* 40, no. 3 (September 1941), 147.

261

NANCY LEE, 1788-1865
Embroidered picture
1804, Dorchester, Massachusetts, silk yarns and
watercolor on silk, signed on front: "Wrought
by Nancy Lee, at Mrs. Saunders & Miss Beach's
Academy Dorchester," signed on back:
"Wrought in 1804, 16 yrs. Nancy Lee born
1788, died 1865"; 18 x 14 in.
Bertram K. and Nina Fletcher Little

The development of numerous female seminaries and academies in and around Boston
from the 1790's onward was an indication of the
changing attitude toward the education of
women in America. Numerous embroideries
that were executed by young women at these
institutions survive today. In many cases a piece
of needlework is the only evidence of the existence of a particular school. At Mrs. Saunders
and Miss Beach's academy in Dorchester,
established in 1803, a number of pupils made
fine silk embroideries. The subjects for the girls'
needlework were taken from Shakespeare or
from classical literature, as in this work with its
description of Petrarch below the picture.

Elegantly framed with a carved and gilt frame
and a glass with eglomisé painting, the glass over
this embroidery is inscribed in the traditional
manner, "Wrought by Nancy Lee." Many such
personalized frames and glasses were ordered
from the Looking Glass Manufactory of John
Doggett in Roxbury. His account book kept between 1802 and 1809 has many entries for Mrs.
Saunders and Miss Beach's, but the frame of
Nancy Lee does not appear in his accounts. It is
refreshing to note that life at the Saunders and
Beach Academy was not all work. There are
numerous entries in the Doggett account book
for the school buying casks and "cegs" of beer.

Refs.: Betty Ring, "Memorial Embroideries by
American Schoolgirls," *Antiques* 50 (October 1971),
570-575. Joseph Downs Microfilm and Manuscript
Collection, the Henry Francis duPont Winterthur
Museum, Account Book of John Doggett, Looking
Glass Manufactory, Roxbury, 1802-1809.

Petrarch recommended himself to the confidence of Cardinal Colonna, by his candour and strict regard to truth. A violent quarrel occurred in the household of this nobleman. He wished to know the foundation of this affair, and that he might decide with justice he obliged all his people by a most solemn oath on the gospels, to declare the truth. Even the Bishop of Luna was not excused. But when Petrarch presented himself to take the oath, the Cardinal closed the book, and said, "As to you, Petrarch, your word is sufficient."

Executed by
Sarah Chandler
In The Year
1808

At Mrs Dobls
Seminary In
Boston

A BC DEFGHJK LMN
OPQRSTUVWXYZ

Filial Love

Next Unto God Dear Parents I Addrefs
Myself to You In Humble Thankfulnefs
For All Your Care and Charge on me Bestowed
The Means of Learning Unto me Allowed
Go on I Pray and Let me Still Pursue
The Golden Art the Vulgar Never Knew

262
SARAH CHANDLER
Embroidered sampler
1808, Boston, silk yarns on linen, signed upper
left and upper right: "Executed by Sarah
Chandler In The Year 1808 At Mrs. Dobls
Seminary In Boston"; 21⅞ x 20¼ in.
New England Historic Genealogical Society,
Boston

This simply worked silk-embroidered alphabet
sampler is one of the few evidences of the
existence of Mrs. Dobls' Seminary in Boston.
In the Boston Directories for 1796 and 1798 a
Mary Doble is listed as a schoolmistress first on
Bennett Street and then on Middle Street.
Possibly this is the same Mrs. Dobls who later
operated the seminary where this sampler was

"Executed by Sarah Chandler In The Year
1808." In an expression of filial love and devo-
tion, young Miss Chandler has honored her
parents in "Humble Thankfulness" with a
charming verse neatly stitched above a pastoral
scene that may picture her own home with a
duck pond.

264
ANONYMOUS ARTIST
Memorial picture
1818, Boston area, watercolor on paper,
inscribed on tomb: "IN MEMORY OF Mʳ JOHN
COGSWELL Who died 30 Janʸ 1818 AE 80 Yr's";
18 x 22 in.
Bertram K. and Nina Fletcher Little

Painting was among the many skills taught to
young women in academies, and often it was
done in a manner that simulated embroidery.
The beginning of the nineteenth century brought
a great vogue for mourning memorabilia
honoring the beloved deceased. This brilliantly
colored and delicately painted urn upon
pedestal situated amidst lush flora memorializes
the eminent cabinetmaker John Cogswell, who
worked in Boston and died in 1818. Most likely
this watercolor was executed by a member of
Cogswell's own family, but the artist is
unknown.

265
JOHN COGSWELL, 1738-1818
Chest-on-chest
1782, Boston, mahogany with white pine, inscribed on top of the lower section: "Made By John Cogswell in midle Street Boston 1782"; H. 97 in., W. 44¼ in., DEPTH 23½ in.
Museum of Fine Arts, William Francis Warden Fund. 1973.289

This exceptional bombé chest-on-chest not only is a tribute to the fine craftsmanship exhibited by Boston's cabinetmakers immediately after the Revolution but also is a major document in the study of American furniture because of its signature and date. According to family tradition, this piece of furniture was originally made for John Derby, the son of Elias Hasket Derby. It remained in the Derby family until it was purchased by the Museum of Fine Arts two years ago.

This is the only fully documented piece of work by Cogswell. It demonstrates the conservative nature of New England taste. Made well after the rococo mode went out of fashion abroad, it continues and lifts to new heights a form brought to this country in the 1750's. The chest-on-chest also foreshadows the neoclassical style with its restraint of line and refinement of carved ornamentation. Living on Middle Street in the North End, Cogswell was a close neighbor of Revere's and the two men surely must have known one another in the extensive circle of artisans and mechanics who inhabited that area. Cogswell held town offices from 1778 until 1809, acting as surveyor of mahogany for the port of Boston in 1809. Between 1809 and 1812 one of his sons was in partnership with Thomas Seymour. When Cogswell died in 1818 he left an estate valued at $4218.65, his house in Middle Street, and one pew in the Reverend Dr. Parkman's Meeting House. As one of Boston's leading cabinetmakers, Cogswell created furniture superior in quality of design and craftsmanship to any other produced in Boston.

Refs.: Joseph Downs, "John Cogswell, Cabinetmaker," *Antiques 61* (April 1952), 322-324. Gilbert T. Vincent, "The Bombé Furniture of Boston," in *Boston Furniture of the Eighteenth Century,* Boston, Colonial Society of Massachusetts, 1974, pp. 137-196.

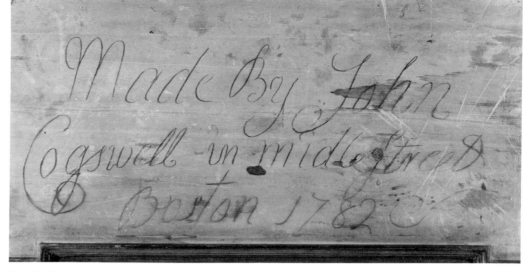

Inscription on 265

266
STEPHEN BADLAM, 1751-1815
Side chair
1790-1800, Dorchester, Massachusetts, mahogany, secondary woods unexamined, stamped: "S. BADLAM" on outside back seat rail; H. 38⅜ in., W. 21½ in., DEPTH 21½ in.
Mr. and Mrs. Bertram D. Coleman

This shield-back chair with central pierced splat represents a transition from the Chippendale style to the neoclassicism of the Federal period. The ornaments on this chair—stopped-fluting, a pierced splat, and carved motifs—are similar to late Chippendale features and stylistically place it early in the Federal period. This chair was made and branded by Stephen Badlam, a noted cabinetmaker with an extensive shop in Dorchester Lower Mills. Badlam had served in the army during the Revolution, and in 1776 he was commissioned by John Hancock a "Captain of a Company in the Regiment of Artillery commanded by Colonel Henry Knox."

Refs.: Charles F. Montgomery, *American Furniture: The Federal Period, 1788-1825,* New York, Viking Press for the Winterthur Museum, 1966, pp. 86-87. Mabel Swan, "Boston's Carvers and Joiners," *Antiques* 53 (March-April 1948), 281.

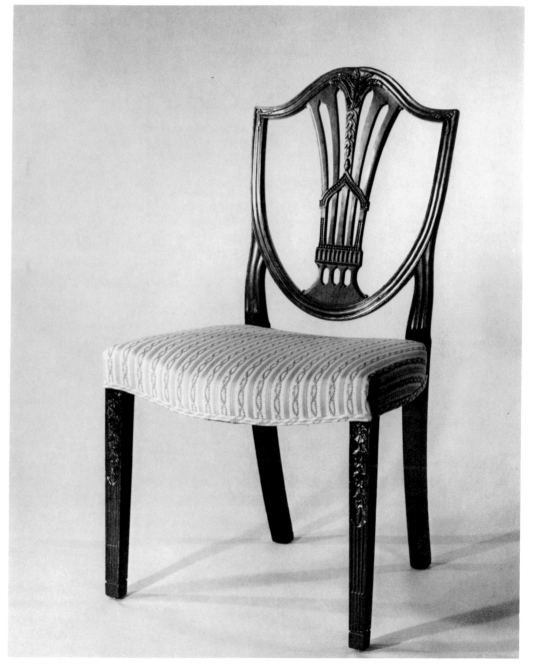

278

AARON WILLARD, 1757-1844
Shelf clock

1817, mahogany with pine, brass, painted glass, inscribed on upper glass panel in gold on red ground: "Aaron Willard BOSTON"; H. 36 in., W. 13½ in., DEPTH 5⅞ in.
Museum of Fine Arts, gift of Mrs. Anna R. B. Wilson in memory of Charles H. Wilson, of Hingham, Massachusetts

Shelf clocks were very popular in the early decades of the nineteenth century, along with other specialized clock forms like the banjo, girandole, and lighthouse. This clock was bought by Louisa Adams for $50 in 1817, the year of her marriage to William Wilson in Quincy, Mass. It descended in the Wilson family until it was given to the museum in 1964. The painted and stenciled glass panels were decorated in much the same manner as fashionably painted and stenciled polychrome furniture of the same period. The panels are similar to the painted leafage and shells on the massive Seymour commode (no. 280), and the painted work box (no. 257). John Ritto Penniman may have painted this clock also. However, Aaron Willard, Jr., was an ornamental painter as well as a clockmaker, and it is more likely that he decorated this clock in his father's shop.

Refs.: Dean A. Fales, Jr., *American Painted Furniture 1660-1880,* New York, E. P. Dutton, 1972, pp. 172-173, no. 276. Richard Randall, Jr., *American Furniture in the Museum of Fine Arts, Boston,* Boston, Museum of Fine Arts, 1965, pp. 254-255, no. 211.

268

JACOB FORSTER, 1764-1838

Side chair

1790-1800, Charlestown, Massachusetts, mahogany with satinwood inlay and birch, labeled on inside rear seat rail: "J. Forster, Charlestown; Massa. 179"; H. 37½ in., DEPTH 20¾ in. Private collection

This shield-back chair made and labeled by Jacob Forster of Charlestown is similar in overall form to the branded Badlam side chair, yet quite different in the manner of ornamentation and execution. A piece of furniture in the full-blown neoclassical style of the Federal period, this chair is ornamented with string inlay as well as oval paterae and fan motifs. The single vertical splat in the Badlam chair is heavy by contrast. The back of the Forster chair is separated into three vertical slats that create an even interplay of solids and voids across the entire shield-back. Instead of carving and stopped-fluting on the outside face of the legs, Forster has employed a simple stringing to call attention to the flat tapering surface. The label on this chair is the shorter one of two used by Forster, and virtually identical to the label of Stone and Alexander, another Boston maker.

Refs.: Mabel M. Swan, "Furnituremakers of Charlestown," *Antiques* 46, (October 1944), 203-206. Charles F. Montgomery, *American Furniture: The Federal Period 1788-1825,* New York, Viking Press for the Winterthur Museum, 1966, pp. 87-88 (for a similar chair).

271
THOMAS FOSTER
Card table
1790-1800, Boston, mahogany, mahogany
veneer on pine, maple gate, labeled on back:
"Thomas Foster Cabinet-Maker BSOTON";
H. 29 in., W. 35½ in., DEPTH (closed) 17 in.
Mr. and Mrs. George M. Kaufman

Thomas Foster was one of the little-known
cabinetmakers who worked in Boston after the
Revolution. He is not, however, recorded in any
twentieth century list of American cabinetmakers, including a recently compiled one of
Boston cabinetmakers working before 1800.
The form and handsomely veneered surface of
this table is typical of the Federal period, but the
inlaid motif is unique. The swag and tassel motif
repeated three times across the skirt is an
appropriate neoclassical inlay. Other sections of
the inlay are innovative for a Boston craftsman
of the Federal period.

273
BENJAMIN FROTHINGHAM, JR., 1734-1809
Slant-top desk
1785-1800, Charlestown, Massachusetts, ma-
hogany with pine, labeled on inside interior
drawer with fan inlay: "Benjⁿ Frothingham
Cabbinet Maker Charles-Town. N.E.";
H. 43 in., W. 40⅞ in., DEPTH 21⅜ in.
The Currier Gallery of Art, Manchester,
New Hampshire

This serpentine-front desk is a good example of
the continuation of an earlier furniture form.
The heavy, late Chippendale slant-top desk with
large brasses and shaped bracket feet disap-
peared with the introduction of the lighter
neoclassical furniture of the 1790's. The only
indication that this desk was made after 1785-
1790 appears on the interior, where there is
stringing and an inlaid fan motif on the top
central drawer front. When the drawer below
this one is opened, the label of Benjamin Frothingham engraved by Nathaniel Hurd can be
seen with its scrolled rococo surround.

Benjamin Frothingham, Jr., had grown up in
Boston, where his father had a cabinetmaking
shop on Milk Street. About 1754 he moved to
Charlestown, and from that date on he served
in the militia. During the Revolution he reached
the rank of major and served under General
Washington. This service entitled him to membership in the Society of the Cincinnati, for
which he received the customary certificate.

Refs.: Richard H. Randall, Jr., "Benjamin Frothing-
ham," *Boston Furniture of the Eighteenth Century*,
Boston, Colonial Society of Massachusetts, 1974,
pp. 223-249. Brock Jobe, "A Desk by Benjamin
Frothingham of Charlestown," *Currier Gallery of
Art Bulletin* 2 (1975), in press.

Label in 273

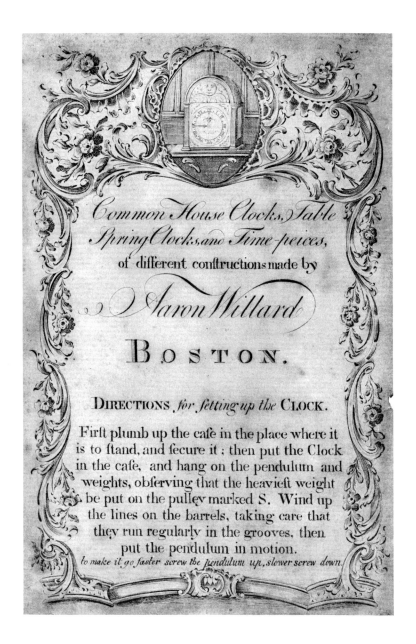

276
PAUL REVERE II, 1735-1818
Clock label of Aaron Willard
Ca. 1781, Boston, line engraving; 6⅝ x 4⅞ in.
American Antiquarian Society, Worcester,
Massachusetts

The Willards were well-known clockmakers
during Revere's lifetime. Four of the sons of
Benjamin Willard, Sr., worked in Grafton, Med-
ford, Roxbury, and Boston. In the 1780's Paul
Revere engraved labels for the tall clocks and
small round watches made by Aaron Willard.
There are three charges in Revere's daybooks
against Simon Willard in 1781, the last entry of
which notes "To 100 prints for your Br Aron
for Watches 0-6-0."

Three versions of the Aaron Willard tall clock
label are known; one places him working in
Roxbury and two in Boston. This label, with
its ornate rococo floral scroll border and shelf
clock surmounting the top, was used by Aaron
when he returned to Boston after 1792 and
managed a large shop there.

As fellow mechanics, Revere and the Willards
had close ties. In the 1780's Simon Willard in
Roxbury was making "patent jacks" and mar-
keting them in New York through Revere. And
there is evidence that on several occasions Simon
asked Revere to lend him money.

Ref.: Clarence S. Brigham, *Paul Revere's Engravings,* New York, Atheneum, 1969, pp. 176-179.

277
AARON WILLARD, 1757-1844
Tall clock
1806, Boston, mahogany, mahogany and satin-
wood veneers and inlay, with pine. Dial reads:
"Warranted for Mr. Joshua Seaver 1806 Aaron
Willard Boston"; H. 94 in., W. 19 in., DEPTH
19½ in.
Private collection

This clock, made in Boston in 1806, bears
Revere's engraved label (no. 276) used by Aaron
Willard. While Willard made the works, the
case is obviously from the hand of a highly
skilled furniture craftsman. The painted dial and
picture is the work of an ornamental painter,
possibly John Ritto Penniman. The exceptional
quality of this case is visible in the masterful use
of a variety of patterned veneers and inlays that
create a dramatic play of surfaces. This pattern-
ing relieves the extreme verticality of the form.
The engaged fluted quarter columns surmounted by freestanding small columns, all with
brass capitals and stopped-fluting, are additional
attributes that mark this clock case as one of
the finest. The case may have come from the
Cabinet Warehouse of Thomas Seymour, who
in 1805 had his warehouse at the bottom of the
Mall on Common Street. Willard was located
on Washington Street near Boston Neck. Since
they worked in close proximity, there is a strong
possibility that there was some collaboration
between them.

Ref.: John Ware Willard, *A History of Simon
Willard,* Boston, E. O. Cockayne, 1911.

279 *(overleaf)*
JOHN DOGGETT, 1780-1857
Looking-glass (one of a pair)
1800-1815, Roxbury, Massachusetts, carved and
gilt pine, reverse painting on glass, label on back
reads: "John Doggett, Gilder, Looking Glass &
Picture Frame Manufacturer. Roxbury. Con-
stantly for sale a large assortment of Looking
Glasses"; H. 57 in., W. 25 in.
Mrs. Charles L. Bybee

The development of large cabinet shops and
furniture manufactories in the early nineteenth
century is demonstrated in the business and
account books of John Doggett of Roxbury,
who is primarily known for the manufacture of
elaborate gilt mirrors such as this one. Between
1802 and 1809 he assiduously recorded his
transactions with a variety of customers who
bought finished goods and supplies for making
and finishing furniture. Stephen Badlam, William Fiske, Harrison Gray Otis, James Swan,
and John Ritto Penniman are all familiar names
found in the account books.

Doggett also bought his supplies from other
craftsmen. In 1803, he even credited Penniman
with $2.55 for "painting my sign." He may have
purchased the tablet, or reverse painting on
glass, which appears over the top of this mirror
from Penniman. This looking-glass is among the
largest Doggett is known to have made. His
account book records another pair of similar
size, 57 inches by 31 inches, made for Andrew
Cunningham in 1807. Doggett charged Cunningham $327, the highest price he ever
recorded for looking-glasses. The simple recti-
linear form of this glass, with its heavy entabla-
ture, overhanging cornice, and gilt balls, was
popular during the first thirty years of the nineteenth century. Another popular form of looking-glass, the circular girandole, appears on
Doggett's label, surmounted with scrolled
leafage, strings of gilt balls, and a dominant
eagle.

Refs.: Jonathan L. Fairbanks, "American Antiques
in the Collection of Mr. and Mrs. Charles L. Bybee,
Part II," *Antiques* 93 (January 1968), 82. The Henry
Francis du Pont Winterthur Museum, Joseph Downs
Manuscript and Microfilm Collection, John Doggett
Account Book, 1802-1809, p. 4.

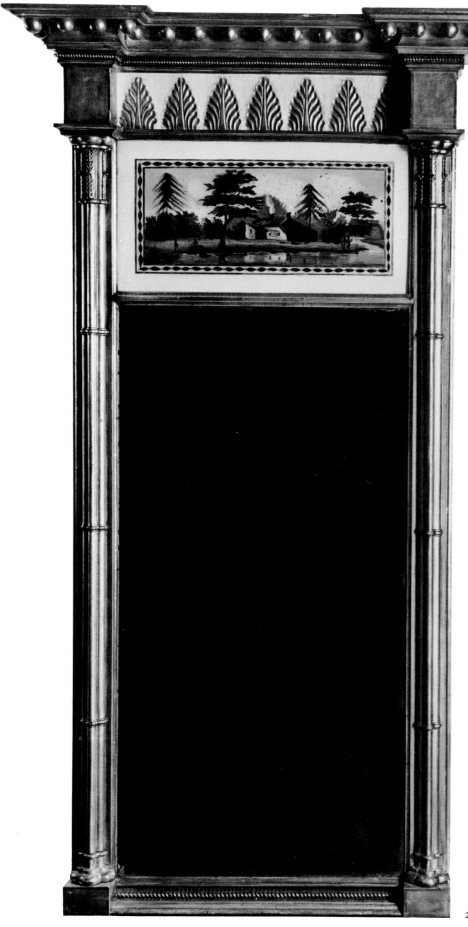

281-284
Attributed to JOHN SEYMOUR, ca. 1738-1818
or THOMAS SEYMOUR, 1771-1848
Nest of tables
1800-1815, Boston, painted curly maple;
H. 29¼ in., W. 7¾ in., DEPTH 12¾ in.
Mr. and Mrs. George M. Kaufman

This nest of tables with painted decoration is unusual in American Federal furniture. A direct English source for this form can be found in Thomas Sheraton's 1803 book, *The Cabinet Dictionary*. Plate 75 illustrates a "Quartetto Table," which he describes as "A kind of small work table made to draw out of each other, and may be used separately, and again inclosed within each other when not wanted." The only other related American table is a curly maple work table. The lightness and delicacy of these tables is heightened by the use of highly striped maple, which functions in much the same way as an elaborately grained veneer. The striped effect of the grain is accented on the legs by three thinly turned, evenly spaced rings. At the top and bottom of each leg the ring turning is repeated in a cluster of three, ending in a block form.

While the form of these tables is simple, the execution is masterful. The painted decoration on the top and sides of each table is related to the known work of John Ritto Penniman, but specific evidence of its authorship is not known to exist. These tables have a history of ownership by Elias Hasket Derby and remained in that family until sold by Martha Codman Karolik of Newport, Rhode Island.

Refs.: Vernon C. Stoneman, *A Supplement to John and Thomas Seymour, Cabinetmakers in Boston 1794-1816*, Boston, Special Publications, 1965, p. 93, no. 67 (also see p. 80, no. 54, for a related sewing table). Thomas Sheraton, *The Cabinet Dictionary* vol. 2, Charles F. Montgomery, ed., New York, Praeger, 1970, p. 293, pl. 75.

279. JOHN DOGGETT. *Looking Glass*, (see p. 183)

288
PAUL REVERE II, 1735-1818
Teapot
1783, Boston, silver with replaced wooden
handle, marked: "·REVERE" in rectangle on
bottom, inscribed on pourer's side in script
monogram "MRH"; H. 6½ in., DIAM. (base)
4¼ in., DIAM. (lip) 3 in.
Private collection

289
PAUL REVERE II, 1735-1818
Creampot
1783, Boston, silver, marked: "·REVERE" in
rectangle at left of handle, inscribed in script
monogram "MRH" under spout; H. 5¼ in.,
DIAM. (base) 2⅜ in.
Private collection

Revere's daybooks indicate that after the Revolution he had resumed his goldsmithing activities on a full scale by 1781. At this time
Revere was already familiar with the new linear
neoclassical approach to design. The body of
this teapot was raised in the traditional manner.
New technology soon would afford the luxury
of rolled sheets of silver. This permitted silver to
be more easily fashioned in the new neoclassical
forms. The pear-shaped creampot also reveals
a more classical vase or urn-shaped form. This
teapot and creamer, made for Moses and Rachel
Hays, are an early example of Revere's use of
totally new form and decoration. The decorative
motifs on the creampot combine older style
gadrooning with the more avant-garde beading.
In 1782 Revere had made an identical teapot for
his cousin Thomas Hitchborn using gadrooned
bands of decoration and a less distinguished ball
finial. The engraved script initials in leafy oval
are also in a new style. Also in 1782, Revere had
used a similar engraved pattern on a pair of
gilt-lined goblets made for Nathaniel Tracy of
Newburyport.

One of Boston's few Jewish citizens, Moses
Hays was a constant client of Revere's, as well
as a fellow Mason and one-time Grand Master
of the Grand Lodge of Massachusetts. Hays was
married to Rachel Myers, the sister of the New
York silversmith Myer Myers. Among the other
items that Revere fashioned for Hays were four
goblets, two pairs of butter or sauce boats with
beaded decoration, and "Two silver Ragout
spoons."

Refs.: Buhler, *American Silver in the Museum of
Fine Arts,* vol. 2, pp. 420-421, no. 368. Kathryn C.
Buhler and Graham Hood, *American Silver, Garvan
and Other Collections in the Yale University Art
Gallery,* New Haven, Conn., Yale University Press,
1970, vol. 1, pp. 189-190, no. 244. Sotheby Parke
Bernet, New York, catalogue, sale no. 3490,
American, English and Continental Silver, March
28, 1973, p. 32, lot 161, Revere sauceboats. Jane
Bortman, "Moses Hays and His Revere Silver,"
Antiques 66 (October 1954), 304-305.

286 *(overleaf)*
Attributed to THOMAS SEYMOUR, 1771-1848
Pedimented tambour desk
1790-1810, Boston, mahogany with mahogany
veneer and satinwood veneer and pine, portrait
of man in pencil on rear boards; H. 65½ in.,
W. 36 in., DEPTH 18½ in.
Mr. and Mrs. George M. Kaufman

This unusual pedimented tambour desk is one
of less than half a dozen labeled or well-documented pieces of furniture made by John and/or
Thomas Seymour. Only three tambour desks
with an arched pediment top are known. This
desk originally belonged to Eliza and Benjamin
Proctor, who lived on Marlborough Street in
Boston in 1802. Thomas Seymour and Benjamin
Proctor were recorded as partners in a 1799
purchase of land from Diana Ring of Boston.
While this connection between Proctor and Seymour is not conclusive evidence of Seymour's
authorship of this desk, it does establish a close
business relationship between them. Further
comparison of this desk with two known tambour desks with the label of John Seymour and
Son further suggest its authorship. An unex-
plained feature on the back of this desk is an
oval portrait bust of a man with some
undecipherable writing below it.

Ref.: Vernon C. Stoneman, *John and Thomas
Seymour, Cabinetmakers in Boston 1794-1816,*
Boston, Special Publications, 1959, pp. 82-85;
supplement, 1965, p. 10, no. 4.

286. Attributed to THOMAS SEYMOUR. *Pedimented Tambour desk* (see p. 187)

340

PAUL REVERE II, 1735-1818

Teapot and stand

1787, Boston, silver with wooden handle and finial on teapot, marked: on teapot, first stroke of "•REVERE" visible under "J•AUSTIN" stamped over in opposite direction on bottom; on stand, "•REVERE" on bottom, inscribed with script monogram "HC" in ellipse on pourer's side; teapot H. 5½ in., L. 10¾ in., stand H. 1 in., L. 6¾ in.

Museum of Fine Arts, gift of the estates of the Misses Eunice McLelland and Frances Cordis Cruft. 42.377-378

This silver teapot, made in 1787 for Hannah Carter, is one of four similar paneled teapots made by Revere in the late 1780's. During this period Revere developed variations in style of the straight-sided oval teapot form. The paneled form of this teapot is more sophisticated than a straight-sided one made for Dr. John Warren in 1785 but simpler than the fluted form made for Hannah Rowe in 1791.

Hannah Carter's teapot was not only marked by Revere but also by "J•AUSTIN." Apparently the goldsmith Nathaniel Austin bought silver pieces from Revere, marked them with his brother James' mark presumably, and resold them. Revere did record in his daybook a charge to Nathaniel Austin in 1787, the year of Hannah Carter's marriage, for twelve scalloped teaspoons, twelve silver teaspoons, a pair of silver sugar tongs, and the cost of engraving twenty-five ciphers. Six of those scalloped teaspoons, marked "J•AUSTIN" are now owned by Yale University.

Refs.: Buhler, *American Silver in the Museum of Fine Arts*, vol. 2, pp. 430-431, no. 381. Kathryn C. Buhler and Graham Hood, *American Silver: Garvan and Other Collections in the Yale University Art Gallery*, New Haven, Conn., Yale University Press, 1970, vol. 1, p. 191, no. 248.

296

PAUL REVERE II, 1735-1818
Waiter
1797, Boston, silver, marked: "REVERE" in
rectangle with clipped lower corner and uneven
lower line on bottom, inscribed "EHD" on face;
W. 13¼ in., L. 17 in.
Yale University Art Gallery, New Haven, Connecticut, the Mabel Brady Garvan Collection

The prosperous Salem merchant Elias Hasket
Derby purchased much of his furniture and
furnishings from Boston craftsmen. He and his
wife not only bought furniture from Thomas
Seymour and John Doggett but also patronized Paul Revere II for some very impressive
pieces of silver. This outstanding silver tray, or
waiter, as Revere called it in his daybook, was
made in 1797 for Derby. Revere charged him
£14:13:19 for the silver (41 oz. 11 dwt.) that
went into it, as well as £12:06:00 for the
making, and £00:15:00 for the engraving. The
scalloped border is reminiscent of salvers made
by Revere for the Chandler and Tyng families
in the early 1760's, yet this waiter exhibits a
more simple and refined version of the rococo
style found on earlier salvers. The engraved
decoration of the central portion with oval
medallion and trailing bowknot was very
fashionable in the neoclassical period. One of
Revere's small occasional account books contains several sketches of a similar design
labeled "waiter." These sketches must have been
preliminary drawings for the motifs on this piece
of silver.

Ref.: Kathryn C. Buhler and Graham Hood,
*American Silver, Garvan and Other Collections in
the Yale University Art Gallery,* New Haven, Conn.,
Yale University Press, 1970, vol. 1, pp. 198-199,
no. 259.

297

DENIS COLOMBIER, active in Paris 1776-1809
Cup (from a set of four)
1789, Paris, silver, maker's marks on bottom;
H. 2¾ in., DIAM. (base) 2 in., DIAM. (rim) 2¾ in.
Sheldon Arpad

298-299

PAUL REVERE II, 1735-1818
Two cups (from a set of eight)
1795, Boston, silver, marked: "REVERE" on
bottom; H. 2¾ in., DIAM. (rim) 2¾ in.
Sheldon Arpad (no. 298)
David Saltonstall (no. 299)

Although craftsmen were often asked to copy
models or illustrations that clients brought to
them, few documented instances of this are
known. However, these cups by Paul Revere II
are an exception. In 1795 Elias Hasket Derby
asked Revere to make him eight cups, supplying
as a model one of four cups that he had
acquired from Paris in 1789. The French cup
(no. 297) was made by the goldsmith Denis
Colombier. It was very plain with the exception
of an engraved motif around the outside just
below the lip. Revere easily fashioned the eight
cups and was able to simulate the engraved
motif, though not copy it exactly. He charged
Derby thirty-six shillings each for the "8 Silver
Cups Engrav[d]." These twelve cups were listed
in Derby's 1799 inventory along with twelve
tumblers that Revere made for him in 1797 at
the same time that the silver waiter (no. 296)
was ordered. Today three of the Colombier cups
and seven of the Revere cups are known. The
tumblers are still undiscovered.

Ref.: Martha Gandy Fales, *Early American Silver for
the Cautious Collector,* New York, 1970, E. P.
Dutton, 1973, pp. 122-125, nos. 122 and 123.

302

JOHN SCHOFIELD, active 1778-1796
Urn
1786, London, silver, maker's marks under
plinth and three on bezel of cover, inscribed
monogram on front "OAW"; H. 20½ in.,
W. 11¼ in.
Museum of Fine Arts, bequest of Mrs. M. A.
Elton. 88.291

The classical urn form was introduced into
America by the late 1780's. This large tea or
coffee urn, containing over 91 ounces of silver,
was made in England in 1786 and is among the
earliest instances of this new form being imported and owned in Boston. The applied beading, bright-cut decoration, and trailing bowknot
above the oval with engraved cipher are all
motifs introduced in the neoclassical style. The
initials OAW encircled by the oval band stand for
Abigail and Oliver Whipple of Boston. They
were married on November 15, 1774, later
divorced, and remarried February 18, 1797.
Mrs. Whipple was the daughter of Sylvester
Gardiner, a Boston Loyalist. It is not known
what prompted the purchase of this urn in 1786,
but the Whipples also acquired other pieces of
silver made in London, including a teapot, a
pair of salt dish frames, a ewer, and a sugar
basket.

304 *(overleaf)*

PAUL REVERE II, 1735-1818
Urn
1800, Boston, silver with ivory spigot handle,
marked: "REVERE" in rectangle on side of
plinth, inscribed on front: "TO/PERPETUATE/
The Gallant defence/Made by/Capt GAMALIEL
BRADFORD./in the Ship Industry on the 8th July
1800/when Attacked by four French Privateers/
in the Streights of Gibralter./This URN is
Presented to him/by/SAMUEL PARKMAN.";
H. 19 in., W. 10¼ in., DIAM. (rim) 6½ in.
Massachusetts Historical Society, Boston

Revere was quick to adopt new forms and
fashions and to accommodate his work to the
desires of his clients. By 1791 he was making
large, distinguished urn forms. In that year he
billed Hannah Rowe, at a total of £84:12:04,
for "a Silver Tea Urn" weighing 111 ounces, and
the making and cost of the ivory key, which
controlled the flow through the spigot. Two
years later Revere made "a Silver fluted &
Engr^d Coffe Urn Wt oz 50-8" for Burrell Carnes
of Lancaster, Massachusetts. The Rowe and
Carnes urns are very similar.

The urn form continued in popularity, and
almost a decade later Revere made this silver
one for Samuel Parkman as a gift to Captain
Gamaliel Bradford. As the inscription indicates,
French privateers were still plaguing the merchants of Boston. But by this time the trouble
was in the "Streights of Gibralter" instead of the
coastal waters off Massachusetts. This urn
weighs 61 ounces 18 dwt., and while it is related
in form to the Rowe tea urn, the proportions,
decoration, and fashioning of the top, including
an urn instead of pineapple finial, are different.

Refs.: Kathryn C. Buhler, *American Silver in the
Museum of Fine Arts*, vol. 2, pp. 442-443, no. 392.
Mary Glaze and Marilynn Johnson Bordes, "Two
American Wing Exhibitions," *Metropolitan
Museum of Art Bulletin* 30 (April-May 1972),
248-249.

304. PAUL REVERE II. *Urn (see p. 193)*

287
Gaming table
1790-1805, Boston, mahogany with satinwood
veneer; H. 30 in., W. 20 in., DEPTH 30 in.
Mr. and Mrs. George M. Kaufman

Thomas Sheraton would have called this an
"occasional table," which he said was "so plain
as to require little or no description." In plate
59 of his *Cabinet Dictionary* he illustrated an
occasional table that had a reversible rec-
tangular top similar in concept to the one seen
on this handsome game table. Sheraton noted:
"To the stranger, however, it may be necessary
to observe, that the top shewn partly out may
be turned over, and pushed in so as to inclose
the whole, and hide the chess board." The
central section of the top of this table is designed
in this manner. In the well inside the table there
is a patterned backgammon board, just as in
Sheraton's illustration. The turned and carved
wooden chess pieces on this table are believed
to be original. The drawers, or compartments,
on either end of the table are hinged on one
side and swing out to hold the chess and backgammon pieces.

This table is a singular example among American furniture from the Federal period. The
finely turned and reeded legs and the elaborately
grained veneer and inlay mark this table as
chastely simple yet with superb craftsmanship
in both design and execution.

Ref.: Thomas Sheraton, *The Cabinet Dictionary,*
Charles F. Montgomery, ed., New York, Praeger,
1970, vol. 2, p. 277, pl. 59.

305

Charles Balthazar Julien Fevret de Saint-Memin, 1770-1852
Paul Revere, 1735-1818
Ca. 1800, Philadelphia, chalk on paper;
20¼ x 14¼ in.
Museum of Fine Arts, gift of Mrs. Walter Knight
(Patricia Riddle Knight). 47.1055

Revere was well past the turbulent days of the Revolution when he sat for the artist Saint-Memin in Philadelphia. As a respected goldsmith, foundryman, producer of rolled copper, and honored Mason, Revere is shown here as a successful man of business, with the dignity of appearance befitting his station, at the start of the nineteenth century.

Drawing with the aid of a phisiognotrace, a mechanical device for tracing profiles, the French emigrant artist Saint-Memin carefully recreated a life-size image of Paul Revere II around his sixty-fifth year. This drawing was made in preparation for a small mezzotint print made and sold to the sitter by Saint-Memin along with the drawing. About a dozen prints were usually pulled from one of Saint-Memin's copperplates. The customer usually paid about $33 for the plate, prints, and original framed drawing.

Refs.: *The St.-Memin Collection of Portraits,* New York, Elias Dexter, 1862, pp. 40-41, pl. 201. Esther Forbes, *Paul Revere and the World He Lived In,* Boston, Houghton Mifflin, 1969, p. 469.

Revere after the Revolution: Entrepreneur and Businessman

THE REVERE FAMILY suffered many hardships and even periods of long separation during the war years. After his heroic ride on the evening of April 18, Revere's movements in and about Boston had to be carefully planned, as he continued to ride for five shillings a day for the Committee of Safety. By the first week of May 1775, Rachel and the children had left Boston, and Revere settled his family in Watertown, which became the capital of Massachusetts for over a year. During this time Revere's only income was from his riding and printing paper currency for the colony. Once the British evacuated Boston, in March 1776, Rachel and the children returned to Boston, but by that fall Revere was a lieutenant colonel in the army and commander of Castle William in Boston Harbor. Revere's family remained in Boston, rather than join him on the island, so his contact with them was limited. Rachel had to manage as best she could until Revere finally returned home late in 1779 after the ill-fated Penobscot expedition. Often alone and caring for seven Revere children (six from Paul's first marriage), Rachel bore three more children during the difficult years between 1775 and 1780. Their son Joseph Warren Revere (b. 1777) was the only one to survive, as the other two died in infancy.

With the war almost over in 1780, prospects for gainful employment and self-betterment were looking brighter for Revere and his fellow Americans. In 1780 Revere was forty-five years old and ready to pursue every opportunity for success offered by the flexibility of American society. Through the 1780's and 1790's he would rise from a highly skilled artisan and goldsmith to a businessman and entrepreneur, and by 1800 he would become a well-to-do manufacturer and landowner.

Anxious to resume his trade and once again to have a steady income to support his growing family, Revere entered the new decade with renewed vigor. His daybooks indicate a definite break in work from April 1, 1775, until the beginning of 1779 and then again until July and August 1780. The interim entries, before he resumes serious silversmithing in 1781, record the sale of minor items like raisins, rice, wool cards, and loaves of sugar. By 1781 he was working with his familiar tools again and listing accounts with Perez Morton, Simon Willard, Isaiah Thomas, Mungo Mackay, and Michael Moses Hays, among numerous others.

A highly skilled craftsman, Revere was quick to adopt the fashion of new, classically inspired silver forms. He realized that the only way to remain in business was to keep pace with the style trends of the period. By 1782 he was making circular, drumlike teapots with straight spouts. In 1783 he was adding classical beading as a decorative motif to pots of this type (no.

306

GILBERT STUART, 1755-1828
Joseph Warren Revere, 1777-1868
Ca. 1813, Boston, oil on panel; 27¼ x 21¾ in.
Private collection

Joseph Warren Revere was the third child of
Paul and Rachel Revere. He was named after
the popular doctor, Joseph Warren, a good
friend of Revere, who died at the Battle of
Bunker Hill. At the age of twenty-three, Joseph
was already a trained goldsmith, yet he chose
to devote his talent and energies to the Revere
foundries and copper-rolling mills. By the end
of the eighteenth century Joseph was working
in partnership with his father. In 1804 Paul sent
his son to England for the first time to study
bell-casting and copperwork. Shown here as a
man of business in his late thirties, Joseph was
handsome and intelligent. He lived to the age of
ninety and inherited his father's boundless
energy and business acumen. Joseph Warren
Revere was the principal mover in perpetuating
and enlarging the Revere copper works.

Refs.: Lawrence Park, *Gilbert Stuart, An Illustrated
List of His Work,* New York, William Edwin Rudge,
1926, vol. 2, p. 639. Esther Forbes, *Paul Revere and
the World He Lived In,* Boston, Houghton Mifflin,
1969, pp. 418-419.

307

THOMAS CLARKE, active in Boston ca. 1800-1801
Restrike of trade card of Paul Revere and Son
1944, probably Boston, line engraving, signed
bottom center: "T. Clarke Sc."; 3¼ x 4¾ in.
Museum of Fine Arts, gift of the American
Antiquarian Society. M36095

In 1803 the Boston directory listed Paul Revere
and Sons as bell and cannon founders on Lynn
Street. In 1804 the *Columbian Centinel* carried
an advertisement for Paul Revere and Son's Bell
and Cannon Foundry. According to a handwritten note on the back of this print, this trade
card was printed in 1944 from an original steel
plate (no. 308), which formerly belonged to
E. H. R. Revere, of Canton, Mass. Twelve of the
thirty restrikes made at this time were given to
Clarence S. Brigham for distribution to libraries.
The engraver Thomas Clarke was probably the
same man who worked in Philadelphia and
New York City between 1797 and 1800. He also
made at least one other print in Boston in 1801,
a memorial print to George Washington.

309

WILLIAM LYNN, active ca. 1800-1818
ABEL BOWEN, 1790-1850
U.S. Frigate Constitution, *of 44 Guns*
Ca. 1813, Boston, etching and aquatint, touched,
signed lower left: "Drawn by Wᵐ Lynn," signed
lower right: A. Bowen Sc."; 17⅝ x 22⅛ in.
Museum of Fine Arts, bequest of Charles
Hitchcock Tyler. 33.791

Drawn by Wm Lynn.   Boston. Pub.d by Wm Lynn.   A. Bowen Sc.

U. S. FRIGATE CONSTITUTION, of 44 GUNS.

In 1794 Revere was in correspondence with the United States Treasury and War departments negotiating contracts to supply brass cannon presumably for the first frigates of the new American navy. Of the six frigates initially ordered, two were built in the Boston shipyard of Edmund Hartt, very close to Revere's house and shop. The *Constitution* was the most famous of these two ships. Revere furnished the metal that held this ship together in the form of bolts, rudder braces, spikes, staples, and nails. As long as he could find a supply of old or new copper, he vouched that he could do the job "as cheap as anyone and as well." The bill he submitted for the materials for the *Constitution*

totaled $3,820.33. In the mid-nineties when the frigate was built, Revere had not yet attempted to roll sheet copper, so the *Constitution* was bottomed with British copper.

In 1799, when the *Essex* was being built, Revere noted, "My greatest difficulty is to get old Copper, Could I get a sufficient supply of Copper, I would undertake to roll Sheet Copper for Sheathing Ships &c." By 1801 Revere had met the challenge in a mill at Canton where he had succeeded in producing rolled sheet copper. In 1803 when the *Constitution* was in drydock being overhauled, she was rebottomed with Revere copper.

This engraving was produced soon after the *Constitution's* victory over the *Guerriere* during the War of 1812. William Lynn of Boston, the artist who drew the view for Bowen to engrave, was a rigger by trade. His precise delineation of the masts, rigging, and sails gives a sense of the speed and power of which these ships were capable. Bowen was primarily a painter and engraver of book illustrations, and this is the only large folio engraving he did.

Refs.: Esther Forbes, *Paul Revere and the World He Lived In,* Boston, Houghton Mifflin, 1969, pp. 378-380, 409. The Museum of Graphic Art, New York, *American Printmaking, the First 150 Years,* text by Wendy J. Shadwell, New York, 1969, p. 50.

288). He soon began hammering out silver into large sheets, which were then readily fabricated into the new more linear classical shapes.

In 1785 he made, among other items, an oval, straight-sided teapot for Dr. John Warren, which he fashioned from sheet silver, using a vertical seam in the body. Entire tea services were soon being ordered by clients, and on several occasions Revere fashioned large silver urn-shaped vessels (nos. 303 and 304) from which coffee or tea could be served. Sometimes the surfaces of his vessels were broad and smooth, and sometimes they were fluted and ornamented with a delicate engraving called bright-cut decoration.

Occasionally Revere mended silver, broken pieces of porcelain, or even a *"Glass Piramad."* Sometimes he burnished out engraving on old silver to add new monograms, or replaced a handle or lid on tankards and canns. He sold *"setts of bridle buckles and tips"* to harness-makers, and made a silver sword hilt and new scabbard for his friend and fellow Mason Michael Moses Hays. Between 1786 and 1789 Revere kept a shop at 50 Cornhill near the State House, where he sold a ready assortment of "hard" goods, including pewter, brass, copper, ironmongery, Willard's patent jacks, and looking-glasses. At that same address he also carried on the goldsmith's business and made *"all kinds of Plate . . . in the newest taste, and finished in the neatest manner."*[1]

At his shop in Cornhill Revere must have been selling mostly imported hardwares. By the end of the 1780's he decided that the demand was so great for these goods that there was no need to import them. Certainly he could make them as cheaply as the English. By November 1788 he had set up a small air furnace on the tip of the North End. His foundry was conveniently situated near shipyards, and he soon began making castings for ships. Since ships brought to dockside raw material for his use, he negotiated with the Browns of Providence, a prominent shipping family, for a constant supply of pig iron. As an entrepreneur and manufacturer, Revere was already a recognized leader among the artisans of Boston. Once more keeping pace with the demands of the new federal nation, he was prepared to compete with English imports.

In 1792 Revere began casting bells at his Lynn Street foundry. As a youth he had rung bells in various Boston churches. Since the bells had the function of announcing not only meetings and alarms, but also deaths of towns-folk, their tone and quality were important and were judged every day by all. To learn the art of bell-casting, he imported a model bell from the foundry of Warner in Cripplegate, London. In 1804 he sent his son, Joseph Warren, who was then his partner, to visit the principal foundries in England and on the Continent to gather information on casting techniques. In 1815 the Reveres contracted to cast a bell for King's Chapel, and in 1818 it was finally hung, the largest bell they ever cast, weighing 2437 pounds. By 1828, ten years after Revere's death, the company had cast 398 bells.

---

1. Esther Forbes, *Paul Revere and the World He Lived In* (Boston: Houghton Mifflin, 1969), p. 361.

311
PAUL REVERE II, 1735-1818
Teapot and stand
1799, Boston, silver with wooden handle, marked: "REVERE" in rectangle with clipped corner on inside bottom and twice on bottom of teapot and in center of bottom of stand, inscribed with script monogram "EH" on pourer's side, and on the other side: "To/ Edmund Hartt/Constructor of the Frigate BOSTON/Presented by a number of his fellow citizens as a/Memorial of their sense of his Ability, Zeal, and Fidelity/in the completion of that Ornament/of the AMERICAN NAVY./1799"; H. teapot 7¼ in., L. (base) 5 in., overall L. 12⅜ in., H. (stand) 1 in., L. 6⅜ in.
Museum of Fine Arts, gift of James Longley. 96.1 and 96.4

The citizens of Boston were justly proud that both the *Constitution* and the frigate *Boston,* ships of the new American navy, had been produced in a private shipyard in their city. In 1799, upon the completion of the *Boston,* they presented this fine neoclassical style teaset to Edmund Hartt, the owner of the shipyard for his "Ability, Zeal and Fidelity." Paul Revere not only made the copper fittings for both these ships but also fashioned these four pieces of silver from sheet rolled silver. The Greek fret border around the lids of the sugar urn and teapot further emphasize stylistic inspiration from the ancient past.

Ref.: Buhler, *American Silver in the Museum of Fine Arts,* vol. 2, pp. 464-466, nos. 414-416.

202

314, 315. GILBERT STUART. *Paul Revere* and *Rachel Walker Revere*, (see p. 204)

314

GILBERT STUART, 1755-1828
Paul Revere, 1735-1818
1813, Boston, oil on panel; 28½ x 23¼ in.
Museum of Fine Arts, gift of Joseph W., William
B., and Edward H. R. Revere. 30.782

Painted five years before his death, this portrait
of Paul Revere II shows the aging goldsmith,
patriot, engraver, and entrepreneur in his late
seventies. While the years have softened the
strong form of Revere's face, the alertness of
expression and intense brown eyes reveal full
presence of faculties and commanding personality.

Sympathetically painted by an artist who was
also in his later years, this portrait is instructive
in comparison with the earlier portrait by
Copley of Revere as a young man (no. 5).
Firmly defined hard edges in the Copley
portrait create the effect of youthful vitality and
vigorous presence. In contrast, the loosely
handled pigment in the Stuart portrait is pecul-
iarly appropriate to the age and austerity of
Revere the old man. The scumbled tonality of
warm over cool colors and transparencies of
glazes mixed or overlaid with opaque pigments
was a portrait formula that none of Stuart's
many imitators could match. No portraitist
offered him any serious competition after he
settled in Boston in 1805.

This portrait, along with that of Rachel Revere
(no. 315), was ordered from Stuart by Revere's
son and business partner, Joseph Warren, probably about the time he had his own portrait
painted by Stuart. On June 3, 1813, he paid
Stuart two hundred dollars for the two portraits.

Refs.: Lawrence Park, *Gilbert Stuart, An Illustrated
Descriptive List of His Work,* New York, William
Edwin Rudge, 1926, vol. 2, pp. 639-640. Museum of
Fine Arts, Boston, *American Paintings in the
Museum of Fine Arts, Boston,* Boston, 1969, p. 253,
no. 929.

315

GILBERT STUART, 1755-1828
Rachel Walker Revere (Mrs. Paul), 1745-1813
1813, Boston, oil on panel, signed on back:
"Painted by G. Stuart Esqr. For Joseph W.
Revere In the Spring of 1813"; 28½ x 23¾ in.
Museum of Fine Arts, gift of Joseph W., William
B., and Edward H. R. Revere. 30.783

Rachel Walker Revere was the second wife of
Paul Revere II. Married to Revere in September
1773, she bore eight children between 1774 and
1787. When she died only weeks after this
portrait was finished, four of her eight children
were still living. Stuart serenely posed her in a
white lace cap, fancy collar, and a fashionable,
Empire-style blue-gray silk dress. Stuart's
painterly interchange of transparent warm over
opaque cool pigments in the flesh tones conveys
an almost pearly quality to the soft cheeks of
the aging Mrs. Revere. "While you have nature
before you as a model, paint what you see, and
look with your own eyes," Stuart advised young
artists. Practicing this advanced approach to
portraiture, Stuart shaped the image of Rachel
Revere as a person of serene countenance — an
equal match to Revere's own vitality and
abundant energy.

Refs.: National Gallery of Art, Washington, and
Rhode Island School of Design, Museum of Art,
*Gilbert Stuart, Portraitist of the Young Republic,
1755-1828,* Providence, Museum of Art, Rhode
Island School of Design, 1967, p. 33. Lawrence
Park, *Gilbert Stuart, An Illustrated Descriptive List
of His Work,* New York, William Edwin Rudge,
1926, vol. 2, pp. 640-641. Museum of Fine Arts,
Boston, *American Paintings in the Museum of Fine
Arts, Boston,* Boston, 1969, vol. 1, p. 253, no. 930.

320

PAUL REVERE II, 1735-1818
Covered porringer
Ca. 1773, Boston, silver, inscribed with mono-
gram "PRR" away from bowl; H. (body) 1⅞ in.,
DIAM. (lip) 5⅝ in.
Museum of Fine Arts, Pauline Revere Thayer
Collection. 35.1758

Though this traditional porringer with cover is
unmarked, the script monogram on the handle
"PRR" and its history of descent in the Revere
family confirm its maker as Paul Revere II.
Possibly made as a wedding gift to his new
bride, Rachel, in 1773, this porringer is one of
only a few surviving pieces of silver that the
goldsmith made for use in his own family. Since
porringers with covers are rare, the survival of
this one is a fascinating statement about the
individual preferences of a craftsman who was
capable of producing any desired form. The
source for this unusual American form probably
derives from the French two-handled écuelle,
which more frequently had an accompanying
cover.

Ref.: Buhler, *American Silver in the Museum of
Fine Arts,* vol. 2, p. 416, no. 364.

Revere began negotiations with the United States War and Treasury departments in 1794 and 1795. In those years he contracted to supply the new American navy with all manner of bolts, spikes, dovetails, nails, and cannon for their ships. The one thing Revere could not supply was rolled copper. So the six ships in the new navy were bottomed with British copper. By 1800, however, Revere determined to manufacture rolled copper in large sheets. In a detailed three-page letter in March 1800 Revere wrote to Harrison Gray Otis, then in Congress, telling him of his success in making spikes, nails, dovetails, etc., from maleable copper for the *Constitution, Essex,* and *Boston.* Revere knew he could successfully roll copper into sheets if he could get sufficient raw materials. He wanted Otis to persuade the United States government to back his venture. He wrote: *"I have never tryed to Smelt the Ore, because I could never find any, but I have not a doubt but that I can do it. I wrote the Secretary of the Navy that if Government would send me a quantity of Ore, and pay my expenses, I would build Furnaces, and endeavor to make my self Master of the Business."*[2] Revere put everything he had into this project in 1800 when he bought property and buildings on the Neponset River in Canton. With $25,000 of his own invested, and $10,000 from the United States Government, he began the enterprise. Less than a year later, he wrote to the Secretary of the Navy, Robert Smith, *"I have erected my Works & have Rolled Sheet Copper which is approved of by the best judges as being equal to the best Cold Rolled Copper."*[3] It was not long before Revere was truly *"Master of the Business,"* providing copper sheathing for the *Constitution,* the dome of the new State House, and many other uses.

2. Massachusetts Historical Society, Revere Papers, Paul Revere to Harrison Gray Otis, March 11, 1800.
3. Forbes, *Paul Revere,* p. 409.

324
Pole screen
1760-1790, Boston, mahogany with pine, embroidered panel of wool and silk yarns and paint on linen; H. 64½ in., H. (screen) 27¾ in., W. 22½ in.
Museum of Fine Arts, bequest of Mrs. Pauline Revere Thayer. 35.1845

Throughout the eighteenth century it was customary for a screen of this sort to be used to shield the face from the direct heat of the fire when seated near the hearth. Equally important was its function of displaying the needlework made by the woman of the home. This pole screen has descended in the Revere family. Made of mahogany with delicate carving on the knees and a fluted and reeded central pedestal, the screen stylistically spans the dates of both of Revere's marriages. It is therefore difficult to determine which of his two wives may have done the needlework. The source for the needlework design has been traced to several similar English prints of 1738-1739. In addition, a related needlework scene of a lady and gentleman in a garden is signed and dated 1756, suggesting that possibly the needlework was done by Sara Orne Revere, whom Revere married in 1757. The 1813 household inventory of Revere listed "1 screen $2," presumably old, out of fashion, and worth very little.

Ref.: Richard H. Randall, Jr., *American Furniture in the Museum of Fine Arts, Boston*, Boston, Museum of Fine Arts, 1965, pp. 148-149.

322
PAUL REVERE II, 1735-1818
Pitcher
Ca. 1800, Boston, silver, marked: "REVERE" in rectangle with uneven bottomline, engraved with script *R* below spout, added on base: "Paul and Rachel Revere./Charter Street"; H. 7⅛ in., DIAM. (base) 4¼ in., DIAM. (lip) 4 in.
Museum of Fine Arts, gift of Joseph W. R. Rogers and Mary C. Rogers, 42.462

Ceramic earthenware pitchers made near Liverpool, England, were imported into this country in great numbers in the 1790's and early 1800's. Revere derived the shape of this silver pitcher from that popular English ceramic form. Paul and Rachel Revere owned three pitchers fashioned in this simple yet elegant form. The inventory for their Charter Street house listed "1 Silver Large Pitcher 23 oz. [this one] 1 Silver 2ᵈ Size do 10 oz./1 Silver 3ᵈ Size Do 12½." Today there are eleven pitchers in this form known to have been made by Revere II.

Ref.: Buhler, *American Silver in the Museum of Fine Arts,* vol. 2, p. 470, no. 420.

326
Tambour desk

326

Tambour desk

1790-1805, Boston, mahogany, satinwood inlay with pine; H. 43⅜ in., W. 41¾ in., DEPTH 18¾ in.

Private collection

Less than half a dozen pieces of furniture are known to have survived that were once used by Paul Revere and his family. This tambour secretary desk has a solid Revere family provenance. Tradition states that it was used by Revere at Canton Dale, the country seat he purchased in 1800 located on the east branch of the Neponset River in Canton, Massachusetts. While Revere kept his house in the North End on Charter Street, he seems to have spent much of his time in Canton. In 1804 he wrote to a friend in London: "I have spent the last three years, most of my time in the country, . . . I have my son in partnership with me. He takes care of the business in Boston. I take care at Canton about 16 miles from Boston."

Revere continued his extensive business transactions up until the time of his death in 1818, and this desk must have been well used. Though not the most extravagant desk of this type that could have been purchased, it is of better than average quality. The brilliantly grained mahogany produces two vertical accents across the drawer fronts that counter the overall horizontality of the desk. Simple string inlay with minor accents of single drop bellflowers cap the top of the legs on either side. Original oval brasses and great brass carrying handles emphasize the rugged functionality of this distinctive Federal form.

Ref.: Esther Forbes, *Paul Revere and the World He Lived In*, Boston, Houghton Mifflin, 1969, p. 410.

While Revere was exceedingly busy with his silversmithing, his foundry, and his copper mills from the 1780's onward, he nevertheless found time for active participation in associations of Masons and mechanics. In 1783 in a dispute among members of the Lodge of Saint Andrew, concerning their allegiance to the Grand Lodge of Massachusetts or the Grand Lodge of Scotland, a minority group withdrew and in September 1784 under Revere's leadership formed the Rising States Lodge. These differences were resolved by 1792, and the lodges reunited. From 1795 to 1797 Revere was Grand Master of the Grand Lodge of Massachusetts, an office of supreme honor and esteem. His most lasting and superb material contribution to the Masonic lodge came just after the death of General Washington in December 1799 when he made a small gold urn (no. 338) to enclose a lock of Washington's hair as a symbolic memorial to their most famous brother and the first President of the United States.

Revere had been a leader among artisans and mechanics, and in January 1795 he acted as chairman of the master mechanics of Boston, who met at the Green Dragon Tavern for the "*purpose of consulting on measures for petitioning the General Court to revise and amend the law respecting apprentices.*"[4] By March 1795, under Revere's leadership, a constitution for an association of mechanics had been drawn up. They were called "*The Associated Mechanics and Manufacturers of the Commonwealth of Massachusetts.*" Eighty-three men from a wide variety of professions signed the document, and Paul Revere was elected the first president. Granted incorporation in 1806, as the Massachusetts Charitable Mechanic Association, this organization was an attempt to regulate the apprentice system and give financial aid to craftsmen and laborers in times of need.

Another organization to which Revere contributed was the Massachusetts Historical Society, founded in 1791. Jeremy Belknap, one of the society's founders, was secretary of the society in the last years of the eighteenth century. Several times he had asked Revere to write down the story of the momentous evening of April 18, 1775, for the archives of the society. Revere had already recorded his story both in draft and in finished copy, probably for the Massachusetts Provincial Congress in 1775. But finally, in 1798, he found time to write a more proper copy for the Historical Society, tidying up his English and elaborating upon his original account. Today all three of these manuscripts are held by the Massachusetts Historical Society.

The years following the Revolution were not all filled with joy and success for Revere. Between 1785 and 1813 seven of his twelve surviving children died, and in June of 1813, when he was seventy-eight, his beloved Rachel also died. From 1800, he and Rachel had spent many pleasant and relaxing moments at their home in Canton Dale. They usually spent winters in Boston, in a house they purchased around 1800 on the corner of Charter Street and the present Hanover Street. But Revere loved the country, and truly valued the tranquillity and peacefulness of his abode along the Nepon-

4. *Annals of the Massachusetts Charitable Mechanic Association, 1795-1892* (Boston: Rockwell and Churchill, 1892), p. 1.

327

A view of Canton Dale
Undated, Canton, Massachusetts, pen and ink
sketch; 5½ x 11⅜ in.
Massachusetts Historical Society, Boston

According to family tradition Revere himself
drew this simple sketch of his country seat,
Canton Dale. When he bought the property in
1800 for six thousand dollars it had on it a
frame dwelling house, a triphammer shop
(slitting mill), and a "cole" house. He immediately began to improve it, and presumably this
view was drawn after the improvements. During
his life Revere made many sketches of silver
forms, decorative motifs, and cannon, some of
which survive. It was not out of character therefore that he made this sketch of his property.

Revere loved the peace and tranquillity of his
country abode, and in simple and honest praise
of its joys and pleasures he penned a lengthy
poem (no. 328) composed of nine octaves in
heroic couplets. The first stanza begins:

> Not distant far from *Taunton road*
> In *Canton Dale* is my abode.
> My Cot 'tho small, my mind's at ease,
> My Better Half, takes pains to please,
> Content sits lolling in her chair,
> And all my friends find welcome there
> When they git home they never fail,
> to praise the charms of *Canton Dale*.

Paul and Rachel were probably never happier
than during the years that they spent in Canton,
entertaining old friends and delighting in the
sweet songs of birds, the grassy fields, and a
"Chearfull Glass" now and then.

Ref.: Esther Forbes, *Paul Revere and the World He
Lived In*, Boston, Houghton Mifflin, 1969, p. 406.

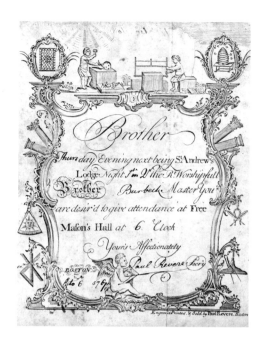

331

PAUL REVERE II, 1735-1818

Notification for the Lodge of Saint Andrew
1767, Boston, line engraving, certificate signed
by Paul Revere as secretary of the lodge, engraving signed lower right: "Engrav'd, Printed
& Sold by Paul Revere, Boston"; 7⅝ x 6 in.
Mrs. Frances Brooks

Revere was an active Mason and member of the
Lodge of Saint Andrew from 1760, when he was
received into the lodge as an active apprentice.
In 1767 and 1769 he was secretary of the lodge,
and in 1770-1771 Master of the lodge. Among
the variety of engraved work that he did for
numerous lodges by 1767 he engraved this notification or summons to meetings for his own
lodge. The certificate is dated October 6, 1767
(Masonic year 5767) and signed by Paul Revere,
secretary. Previously it was thought that this
certificate was engraved in 1784, when a charge
to the lodge appears in Revere's daybooks, but
the discovery of this particular certificate provides evidence for an earlier dating. The rococo
border is identical to the one Revere used on the
trade card of Joseph Webb in 1765 (no. 18).
Webb was also a member of the Lodge of Saint
Andrew. The Free Mason's Hall mentioned in
the summons probably refers to the hall where
they met in the Green Dragon, or Freemason's
Arms.

Ref.: Clarence S. Brigham, *Paul Revere's Engravings*,
New York, Atheneum, 1969, p. 191, pl. 63.

set River. He even drew a sketch of it (no. 327) and wrote a poem about it in
his later years. Joseph Warren Revere, his son, carried on with the bell-
casting and copper-rolling, but his son Paul III, the only son who worked
with him as a goldsmith, died in January 1813. It is not known just when
Revere actually stopped working with silver. His surviving daybooks record
work only as late as 1797. The last dated piece of silver now known by
Revere is a pitcher made for Samuel Gilbert in 1806.[5]

Paul Revere died on Sunday, May 10, 1818, when numerous churches in
Boston and afar were ringing their bells, many cast by Revere and Son. A
man of high intelligence and ingenuity had passed away, yet he left much by
which to be remembered. Certainly Boston had *"sustained an irreparable
loss,"* for few other citizens had so profitably devoted their lives to such
active exertions and useful pursuits *"in performance of acts of disinterested
benevolence or general utility."*[6] Revere would be remembered and respected by many, but especially by the "extensive circle of his own connections," for his industry, perseverance, and sincerity. Few of his
contemporaries thought of Revere merely as a patriot, for his achievements
after the Revolution now overshadowed his earlier career. In every way
Revere had echoed the emergence and growth of the new federal nation, as
he had adapted his talents and faced challenges and great risk. His flexibility,
energy, and ingenuity reflected the expansion not only of his own individual
talents but also those of a vibrant new country.

5. This pitcher is now in the collection of the Paul Revere Insurance Company, Worcester, Mass.
6. Elbridge Henry Goss, *The Life of Colonel Paul Revere* (Boston: Joseph George Cupples, 1891),
   vol. 2, pp. 611-613.

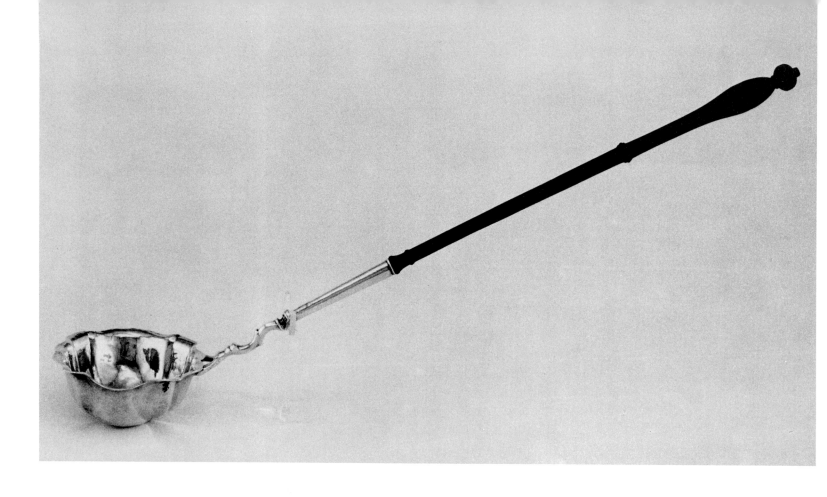

332-333

PAUL REVERE II, 1735-1818

Pair of ladles

1762, Boston, silver with wooden handles, marked: ".REVERE" in rectangle on inside of bowl, inscribed on reverse of bowl (a) "Nº 1/ The Gift of/Bʳ Samˡ Barrett to/Sᵗ Andrew.s Lodge/Nº 82/1762", (b) "Nº 2/The Gift of/Bʳ Samˡ Barrett to/Sᵗ Andrew.s Lodge/Nº 82/1762"; L. (a) 15 in., (b) 14⅛ in. Lodge of Saint Andrew, Boston

On November 19, 1762, Paul Revere recorded the following entry in his daybook:

Mʳ Samuel Barrett Dʳ

	oz
To two Silver Punch Ladles wᵗ 4:0 . . . 1/8	
To the Making at 16/ Each —	1/12
To two Wooding Handles	0/2

This entry recorded the purchase by Samuel Barrett of this pair of silver punch ladles that he presented to his Masonic Lodge, the Lodge of Saint Andrew. The ladles were engraved for presentation and numbered "Nº 1" and "Nº 2," for which Revere did not record any charge.

Samuel Barrett (1738/9-1798) was a Harvard graduate and successful businessman. In 1761 he married Mary Clarke, the daughter of Richard Clarke. Her sister Sukey was the wife of John Singleton Copley. Through the marriage Samuel was connected to the great pre-Revolu-

tionary mercantile families — the Hutchinsons, Winslows, and Olivers. Despite these Loyalist connections, Barrett was known as a Son of Liberty and a member of the Suffolk Convention.

These ladles, hammered by Revere, were shaped with dazzling bowls in a fluted asymmetrical pattern. They are splendid examples of the rococo taste in Boston silver. Two important persons, both Masons, come together in their production — the patron Samuel Barrett and the craftsman Paul Revere II. Over the past two centuries the ladles have been used by the Lodge of Saint Andrew.

Ref.: Buhler, *American Silver in the Museum of Fine Arts,* vol. 2, p. 417, no. 365 (for a similar ladle made for Tyrian Lodge No. 1).

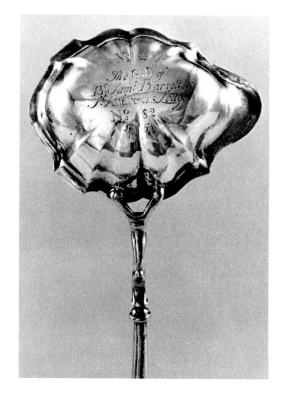

335
Armchair
1765-1785, Boston area, mahogany with maple and gilding, original webbing, liner, and horsehair cover; H. 50½ in., W. 25½ in., DEPTH 19½ in.
Private collection

Few organizations in eighteenth century Boston did more to ferment and develop plans for civil disobedience against the agents of the English crown and laws of Parliament than the Masons. Tracing their heritage back into ancient times, the Masons had a strong belief in a brotherhood that respected certain fundamental human rights. Meeting in secret, the Masons had perfect conditions for organizing in the cause of Liberty.

This chair embodies the authority and rich symbolism of eighteenth century Masonry in and around Boston. While it is not known from which lodge this chair has descended, the shape of the feet, the carving on the knees, and the construction details strongly assert a Boston provenance. The unusual treatment of the back of the chair shows the adaptability of its craftsman to specific needs. The central splat is ornamented with compass, square, and trowel, the customary symbols of the masons' trade. The more secret and mysterious emblems of the moon and sun, and points of the compass are also represented. Columns spanning a grid represent the columns before the entrance to the ancient temple of Solomon.

Among the Revere Papers in the Massachusetts Historical Society there is a bill to Paul Revere from Rea and Johnston, ornamental painters. In August 1786 they charged Revere six shillings "To dº Paintg the Backs of Masonic Chairs." These chairs may have had backs similar to this one.

Refs.: Dean A. Fales, Jr., *American Painted Furniture 1660-1880,* New York, E. P. Dutton, 1972, p. 83, pl. 132. Richard H. Randall, Jr., "The Finest American Masonic Senior Warden's Chair," *Connoisseur* 162, no. 654 (August 1966), pp. 286-287.

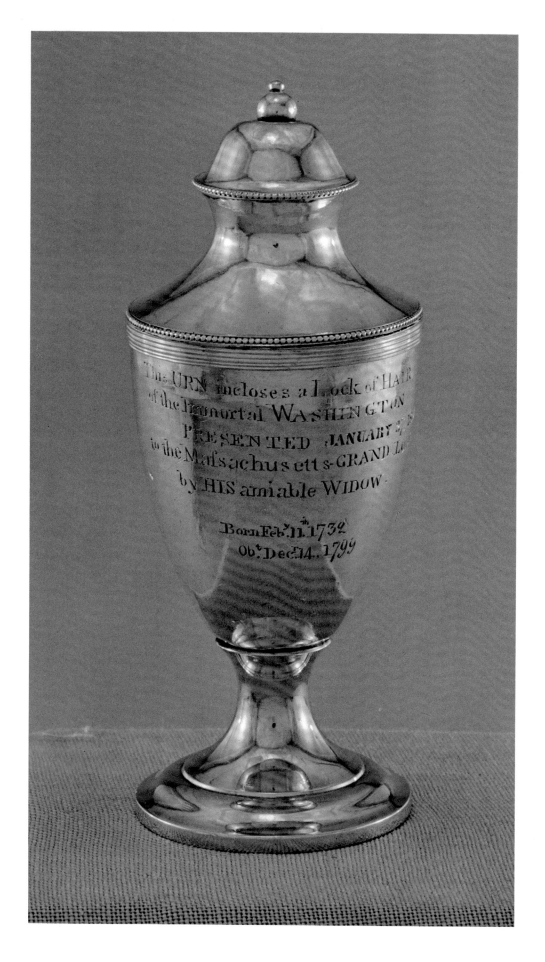

This URN incloses a Lock of HAIR
of the Immortal WASHINGTON
PRESENTED JANUARY
to the Massachusetts GRAND L
by HIS amiable WIDOW.

Born Feb. 11. 1732
Ob. Dec. 14. 1799

338

PAUL REVERE II, 1735-1818

Urn

1800-1801, Boston, gold, inscribed: "This URN
incloses a Lock of HAIR/of the Immortal WASH-
INGTON/PRESENTED JANUARY 27, 1800,/to
the Massachusetts GRAND LODGE/by HIS amiable WIDOW./Born Feby 11th 1732/Ob^t Decr 14.
1799."; H. 3¾ in., DIAM. (base) 1½ in.
The Grand Lodge of Masons in Massachusetts,
Boston

This gold urn, appropriately neoclassical in
style, is a symbol of the respect and high regard
that the Masons of Massachusetts had for their
fellow Mason and first President of the new
nation, George Washington. Shortly after the
death of Washington, the Grand Lodge of Massachusetts held a special meeting at the Concert
Hall to make the necessary preparations for the
"commemoration of the decease of our late
Illustrious Brother, George Washington!" Under
the auspices of the Masons, funeral services
were observed in Boston for Washington, complete with a procession and an oration. Paul
Revere II served as a pallbearer.

John Warren, Paul Revere, and Josiah Bartlett,
all past Grand Masters of the Grand Lodge,
were chosen as a committee to write a letter of
condolence to Mrs. Washington. On January
11, 1800, they wrote: "To their expressions of
sympathy on their solemn dispensation, the
Grand Lodge have subjoined an order that a
Golden Urn be prepared as a deposit for a lock
of hair, an *invaluable* relic of the Hero and the
Patriot whom their wishes would immortalize;
and that it be preserved with the jewels and
regalia of the Society." They further stated,
"Should this favor be granted, Madam, it will
be cherished as the most precious jewel in the
cabinet of the Lodge, as the memory of his virtues will forever be in the hearts of its members." The lodge's favor was granted, and to
this day the gold urn, undoubtedly fashioned by
the goldsmith Revere, has remained the most
cherished possession of the Grand Lodge.

The ancient Greek and Roman urn form (a
cenotaph) became an extremely popular mourning symbol after the death of Washington. This
form appropriately expresses symbolically the
virtues of noble Roman ideals and government.
Even within Washington's own lifetime he was
likened to the celebrated patrician farmer and
Roman consul, Cincinnatus, who as a patriot
won a decisive victory and then abdicated dic-
tatorship to return to the plow.

Refs.: Elbridge Henry Goss, *The Life of Colonel
Paul Revere,* vol. 2, Boston, Joseph George Cupples,
1891, pp. 465-495. Martha Gandy Fales, *Early
American Silver for the Cautious Collector,* New
York, E. P. Dutton, 1973, pp. 164-165.

Bibliography

ADAIR, DOUGLASS, and SCHUTZ, JOHN A., eds. *Peter Oliver's Origin and Progress of the American Rebellion: A Tory View*. San Marino, Calif.: Huntington Library, 1961.

ADAMS, CHARLES FRANCIS, ed. *Familiar Letters of John Adams and His Wife Abigail Adams, during the Revolution*. Boston: Houghton Mifflin, 1875.

American Antiques from Israel Sack Collection. 3 vols. Brochure 1, 1957, to Brochure 17, 1969; Brochure 18, 1970, to Brochure 21, 1972. Highland House Publishers, 1969 and 1972.

ANDREWS, CHARLES M., ed. *Some Cursory Remarks Made by James Birket in His Voyage to North America, 1750-1751*. New Haven, Conn.: Yale University Press, 1916.

BAIL, HAMILTON VAUGHAN. *Views of Harvard; a Pictorial Record to 1860*. Cambridge, Mass.: Harvard University Press, 1949.

BAILYN, BERNARD. *The Ideological Origins of the American Revolution*. Cambridge, Mass.: Harvard University Press, 1967.

_____ *The New England Merchants in the Seventeenth Century*. Cambridge, Mass.: Harvard University Press, 1955.

_____ *The Ordeal of Thomas Hutchinson*. Cambridge, Mass.: Harvard University Press, 1974.

BARBER, SAMUEL. *Boston Common: A Diary of Notable Events, Incidents and Neighboring Occurrences*. Boston: Christopher Publishing House, 1916.

BAXTER, W. T. *The House of Hancock, Business in Boston 1724-1775*. Cambridge, Mass.: Harvard University Press, 1945.

BENEZIT, E. *Dictonnaire critique et documentaire des peintres, sculpteurs . . .* 3 vols. Paris: Ernest Gründ, 1924.

Boston Directories, 1789-1805. Boston: John Norman, 1789; reprinted, 1916, Sampson & Murdock.

Boston Furniture of the Eighteenth Century. Edited by Walter Muir Whitehill, Brock Jobe, and Jonathan Fairbanks. Boston: Colonial Society of Massachusetts, 1974.

BOSTON MUSEUM OF FINE ARTS. *American Paintings in the Museum of Fine Arts, Boston*. Boston: distributed by New York Graphic Society, Greenwich, Conn., 1969.

Boston Prints and Printmakers, 1670-1775. Edited by Walter Muir Whitehill and Sinclair Hutchings. Boston: Colonial Society of Massachusetts, 1973.

BRIDENBAUGH, CARL. *Cities in Revolt, Urban Life in America, 1743-1776*. New York: Alfred A. Knopf, 1955.

_____ *Gentleman's Progress, the Itinerarium of Dr. Alexander Hamilton, 1744*. Chapel Hill: University of North Carolina Press, 1948.

BRIGHAM, CLARENCE S. *Paul Revere's Engravings*. Rev. ed. New York: Atheneum, 1969.

BROWN, JOHN HULL. *Early American Beverages*. New York: Bonanza Books, 1966.

BUHLER, KATHRYN C. *American Silver, 1655-1825, in the Museum of Fine Arts, Boston*. 2 vols. Boston: Museum of Fine Arts, 1972.

_____ *Massachusetts Silver in the Frank L. and Louise C. Harrington Collection*. Worcester, Mass.: Barre Publishers, 1965.

_____ and HOOD, GRAHAM. *American Silver, Garvan and Other Collections in the Yale University Art Gallery*. 2 vols. New Haven, Conn.: Yale University Press, 1970.

BULFINCH, CHARLES. *The Life and Letters of Charles Bulfinch*. Edited by Ellen Susan Bulfinch. New York: B. Franklin, 1973.

BURROUGHS, ALAN. *John Greenwood in America 1745-1752*. Andover, Mass.: Addison Gallery of American Art, 1943.

BUTTERFIELD, L. H., ed., et al. *Diary and Autobiography of John Adams*. 4 vols. Cambridge, Mass.: Harvard University Press, 1961.

CALHOON, ROBERT MCCLUER. *The Loyalists in Revolutionary America, 1760-1781*. New York: Harcourt Brace Jovanovich, 1973.

CHAMBERLAIN, ALLEN. *Beacon Hill: Its Ancient Pastures and Early Mansions*. Boston: Houghton Mifflin, 1925.

CHICKERING, JESSE. *A Statistical View of the Population of Massachusetts from 1765-1840*. Boston: Charles C. Little and James Brown, 1846.

CLAS, H. A., and VAILLE, F. O. *The Harvard Book, Historical, Biographical and Descriptive Sketches*. 2 vols. Cambridge, Mass.: Welch, Bigelow & Company, 1875.

CODMAN, MARTHA, ed. *The Journal of Mrs. John Amory with Letters from Her Father Rufus Greene*. Boston: privately printed, 1923.

CRAWFORD, RICHARD, and MCKAY, DAVID P. "Music in Manuscript: A Massachusetts Tunebook of 1782." *Proceedings of the American Antiquarian Society* 84, part 1 (April 1974), 43-64.

CUNNINGHAM, ANNE ROWE, ed. *Letters and Diary of John Rowe, Boston Merchant*. Boston: W. B. Clarke, 1903.

CUNNINGHAM, HENRY WINCHESTER. *Christian Remick: An Early Boston Artist*. Boston: Club of Odd Volumes, 1904.

DETROIT INSTITUTE OF ARTS. *The French in America, 1520-1880*. Detroit, 1951.

DOGGETT, JOHN. "Account Book of Looking Glass Manufactory, Roxbury 1802-1809." Joseph Downs Microfilm and Manuscript Collection, Henry Francis duPont Winterthur Museum, Winterthur, Del.

DOW, GEORGE FRANCIS. *The Arts and Crafts in New England 1704-1775*. Topsfield, Mass.: Wayside Press, 1927.

_____ *Every Day Life in the Massachusetts Bay Colony*. Topsfield, Mass.: Wayside Press, 1935.

DOWNS JOSEPH. *American Furniture Queen Anne and Chippendale Periods in the Henry Francis duPont Winterthur Museum*. New York: Macmillan, 1952.

_____ "John Cogswell, Cabinetmaker." *Antiques* 61 (April 1952), 322-324.

DRESSER, LOUISA. "Christian Gullager, an Introduction to his Life and Some Representative Examples of His Work." *Art in America* 37 (July 1949), 105-179.

EARLE, ALICE MORSE. *Child Life in Colonial Days*. New York: Macmillan, 1899.

_____ *Colonial Dames and Goodwives*. Boston: Houghton Mifflin, 1895.

_____ *Customs and Fashions in Old New England*. New York: Charles Scribner's Sons, 1893.

_____ ed. *Diary of Anna Green Winslow: A Boston School Girl of 1771*. Cambridge, Mass.: Riverside Press, 1894.

_____ *Home Life in Colonial Days*. New York: Grossett and Dunlap, 1908.

Early New England Printmakers. Worcester, Mass.: Worcester Art Museum, 1940.

ELIOT, SAMUEL A. *A Sketch of the History of Harvard College*. Boston: Charles C. Little and James Brown, 1848.

ELLIS, MILTON, and PENDLETON, EMILY. *Phileria, the Life and Works of Sarah Wentworth Morton, 1759-1846*. University of Maine Studies, series 2, no. 20. Orono: University of Maine, 1931.

FALES, DEAN A., JR. *American Painted Furniture 1660-1880*. New York: E. P. Dutton, 1972.

FALES, MARTHA GANDY. *Early American Silver for the Cautious Collector*. New York: E. P. Dutton, 1973.

FANEUIL, PETER. "Letterbook, 1737-1739." Hancock Papers, Baker Library, Harvard University.

FISHER, WILLIAM ARMS. *Notes on Music in Old Boston*. Boston: Oliver Ditson, 1918.

FLEXNER, JAMES THOMAS. *First Flowers of our Wilderness*. New York: Houghton Mifflin, 1947, pp. 201, 349.

FLYNT, HENRY N., and FALES, MARTHA GANDY. *The Heritage Foundation Collection of Silver with Biographical Sketches of New England Silversmiths, 1625-1825*. Deerfield, Mass.: Heritage Foundation, 1968.

FOOTE, HENRY WILDER. *John Smibert Painter*. Cambridge, Mass.: Harvard University Press, 1950.

_____ "Musical Life in Boston in the Eighteenth Century." *Proceedings of the American Antiquarian Society*, New series. 49 (April 19, 1939-October 18, 1939), 293-313.

FORBES, ALLAN. *Taverns and Stagecoaches of New England*. 2 vols. Boston: Rand Press for State Street Trust Company, 1954, pp. 18-27.

FORBES, ESTHER. *Paul Revere and the World He Lived In*. Boston: Houghton Mifflin, 1969.

FRENCH, HOLLIS. *Jacob Hurd and His Sons Nathaniel and Benjamin, Silversmiths, 1702-1781.* Cambridge, Mass.: Riverside Press, 1939.

GARRETT, WENDELL D. *Apthorp House 1760-1960.* Cambridge, Mass.: Harvard University Press, 1960.

"Gawen and Mather Brown." *Proceedings of the Massachusetts Historical Society* 47 (March-April 1914), 289-293.

GIFFEN, JANE C. "Susanna Rowson and Her Academy." *Antiques* 98 (September 1970), 436-440.

GOSS, ELBRIDGE HENRY. *The Life of Colonel Paul Revere.* 2 vols. Boston: Joseph George Cupples, 1891.

GREENWOOD, ISAAC JOHN. *The Greenwood Family of Norwich, England, in America.* Concord, N.H.: Rumford Press, 1934.

GROCE, GEORGE C., and WALLACE, DAVID H. *The New-York Historical Society's Dictionary of Artists in America, 1564-1860.* New Haven, Conn.: Yale University Press, 1957.

HARRIS, PAUL S. "Gilbert Stuart and a Portrait of Mrs. Sarah Apthorp Morton." In *Winterthur Portfolio One,* Charlottesville: University Press of Virginia, 1964, pp. 198-220.

HENRETTA, JAMES A. "Economic Development and Social Structure in Colonial Boston." *William and Mary Quarterly.* 3rd series 22 (January 1965), 75-92.

HEWITT, BERNARD. *Theater U.S.A., 1665-1957.* New York: McGraw-Hill, 1959.

HIPKISS, EDWIN J. *Eighteenth-Century American Arts, the M. and M. Karolik Collection.* Cambridge, Mass.: Harvard University Press, 1941.

"Historic Processions in Boston." *Publications of the Bostonian Society* 5 (1908), 65-119.

Historical Records Survey, Works Progress Administration. *American Portraits 1620-1825 Found in Massachusetts.* 2 vols. Boston, 1939.

HITCHINGS, SINCLAIR. "Eighteenth-Century Views of Boston." Unpublished list, Print Department, Boston Public Library, Boston.

HOWAY, FREDERIC W., ed. *Voyages of the "Columbia" to the Northwest Coast, 1787-1790, and 1790-1793.* Collections, 79. Boston: Massachusetts Historical Society, 1941.

HUTCHESON, MAUD M. "Mercy Warren, 1728-1814," *William and Mary Quarterly* 3rd series. 10 (July 1953), 378-402.

HUTCHINSON, PETER ORLANDO, ed. *The Diary and Letters of His Excellency Thomas Hutchinson.* 2 vols. Boston: Houghton Mifflin, 1884-1886.

KATZ, WILLIAM LOREN. *Eyewitness: The Negro in American History.* 3rd ed. New York: Pittman, 1974.

KIRKER, HAROLD. *The Architecture of Charles Bulfinch.* Cambridge, Mass.: Harvard University Press, 1969.

_____ and KIRKER, JAMES. *Bulfinch's Boston.* New York: Oxford University Press, 1964.

KULIKOFF, ALLAN. "The Progress of Inequality in Revolutionary Boston." *William and Mary Quarterly.* 3rd series, 28 (July 1971), 375-412.

LABAREE, BENJAMIN WOODS. *The Boston Tea Party.* New York: Oxford University Press, 1964.

Letters and Papers of John Singleton Copley and Henry Pelham, 1739-1776. Collections, no. 71. Boston: Massachusetts Historical Society, 1914.

List of Maps of Boston Published Between 1614-1822. Boston: Municipal Printing Office, 1902.

LONGFELLOW, HENRY WADSWORTH. *Tales of the Wayside Inn.* Boston: Tichnor and Fields, 1863.
LORD, ROBERT H. "Jean Lefebvre de Cheverus, First Catholic Bishop of Boston." *Proceedings of the Massachusetts Historical Society* 65 (January 1933), 64-79.

MACKEY, ALBERT G., HUGHAN, WILLIAM J., and HAWKINS, EDWARD L. *An Encyclopedia of Freemasonry,* rev. ed. 2 vols. New York: Masonic History Company, 1915.

MAIER, PAULINE. "John Wilkes and American Disillusionment with Britain." *William and Mary Quarterly.* 3rd series, 20 (1963), 373-395.

MIDDLEKAUFF, ROBERT. *Ancients and Axioms: Secondary Education in Eighteenth-Century New England.* New Haven, Conn.: Yale University Press, 1963.

MONTGOMERY, CHARLES F. *American Furniture: The Federal Period.* New York: Viking Press for the Henry Francis duPont Winterthur Museum, 1966.

MOOZ, R. PETER. "Colonial Art," in *The Genius of American Painting.* Edited by John Wilmerding, London: Weidenfeld and Nicholson, 1973.

MORGAN, EDMUND S. and MORGAN, HELEN M. *The Stamp Act Crisis, Prologue to Revolution.* New York: Collier Books, 1962.

MORISON, SAMUEL ELIOT. *Harrison Gray Otis, 1765-1848: Urbane Federalist.* Boston: Houghton Mifflin, 1969.

_____ *Three Centuries of Harvard, 1636-1936.* Cambridge, Mass.: Harvard University Press, 1936.

MORSE, JOHN D., ed. *Winterthur Conference Report 1970: Prints in and of America to 1850.* Charlottesville: University Press of Virginia, 1970.

MUDGE, JEAN McCLURE. *Chinese Export Porcelain for the American Trade 1785-1835.* Newark, N.J.: University of Delaware Press, 1962.

MUNSTERBERG, MARGARET. "Early Views of Beacon Hill." *Boston Public Library Quarterly* 8 (October 1956), 171-180.

MUSEUM OF GRAPHIC ART. *American Printmaking, the First 150 Years.* New York, 1969.

NICHOLS, ARTHUR H. "The Bells of Paul and Joseph W. Revere." *Essex Institute Historical Collections* 47 (October 1911), 293-316.

NORTON, MARY BETH. *The British-American: The Loyalist Exiles in England, 1774-1789.* Boston: Little, Brown, 1972.

OLIVER, ANDREW, comp. *Faces of a Family.* Boston: privately printed, 1960.

_____ *Portraits of John and Abigail Adams.* Cambridge, Mass.: Harvard University Press, 1967.

PARK, LAWRENCE. "An Account of Joseph Badger, and a Descriptive List of his Work." *Proceedings of the Massachusetts Historical Society* 51 (1917-1918), 158-201.

_____ *Gilbert Stuart, an Illustrated Descriptive List of his Work.* 4 vols. New York: William Edwin Rudge, 1926.

_____ "Joseph Blackburn — Portrait Painter." *Proceedings of the American Antiquarian Society* 32 (1922), 270-329.

PARKER, BARBARA NEVILLE, and WHEELER, ANNE BOLLING. *John Singleton Copley, American Portraits in Oil, Pastel, and Miniature.* Boston: Museum of Fine Arts, 1938.

Paul Revere's Three Accounts of his Famous Ride. Introduction by Edmund S. Morgan. Boston: Massachusetts Historical Society, 1968.

PROWN, JULES DAVID. *John Singleton Copley.* 2 vols. Cambridge, Mass.: Harvard University Press, 1966.

QUIMBY, IAN M. G. "The Doolittle Engravings of the Battle of Lexington and Concord." In *Winterthur Portfolio Four.* Charlottesville: University Press of Virginia, 1968, pp. 83-108.

_____ ed. *Winterthur Conference Report 1971: American Painting to 1776: A Reappraisal.* Charlottesville: University Press of Virginia, 1971.

RANDALL, RICHARD R., JR. *American Furniture in the Museum of Fine Arts, Boston.* Boston: Museum of Fine Arts, 1965.

_____ "George Bright, Cabinetmaker." *Art Quarterly* 27 (1964), 135-149.

"Revere Papers." Unpublished manuscript, Massachusetts Historical Society.

RHOADES, ELIZABETH, and JOBE, BROCK. "Recent Discoveries in Boston Japanned Furniture." *Antiques* 105 (May 1974), 182-191.

RICHARDSON, E. P. "Stamp Act Cartoons in the Colonies." *Pennsylvania Magazine of History and Biography* 96 (July 1972), 275-297.

RING, BETTY. "Memorial Embroideries by American Schoolgirls." *Antiques* 50 (October 1971), 570-575.

ROTH, RODRIS. "Tea Drinking in 18th Century America: Its Etiquette and Equipage." Bulletin 225, Paper 14 (1961), 63-89.

SADIK, MARVIN S. *Colonial and Federal Portraits at Bowdoin College.* Brunswick, Maine: Bowdoin College Museum of Art, 1966.

The St.-Memin Collection of Portraits . . . New York: Elias Dexter, 1862.

SCHUTZ, JOHN A. *William Shirley, King's Governor of Massachusetts.* Chapel Hill: University of North Carolina Press, 1961.

Sibley's Harvard Graduates: Biographical Sketches of Those Who Attended Harvard College . . . 16 vols. Boston: Massachusetts Historical Society, 1873-19 —.

SLADE, DENISON ROGERS. "Henry Pelham, the Half-Brother of John Singleton Copley." *Transactions of the Colonial Society of Massachusetts* 5 (1897-1898), 193-211.

SMIBERT, JOHN. *The Notebook of John Smibert. With Essays by Sir David Evans, John Kerslake and Andrew Oliver. And with Notes Relating to Smibert's American Portraits by Andrew Oliver.* Boston: Massachusetts Historical Society, 1969.

STARK, JAMES H. *The Loyalists of Massachusetts.* Boston: James H. Stark, 1910.

_____ *Stark's Antique Views of Ye Towne of Boston.* Boston: James H. Stark, 1901.

STICKNEY, EDWARD C. *Revere Bells.* Bedford, Mass.: privately printed, 1956.

STOKES, ISAAC NEWTON. *American Historical Prints.* New York: New York Public Library, 1933.

STODDARD, RICHARD. "A Reconstruction of Charles Bulfinch's First Federal Street Theatre, Boston." In *Winterthur Portfolio Six.* Charlottesville: University Press of Virginia, 1970, pp. 185-208.

STONEMAN, VERNON C. *John and Thomas Seymour, Cabinetmakers in Boston 1794-1816.* Boston: Special Publications, 1959.

_____ *A Supplement to John and Thomas Seymour, Cabinetmakers in Boston, 1794-1816.* Boston: Special Publications, 1965.

SWAN, MABEL M. "Boston's Carvers and Joiners, Part I." *Antiques* 53 (March 1948), 198-201.

_____ "Boston's Carvers and Joiners, Part II." *Antiques* 53 (April 1948), 281-283

_____ "Furniture of the Boston Tories." *Antiques* 41 (March 1942), 186-189.

_____ "Furnituremakers of Charlestown." *Antiques* 46 (October 1944), 203-206.

THIEME, DR. ULRICH, and BECKER, DR. FELIX. *Allgemeines Lexikon der Bildenden Künstler.* 37 vols. Leipzig: E. A. Seeman Verlag, 1908.

THWING, ANNIE H. "Boston Inhabitants." Unpublished card file, Massachusetts Historical Society.

_____ *The Crooked and Narrow Streets of the Town of Boston, 1630-1822.* Boston: Marshall Jones, 1920.

VOLZ, ROBERT L. *Governor Bowdoin and His Family.* Brunswick, Maine: Bowdoin College, 1969.

Warren-Adams Letters. Collections, no. 72. Boston: *Massachusetts Historical Society,* 1917.

WARREN, CHARLES. "Samuel Adams and the Sans Souci Club in 1785." *Proceedings of the Massachusetts Historical Society* 60 (1926-1927), 318-344.

WATKINS, WALTER K. *Old Boston Taverns and Tavern Clubs.* Boston: W. A. Butterfield, 1917.

WEEDEN, WILLIAM B. *Economic and Social History of New England 1620-1789.* 2 vols. Boston: Houghton Mifflin, 1891.

WHEATLAND, DAVID P. *The Apparatus of Science at Harvard, 1765-1800.* Cambridge, Mass.: Harvard University Press, 1968.

WHITEHILL, WALTER MUIR. *Boston: A Topographical History.* 2nd ed. Cambridge, Mass.: Harvard University Press, 1968.

WILLARD, JOHN WARE. *A History of Simon Willard.* Boston: E. O. Cockayne, 1911.

WINSOR, JUSTIN, ed. *The Memorial History of Boston.* 4 vols. Boston: Ticknor, 1881.

ZOBEL, HILLER B. *The Boston Massacre.* New York: W. W. Norton, 1970.

Checklist

Dimensions are to nearest one-eighth inch. An asterisk indicates that the work is illustrated in the catalogue.

1, 2
Pair of garden figures
Eighteenth Century, France, polychromed lead, H. (woman) 51¾ in., H. (man) 48 in.
Massachusetts Historical Society, Boston

3*
Shem Drowne, 1683-1774
Indian weathervane
Ca. 1716-1720, Boston, gilded copper, H. 54½ in., W. 47½ in.
Massachusetts Historical Society, Boston

4*
Carved plaque of royal arms
Eighteenth century, Boston, carved and painted wood, H. 31 in., W. 36½ in.
Massachusetts Historical Society, Boston

5*
John Singleton Copley, 1738-1815
Paul Revere, 1735-1818
Ca. 1768-1770, Boston, oil on canvas, 35 x 28½ in.
Museum of Fine Arts, gift of Joseph W., William B., and Edward H. R. Revere. 30.781

6
William Burgis, active ca. 1716-1731
Thomas Johnston, ca. 1708-1767
Boston in New England
1728, Boston, line engraving, signed in shield, "Will Burgiss," and signed lower right, "Engraven By Thos Iohnson Boston"; 10¼ x 14¼ in.
The Boston Athenaeum

7*
Paul Revere II, 1735-1818
Teapot
Ca. 1770, Boston, silver with wooden handle, marked: "• REVERE" in rectangle on bottom, engraved with Parsons arms on pourer's side, inscribed on other side, not by Revere: "TSP/to/SP"; H. 6¾ in., DIAM. (base) 3⅛ in.
Museum of Fine Arts, bequest of Mrs. Beatrice Constance (Turner) Maynard in memory of Winthrop Sargent. 61.1160

8*
Paul Revere II, 1735-1818
Creampot
1761, Boston, silver, marked: "• REVERE" and script "PR" on bottom, engraved on pourer's side with Chandler coat of arms and crest; H. 4⅜ in.
Museum of Fine Arts, Pauline Revere Thayer Collection. 35.1782

9*
Paul Revere II, 1735-1818
Sugar Bowl
1761, Boston, silver, marked: "• REVERE" and script "PR" on bottom, and script "PR" at base of finial, engraved with Chandler coat of arms and crest on front of bowl and inscribed in semiscript under foot "B. Greene to L. Chandler"; H. 6½ in., DIAM. (base) 3¼ in., DIAM. (rim) 4¼ in.
Museum of Fine Arts, Pauline Revere Thayer Collection. 35. 1781

10
Paul Revere II, 1735-1818
Salver
1761, Boston, silver, marked: "• REVERE" (chattered stamp) on back, engraved in center with Chandler coat of arms, inscribed on back in semiscript: "L. Chandler" below maker's mark; H. 1⅞ in., DIAM. 13⅛ in.
Museum of Fine Arts, gift of Henry Davis Sleeper in memory of his mother, Maria Westcote Sleeper. 25.592

11*
Paul Revere II, 1735-1818
Bookplate of Gardiner Chandler
Ca. 1760-1770, Boston, line engraving, signed lower right: "P Revere Sculp"; H. 3⅜ in., W. 2¾ in.
Private collection

12
Paul Revere II, 1735-1818
Cann
1760-1770, Boston, silver, marked: "• REVERE" in rectangle at left of handle, engraved with Hutchinson arms on front; H. 5¼ in., DIAM. (base) 3½ in., DIAM. (lip) 3⅛ in.
Private collection

13*
Paul Revere II, 1735-1818
Tankard
1769, Boston, silver, marked: "• REVERE" in rectangle engraved with Goodwin coat of arms on side and inscribed "Joseph Goodwin" on scrolls below, engraved with Goodwin crest on cover; H. 8⅞ in., DIAM. (base) 6¼ in., DIAM. (lip) 2¾ in.
Private collection

14*
Paul Revere II, 1735-1818
Sauceboat
1760-1770, Boston, silver, marked: "• REVERE" in rectangle on slant below initials, inscribed on bottom: "Z^I^E"; H. 5⅛ in., L. 8 in.
Museum of Fine Arts, Pauline Revere Thayer Collection. 35.1771

15
Paul Revere II, 1735-1818
Sauceboat
1760-1770, Boston, silver, marked: "• REVERE" in rectangle on slant below initials, inscribed on bottom: "Z^I^E"; H. 5 in., L. 8⅛ in.
Museum of Fine Arts, Pauline Revere Thayer Collection. 35.1772

16
Paul Revere II, 1735-1818
Coffee pot
1755-1760, Boston, silver with wooden handle, marked: "• REVERE" in rectangle on bottom, engraved with Flynt coat of arms and crest on pourer's side; H. 10¾ in., DIAM. (base) 4⅞ in.
Museum of Fine Arts, gift of Patrick Tracy Jackson. 59.34

17
Paul Revere II, 1735-1818
Coffee pot
1772, Boston, silver with wooden handle, marked: "• REVERE" in rectangle at left of handle, inscribed on bottom: "I^D^E"; H. 8⅛ in., DIAM. (rim) 3½ in.
Mrs. Charles Townsend

18*
Paul Revere II, 1735-1818
Trade card of Joseph Webb
1765, Boston, line engraving, signed lower right: "Paul Revere Sculp"; 7⅜ x 5⅞ in.
American Antiquarian Society, Worcester, Mass.

19
Paul Revere II, 1735-1818
Trade card of Isaac Greenwood
1760-1775, Boston, line engraving, signed lower right: "P Revere Sculp"; 6⅜ x 5 in.
American Antiquarian Society, Worcester, Mass.

20
Paul Revere II, 1735-1818
Philip. King of Mt. Hope.
1772, Boston, line engraving, signed lower right: "P Revere Sc"; 6¼ x 3⅜ in.
Museum of Fine Arts, the M. and M. Karolik Collection. 1971.263

21*
Paul Revere II, 1735-1818
History of Lauretta
1775, Boston, line engraving, signed lower right: "P Revere Sc"; 6⅜ x 3½ in.
Private collection

22
Paul Revere II, 1735-1818
Notice of Relief Society meetings
1782, Boston, line engraving, signed lower right: "P Revere sculp"; 5½ x 7 in.
American Antiquarian Society, Worcester, Mass.

23*
William Burgis, active 1716-1741, and revised by William Price, 1684-1771
John Harris, active 1686-1740
A South East View of ye Great Town of Boston in New England in America
1743, Boston, line engraving, signed lower left: "W. Burgis Delin.," lower left: "I. Harris Sculp."; 23⅛ x 51⅛ in.
American Antiquarian Society, Worcester, Mass.

24
Nathaniel Hurd, 1729-1777
Thomas Dawes, Jr., 1731-1809
South Prospect of the Court House in Boston
1751, Boston, line engraving, signed lower right: "N Hurd Sculp," and lower left: "T. Dawes Junr del."; 7⅜ x 9¾ in.
Miss Eleanor Appleton Fayerweather

25
THOMAS DAWES, JR., 1731-1809, or a copyist
The South Prospect of the Court House in Boston
1748 or later than 1751, Boston, pen and ink, signed
center bottom: "Drawn By T. D. aives Cambridge";
9¼ x 8¼ in.
The Boston Athenaeum, Boston

26*
JOHN SMIBERT, 1688-1751
Peter Faneuil, 1700-1742/3
Ca. 1742, Boston, oil on canvas, 49 x 39 in.
Massachusetts Historical Society, Boston

27*
WILLIAM BURGIS, active ca. 1716-1731
View of the Lighthouse
1729, Boston, line engraving, signed lower right
under picture: "W. Burgis del et fecit"; 9⅞ x 12⅜ in.
The Mariners Museum, Newport News, Va.

28
C. RANDLE, active 1774-1816
S.S.E. View of Boston Lighthouse
1775, Boston, watercolor, signed center bottom:
"C. Randle 1775"; 5¼ x 11½ in.
Private collection

29
NATHANIEL HURD, 1729/30-1777
Seal
1754, Boston, silver, marked: "N.Hurd" in rectangle
engraved with ship arriving at port with sun break-
ing through storm clouds; DIAM. 1⅞ in., L. 4½ in.
Boston Marine Society, Boston

30*
JACOB HURD, 1702/3-1758
Admiralty oar
1740-1750, Boston, silver, marked: "HURD" in small
rectangle on blade, engraved with royal arms on
one side, admiralty anchor on the other; L. 23¼ in.
Massachusetts Historical Society, Boston

31*
ANONYMOUS ARTIST
Commodore Edward Tyng, 1683-1755
Ca. 1725-1750, probably Boston, oil on canvas,
49¾ x 40⅜ in.
Yale University Art Gallery, New Haven, Conn.,
the Mabel Brady Garvan Collection

32*
JACOB HURD, 1702/3-1758
Two-handled covered cup
1744, Boston, silver, marked: "HURD" in small
rectangle at lip and twice on bezel of cover, and
"Jacob Hurd" in two lines in cartouche on bottom;
inscribed in semiscript and block letters on front:
"To/EDWARD TYNG Esqr./Commander of ye
SNOW/Prince of Orange/As an Acknowledgement
of/his good Service done the/TRADE in Taking
ye First/French Privateer/on this Coast the 24th of
June/1744 This Plate is presented BY Several of ye
Merchts./in Boston New/England"; H. 15⅛ in.,
w. 13¾ in., DIAM. (base) 6¼ in., DIAM. (lip) 7¾ in.
Yale University Art Gallery, New Haven, Conn.,
the Mabel Brady Garvan Collection

33*
JOSEPH BADGER, 1708-1765
James Bowdoin, 1676-1747
1746-1747, Boston, oil on canvas, 51⅛ x 40⅛ in.
The Detroit Institute of Arts, Gibbs-Williams Fund

34*
ROBERT FEKE, active 1741-1750
James Bowdoin II, 1726-1790
1748, Boston, oil on canvas, signed and dated lower
left: "R F Pinx/1748"; 50 x 40 in.
Bowdoin College Museum of Art, Brunswick,
Maine, bequest of Mrs. Sarah Bowdoin Dearborn

35*
CHARLES-LOUIS SPRIGMAN, active ca. 1776-1783
Covered tureen with liner
1775, Paris, France, silver, marked on cover, tureen,
and liner with maker's marks; engraved with
Bowdoin crest; H. 10¼ in., L. 15¼ in., w. 8½ in.
Bowdoin College Museum of Art, Brunswick,
Maine, gift of Miss Clara Bowdoin Winthrop for the
children of Mr. and Mrs. Robert C. Winthrop, Jr.

36
Tray
Ca. 1774-1780, Paris, France, silver, marked on edge
of rim with bull's head; L. 18⅜ in., w. 12¼ in.
Bowdoin College of Art, Brunswick, Maine, gift of
Miss Clara Bowdoin Winthrop for the children of
Mr. and Mrs. Robert C. Winthrop, Jr.

37*
JOHN SMIBERT, 1688-1751
Thomas Hancock, 1703-1764
Ca. 1730, Boston, oil on canvas, 30 x 25 in.
Museum of Fine Arts, gift of Miss Amelia Peabody.
65.1712

38-39
JACOB HURD, 1702/3-1758
Pair of chafing dishes
Ca. 1730-1740, Boston, silver, marked: "I Hurd" in
cartouche on bottom of each, engraved with
Henchman coat of arms and crest on side;
H. 3⅝ in., DIAM. (lip) 6 in.
Yale University Art Gallery, New Haven, Conn.,
the Mabel Brady Garvan Collection

40
JACOB HURD, 1702/3-1758
Sugar bowl
1730-1740, Boston, silver, marked: "Hurd" in
semiscript in ellipse in handle of cover and inside
foot on bottom, engraved with Henchman coat of
arms with crest; H. 3⅞ in., DIAM. (base) 2⅞ in.,
DIAM. (lip) 5⅜ in.
Museum of Fine Arts, gift of Mrs. Horatio A. Lamb.
41.222

41*
JOHN SINGLETON COPLEY, 1738-1815
Thomas Hancock, 1703-1764
1764-1766, Boston, oil on canvas, 95⅝ x 59½ in.
Harvard University Portrait Collection

42*
JOHN COBURN, 1725-1803
Communion dish
1764, Boston, silver, marked: "J. COBURN" on
bottom at center point and upside down on rim in
left wing framing cherub; engraved with Hancock
arms and crest, and inscribed in semiscript and

block letters on rim: "The Gift of the Honᵇˡᵉ
THOMAS HANCOCK ESQᴿ/to the CHURCH
in Brattle Street Boston 1764."; DIAM. 13¼ in.
Museum of Fine Arts, gift of the Benevolent
Fraternity of Churches. 13.394

43
Dropleaf table
1730-1750, Boston, walnut with maple and pine;
H. 27¼ in., L. (open) 29¾ in., w. 28¾ in.
Peter W. Eliot

44*
ROBERT FEKE, active 1741-1750
Charles Apthorp, 1698-1758
1748, Boston, oil on canvas, signed and dated lower
right: "R F 1748"; 50 x 40 in.
The Cleveland Museum of Art, gift of the John
Huntington Art and Polytechnic Trust

45
ROBERT FEKE, active 1741-1750
Grizzel Eastwick Apthorp (Mrs. Charles), 1709-1796
1748, Boston, oil on canvas, signed and dated right
edge: "R.F. 1748"; 48½ x 39 in.
Private collection

46
T. DEVONSHIRE and W. WATKINS, active in
partnership from 1756
Teaspoon (one of a set of six)
1759, London, silver, maker's marks on reverse of
stem, inscribed on reverse of tip "S.·.A" over
Apthorp crest; L. 6⅞ in.
Sargent Bradlee

47
T. DEVONSHIRE and W. WATKINS, active in
partnership from 1756
Tablespoon (one of a set of five)
1759, England, silver, maker's marks on reverse of
stem, inscribed on reverse of tip "S.·.A" over
Apthorp crest; L. 8 in.
Sargent Bradlee

48
PAUL REVERE II, 1735-1818
Tablespoon
1759, Boston, silver, marked: "REVERE" on reverse
of stem, inscribed on reverse of tip "S.·.A" over
Apthorp crest; L. 8 in.
Sargent Bradlee

49*
Linen press
1745-1760, England, mahogany with oak and deal,
H. 97 in., w. 46¾ in., DEPTH 25½ in.
Museum of Fine Arts, gift of Albert Sack. 1971.737

50*
BENJAMIN FROTHINGHAM, SR., 1708-1765, or
JR., 1734-1809
Desk and bookcase
1753, Charlestown, Massachusetts, mahogany with
red cedar and white pine, inscribed in pencil in four
places, including date and "Dᵒ Sprage" twice and
"Benjª Frothingham" once; H. 97⅜ in.,
w. 44½ in., DEPTH 24⅝ in.
Department of State, Diplomatic Reception Rooms,
Washington, D.C.

51*
Double chairback settee
1740-1750, England, mahogany, secondary woods unexamined; H. 39½ in., W. 55¼ in., DEPTH 28½ in.
American Antiquarian Society, Worcester, Mass.

52*
Double chairback settee
1770-1780, Boston, mahogany with maple and pine, H. 37½ in., W. 63 in., DEPTH 21¾ in.
Private collection

53*
Side chair
1765-1785, England, mahogany with beech, stamped on back seat rail and front corner brace: "T. HOOPER"; H. 37¼ in., W. (front) 23¼ in., DEPTH 19¼ in.
Museum of Fine Arts, gift of Mrs. Joshua Crane in memory of her husband. 30.726

54*
Armchair
1765-1785, probably Boston, mahogany with soft maple and birch; H. 37¾ in., W. 24¾ in., DEPTH 19⅝ in.
Yale University Art Gallery, New Haven, Conn., gift of Maria Trumbull Dana

55
Settee
Ca. 1750-1775, New England, mahogany with maple, cedar and birch; H. 36¾ in., L. 58½ in., DEPTH 22½ in.
The Metropolitan Museum of Art, New York, the Sylmaris Collection, gift of George Coe Graves, 1930

56*
GEORGE WICKES, active 1721-1742
Two-handled covered cup
Ca. 1740, London, silver, maker's marks on bottom with date letter missing, engraved on front with impaled Hancock-Henchman coat of arms; H. 10⅞ in., W. 10½ in., DIAM. (base) 4½ in., DIAM. (lip) 6⅛ in.
Museum of Fine Arts, gift of the heirs of Samuel May (1723-1794). 30.437

57
ATTRIBUTED TO JOHN COLES, ca. 1749-1809
Coat of Arms of Hancock Family
Ca. 1780-1800, Boston, watercolor, 14 x 10 in.
Bertram K. and Nina Fletcher Little

58*
WILLIAM SHAW and WILLIAM PRIEST, active in partnership 1749-1758
Coffee pot
1751, London, silver with wooden handle, maker's marks on right side of handle, engraved with Faneuil coat of arms on pourer's side and with Faneuil crest on the other; H. 10⅝ in., DIAM. (base) 4⅞ in.
Museum of Fine Arts, gift of General John P. Hawkins in the name of Jane Bethune Craig Hawkins. 13.2857

59*
SAMUEL WOODS, active 1733-1773
Cruet stand
1745, London, silver with glass bottles, marked on back foil of each caster: lion and maker's mark on bezel of casters and handle, engraved with Faneuil coat of arms on plaque of stand and front of each caster, and with Faneuil crest on cylindrical top of each bottle; H. (stand) 8⅛ in., H. (caster) 6¼ in.
Museum of Fine Arts, Boston, gift of Faneuil Suydam and Henry Bethune Weisse. 38.1651

60*
Dressing stand
Ca. 1735-1760, Boston, mahogany with white pine, H. 31¼ in., W. 18⅜ in., DEPTH 11⅝ in.
Mr. and Mrs. Eric M. Wunsch

61*
Miniature chest of drawers
Ca. 1760-1790, Boston, mahogany with white pine, H. 9⅜ in., W. (top) 14¼ in., DEPTH (top) 9⅛ in.
Private collection

62
Kneehole desk
1765-1780, Boston, mahogany with white pine, H. 31½ in., W. (top) 33¾ in., DEPTH 20¾ in.
Private collection

63
Desk
1760-1775, Boston, mahogany with white pine, H. 39¼ in., W. 38¼ in., DEPTH 20⅝ in.
Museum of Fine Arts, the M. and M. Karolik Collection of Eighteenth Century American Arts. 39.85

64*
JOHN SINGLETON COPLEY, 1738-1815
John Amory, 1728-1803
1768, Boston, oil on canvas, 50 x 40 in.
Museum of Fine Arts, the M. and M. Karolik Collection of Eighteenth Century American Arts. 37.37

65*
PETER PELHAM, 1697-1751
Cotton Mather, 1663-1728
1728, Boston, mezzotint, signed lower right: "P. Pelham ad vivum pinxt ab Origin Fecit"; 14 x 10 in.
Massachusetts Historical Society, Boston

66
PETER PELHAM, 1697-1751
Receipt to Mr. Benj. Coleman for the first payment for a subscription to "Cottonus Matherus"
March 29, 1727/8, Boston, print and autograph, signed: "Peter Pelham," 3 x 5⅛ in.
Massachusetts Historical Society, Boston

67
PETER PELHAM, 1697-1751
Mather Byles, 1707-1788
1739, Boston, oil on canvas, 30 x 25 in.
American Antiquarian Society, Worcester, Mass.

68
PETER PELHAM, 1697-1751
Copperplate for "Mather Byles. A.M et V:D.M."
After 1739, Boston, engraved copper, signed lower left in reverse: "P. Pelham ad vivum pinx. & fecit."; 6¼ x 4½ in.
American Antiquarian Society, Worcester, Mass.

69
ATTRIBUTED TO JOSEPH BADGER, 1708-1765
George Whitefield, 1714-1770
Ca. 1743-1765, Boston, oil on canvas, 42 x 32⅞ in.
Harvard University Portrait Collection

70*
PAUL REVERE II, 1735-1818
The Revᵈ Jonathan Mayhew. D.D., 1720-1766
1766, Boston, line engraving, signed lower right: "P Revere sculp"; 5¾ x 4 in.
Prints Division, the New York Public Library, Astor, Lenox and Tilden Foundations

71
JOSEPH BADGER, 1708-1765
Thomas Prince, 1687-1758
Ca. 1750, Boston, oil on canvas, 30 x 25 in.
American Antiquarian Society, Worcester, Mass.

72
PETER PELHAM, 1697-1751
Thomas Prince, A.M., 1687-1758
1750, Boston, mezzotint, signed lower right: "P. Pelham fecit."; 13⅞ x 9⅝ in.
Massachusetts Historical Society, Boston

73
JOHN SINGLETON COPLEY, 1738-1815
Rev. Mr. William Welsteed, 1696-1753
1753, Boston, mezzotint, signed lower left: "J:S: Copley pinxᵗ et fecit."; 13⅝ x 9¾ in.
Museum of Fine Arts, gift of Mrs. Frederick Lewis Gay. M27849

74*
WILLIAM BURGIS, active ca. 1716-1731
A Prospect of the Colledges in Cambridge in New England
1726, Boston, hand-colored line engraving, signed: "W:Burgis" in cartouche at center bottom; 19 x 24⅝ in.
Massachusetts Historical Society, Boston

75*
Embroidered picture of Harvard Hall
First half eighteenth century, Boston area, silk, wool and gilt-silver yarns on linen, 7¾ x 9⅞ in.
Massachusetts Historical Society, Boston

76*
PAUL REVERE II, 1735-1818
JOSEPH CHADWICK, ca. 1721-1783
A Westerly View of the Colledges in Cambridge New England
1767, Boston, line engraving, signed lower right: "P Revere Sculp," signed lower left: "Josʰ Chadwick. del—"; 9¼ x 15¼ in.
Private collection

77*
ATTRIBUTED TO JOHN GREENWOOD, 1727-1792
Henry Flynt, 1675-1760
Ca. 1750, Boston, oil on canvas, 29 x 24½ in.
Harvard University Portrait Collection

78*
JACOB HURD, 1702/3-1758
Teapot
1738, Boston, silver, marked: "Hurd" in semiscript in an ellipse on bottom, engraved with Flynt coat of arms, inscribed below: "Ex dono Pupillorum"; H. 5¾ in., DIAM. (base) 3¼ in.
Museum of Fine Arts, Edward Jackson Holmes Collection, bequest of Mrs. Holmes. 65.385

79
JACOB HURD, 1702/3-1758
Porringer
1730-1740, Boston, silver, marked: "Jacob/Hurd" in cartouche on back of handle, inscribed on handle: "The Gift:of/Henry Flynt/Esqʳ to Hannah/Sprague 1758."; H. 1⅞ in., DIAM. (lip) 5⅛ in., L. (handle) 2⅝ in.
Museum of Fine Arts, the Philip Leffingwell Spalding Collection. Given in his memory by Katherine Ames Spalding and Philip Spalding, Oakes Ames Spalding, Hobert Ames Spalding. 42.238

80*
SAMUEL MINOTT, 1732-1803
Tankard
Ca. 1770, Boston, silver, marked: "M" in semiscript in a square above center point and "Minott" in semiscript in a rectangle below center point, inscribed in front: "HARVARDINATIBUS/Anno Domini MDCCLXX initiatis/Tertium sub ejus tutela annum agentibus,/Hoc poculum acceptum/Refert JOSEPHUS WILLARD."; on bottom within guidelines: "Josephus Willard/Coll:Harv:tutor/Cal:Septembris electus fuit/Anno MDCCLXVI."; H. 8⅞ in., DIAM. (base) 5⅛ in., DIAM. (lip) 4 in.
Museum of Fine Arts, the Philip Leffingwell Spalding Collection. Given in his memory by Katherine Ames Spalding and Philip Spalding, Oakes Ames Spalding, Hobart Ames Spalding. 42.246

81
PAUL REVERE II, 1735-1818
Certificate for the anatomical lectures
1780, Boston, signed lower right; "PR"; 9¼ x 7½ in.
American Antiquarian Society, Worcester, Mass.

82*
Desk
1700-1750, Massachusetts, probably North Shore, painted white pine, signed in ink inside desk: "J. Gyles Merrill's Harvard College 1755"; and "James G. Merrill's Desk Harvard College October 6, 1803."; H. 51¼ in., W. 32½ in., DEPTH, 19¼ in.
Colonial Williamsburg Foundation, Williamsburg, Va.

83*
BENJAMIN MARTIN, 1704-1782
Celestial globe
Ca. 1765, London, paper-covered globe on mahogany stand, H. 35 in., DIAM. (stand) 35½ in., DIAM. (globe) 26¾ in.
Harvard University Collection of Historical Scientific Instruments, Cambridge, Mass.

84*
CHRISTIAN GULLAGER, 1759-1826
James Bowdoin II, 1726-1790 (version B)
Ca. 1791, Boston, oil on panel, 10¾ x 8⅝ in.
Bowdoin College Museum of Art, Brunswick, Maine, bequest of Sarah Bowdoin Dearborn

85*
JOHN SINGLETON COPLEY, 1738-1815
Ebenezer Storer II, 1730-1807
1767-1769, Boston, pastel on paper, 28 x 22 in.
Private collection

86
JOHN SINGLETON COPLEY, 1738-1815
Elizabeth Green Storer (Mrs. Ebenezer II), 1734-1774
1767-1769, Boston, pastel on paper, 28⅝ x 22½ in.
Private collection

87
HANNAH STORER, 1739-1811
Embroidered sampler
1747, Boston, silk yarns on linen, inscribed: "Hannah Storer her Sam/pler Aged Eight Years."; 15½ x 11¾ in.
Massachusetts Historical Society, Boston

88*
Chest of drawers
1765, Boston, mahogany with white pine, H. 30 in., W. 36 in., DEPTH 20 in.
Department of State, Diplomatic Reception Rooms, Washington, D.C.

89
ZACHARIAH BRIGDEN, 1734-1787
Chocolate pot
Ca. 1755, Boston, silver, marked: "Z. Brigden" in cartouche on bottom and left of handle, and "Z•B" in a rectangle on edge of cover, engraved with coat of arms used by Ebenezer Storer; H. 9⅞ in., DIAM. (base) 4¾ in.
Museum of Fine Arts, gift of the Misses Rose and Elizabeth Townsend. 56.676

90
JACOB HURD, 1702/3-1758
Teapot
1730-1735, Boston, silver, marked: "Hurd" in semiscript in ellipse on cover, and "Jacob/Hurd" in cartouche between engravings on bottom, engraved with Sturgis coat of arms and crest; H. 5 in., DIAM. (base) 3¼ in.
Museum of Fine Arts, gift of William S. Eaton in the name of Miss Georgiana G. Eaton. 13.558

91
SETH STORER COBURN, 1744-after 1790
Nutmeg grater
Ca. 1770, Boston, silver, marked: "S.S.C." in cartouche on bottom and in cover, inscribed "Mary/Storer/1770" on cover, and "MS" on bottom; L. 2⅞ in., DIAM. ⅞ in.
Museum of Fine Arts, gift of Miss Elizabeth Morford in memory of her late partner, Lucy Massenburg. 1973.123

92*
JOHN GREENWOOD, 1727-1792
The Greenwood-Lee Family
Ca. 1747, Boston, oil on canvas, 56 x 68 in.
Promised gift to the Museum of Fine Arts, Boston

93*
BENJAMIN BLYTH, 1746-1787?
Abigail Smith Adams (Mrs. John), 1744-1818
1766, Salem, Massachusetts, pastel on paper, 23 x 17½ in.
Massachusetts Historical Society, Boston

94*
JOHN SINGLETON COPLEY, 1738-1815
Mercy Otis Warren (Mrs. James), 1728-1814
Ca. 1763, Boston, oil on canvas, 51¼ x 41 in.
Museum of Fine Arts, bequest of Winslow Warren. 31.212

95*
Card table
1750-1770, Boston, mahogany with pine and maple and embroidered top made by Mercy Otis Warren; H. 27¼ in., W. 41⅛ in., DEPTH (open) 38½ in.
Collections of the Pilgrim Society, Plymouth, Mass.

96
Embroidered envelope pocketbook
1763, Boston, wool yarns on linen with silk lining, inscribed: "For BENJAMIN/STUART 1763"; H. (closed) 5¼ in., W. 8 in.
Massachusetts Historical Society, Boston

97
MARY FLEET
Embroidered sampler
1743, Boston, silk yarns on linen, inscribed: "Mary Fleet 1743," 17¾ x 17½ in.
Museum of Fine Arts, anonymous gift. 41.493

98
JOSEPH BADGER, 1708-1765
Isabella Duncan Stevenson (Mrs. Thomas), 1744-1775
Ca. 1750, Boston, oil on canvas, 35 x 27 in.
Charles Devens, Jr.

99
ISABELLA DUNCAN STEVENSON, 1744-1775
Embroidered picture
Ca. 1750, Boston, wool, silk and silver yarns and spangles on linen, 16 x 11 in.
Charles Devens, Jr.

100*
Embroidered picture
1756, New England, wool and silk yarns on linen, dated on clock tower: "1756," 20½ x 14¾ in.
American Antiquarian Society, Worcester, Mass.

101*
ATTRIBUTED TO MERCY SCOLLAY, 1741-?, or DEBORAH SCOLLAY, 1736-1794
Embroidered overmantel or chimneypiece
1766, Boston, silk yarns, dated in lower right corner; 21 x 49 in.
Private collection

102*
HANNAH OTIS, 1732-1773
Embroidered picture of Boston Common
Ca. 1755-1760, Boston, silk, wool, and metallic yarns on linen, 24 x 53 in.
Private collection

103*
JOHN GREENWOOD, 1727-1792
Margaret Fayerweather Bromfield (Mrs. Henry),
1732-1761
Ca. 1749-1750, Boston, oil on canvas, 36 x 25½ in.
Museum of Fine Arts, Emily L. Ainsley Fund. 62.173

104*
Side chair
1750-1760, New York, walnut with walnut veneer,
white pine, and maple seat frame, embroidered seat
cover, H. 38½ in., W. 22 in., DEPTH 18⅜ in.
Museum of Fine Arts, gift of Mrs. Jean Frederic
Wagniere in memory of her mother, Henrietta Slade
Warner (Mrs. Henry Eldridge Warner). 68.389

105*
JOHN SMIBERT, 1688-1751
Mary Fitch Oliver (Mrs. Andrew), 1706-1732 and
Andrew Oliver 1731-1799
1732, Boston, oil on canvas, 50¼ x 40¼ in.
Oliver Family

106
JOHN GREENWOOD, 1727-1792
Jersey Nanny (Ann Arnold)
1748, Boston, mezzotint, signed lower left:
"——eenwood ad vivum pinxᵗ et fecit"; 9⅝ x 7¾ in.
Museum of Fine Arts, gift of Dr. Henry L. Shattuck.
1971.715

107*
JOHN SINGLETON COPLEY, 1738-1815
The Copley Family (grisaille study)
1776, England, oil on canvas, 20¾ x 26¼ in.
Private collection

108*
JOSEPH BLACKBURN, active in America 1754-1763
Elizabeth and James Bowdoin III as Children
Ca. 1760, Boston, oil on canvas, 36⅞ x 58 in.
Bowdoin College Museum of Art, Brunswick,
Maine, bequest of Mrs. Sarah Bowdoin Dearborn

109*
THOMAS EDWARDS, 1701-1755
Whistle and bells with coral
Ca. 1722, Boston, silver with coral end, marked:
"TE" in rectangle on side of stem near coral end;
engraved with Fayerweather crest and inscribed with
initials "IF" on side and under whistle; L. 4½ in.
The Art Institute of Chicago, gift of Mrs. J. Ogden
Armour through the Antiquarian Society of Chicago

110
PAUL REVERE II, 1735-1818
Child's whistle
Ca. 1800, Boston, silver with coral broken at
moulded tip, marked: "REVERE" in rectangle near
tip; L. 3⅛ in.
Museum of Fine Arts, gift of Henry Davis Sleeper
in memory of his mother, Maria Westcote Sleeper,
by exchange. 61.406

111
SAMUEL EDWARDS, 1705-1762
Miniature tankard
Ca. 1757, Boston, silver, marked: "SE" in oval at left
of handle and (broken) on base, inscribed:
"M Storer/to/Mary Smith"; H. 2½ in., DIAM.
(base) 1½ in.
The Society for the Preservation of New England
Antiquities, Boston

112
PAUL REVERE I, 1702-1754
Miniature caudle cup
Ca. 1720, Boston, silver, marked: "PR" in rectangle
in pebbling and clear part of leaf on bottom;
H. 1⅜ in., W. 2⅝ in.
Museum of Fine Arts, bequest of Mrs. F. Gordon
Patterson. 56.116

113*
PAUL REVERE I, 1702-1754
Porringer
Ca. 1726-1730, Boston, silver, marked: "PR" in
shield on upper side of bottom, inscribed "D*M"
on handle and "D Mason" on underside of bottom;
H. 1½ in., DIAM. (lip) 3⅞ in., L. (handle) 2¼ in.
Private collection

114
Nursing nipple
Eighteenth Century, possibly Boston, silver, L. 2⅝ in.
The Society for the Preservation of New England
Antiquities, Boston

115
Pin cushion
Ca. 1777, Salem, Massachusetts, metallic threads,
spangles and common pins on silk, obverse reads:
"WELCOME/LITTLE/STRANGER"; reverse reads:
"H.W. 1777/H.W. 1778/I.W. 1781/I.W. 1783/
S.W. 1787/F.W. 1789/M.W. 1792/E.W. 1795";
L. 5¾ in.
The Society for the Preservation of New England
Antiquities, Boston

116
Baby's shirt
Ca. 1764, Boston, linen, L. (back) 7⅞ in.
Mr. and Mrs. Charles Fox Hovey

117-118
Set of sleeve buttons
Ca. 1740-1765, probably Boston, gold,
w. (each) ⅜ in.
Mr. and Mrs. Charles Fox Hovey

119
The School of Good Manners
1715, New London, Connecticut, printed and sold
by T. Green, also sold by B. Eliot at Boston,
inscribed opposite title page "Eunice Treat/Her
Book/Abigail Paine/Her Book/Anno Dom Y
1735"; H. 4½ in., w. 3⅝ in.
Massachusetts Historical Society, Boston

120
The Story of The cruel Giant Barbarico, The good
Giant Benefico, And the little Pretty, Dwarf Mignon
1768, Boston, printed by Mein and Fleeming, H. 4 in.,
w. 2⅝ in.
Massachusetts Historical Society, Boston

121*
JOHN SINGLETON COPLEY, 1738-1815
Dorothy Quincy (Mrs. John Hancock), 1747-1830
Ca. 1772, Boston, oil on canvas, 50 x 39 in.
Museum of Fine Arts, Charles H. Bayley Fund and
partial gift of Anne B. Loring. 1975.13

122*
Tea table
1740-1765, Boston, mahogany with white pine,
H. 27 in., w. 30 in., DEPTH 20 in.
Mr. and Mrs. Eric M. Wunsch

123*
BENJAMIN BURT, 1729-1805
Teapot
Ca. 1765, Boston, silver with wooden handle,
marked: "B. BURT" in rectangle on bottom, en-
graved with Hancock coat of arms on pourer's side;
H. 8½ in., DIAM. (base) 3¾ in., DIAM. (rim) 2¾ in.
Mrs. Harlan P. Hanson

124*
WILLIAM PLUMMER, active 1755-1762
Basket
1760, London, silver, maker's marks on outside
center of one of scroll-cut panels, H. (at end) 3¾ in.,
L. 14⅞ in.
Museum of Fine Arts, Theodora Wilbour Fund in
memory of Charlotte Beebe Wilbour. 66.286

125*
JACOB HURD, 1702/3-1758
Tea kettle on stand
1730-1740, Boston, silver, marked: "I HURD" in
cartouche on bottom at center point and "Hurd" in
ellipse on cover near vent hole, engraved on
pourer's side with coat of arms of Lowell quartering
Leversedge; H. 14⅜ in., DIAM. 7½ in.
Museum of Fine Arts, gift of Esther Lowell Abbott
in memory of her mother, Esther Lowell Cunningham, granddaughter of James Russell Lowell.
1971. 347a, b

126
PAUL REVERE II, 1735-1818
Sugar bowl
1760-1765, Boston, silver, marked: "•REVERE" in
rectangle below center point, engraved with Breck
(?) coat of arms on front, inscribed under foot:
"RᴮS"; H. 6 in., DIAM. (base) 3⅜ in., DIAM. (rim)
4¼ in.
Museum of Fine Arts, Theodora Wilbour Fund in
memory of Charlotte Beebe Wilbour. 68.618

127*
PAUL REVERE I, 1702-1754
Covered milk pot
1730-1750, Boston, silver, marked: "PR" in shield
with line above and below at left of handle and over
center point on bottom; H. 4⅝ in., DIAM. (base) 2⅛
in., DIAM. (lip) 1⅞ in.
Museum of Fine Arts, bequest of Frederick W.
Bradlee. 28.45

128
JACOB HURD, 1702/3-1758
Salver
1730-1740, Boston, silver, marked: "Hurd" in
semiscript in ellipse near rim below arms, engraved
with Oliver coat of arms; H. 2¼ in., DIAM. (base)
3⅛ in., DIAM. (dish) 6⅝ in.
Museum of Fine Arts, gift of Mrs. Ambrose Dawes
in memory of her husband. 13.382

129*
JOHN SINGLETON COPLEY, 1738-1815
Nicholas Boylston, 1716-1771
Ca. 1767, Boston, oil on canvas, 50¼ x 40¼ in.
Museum of Fine Arts, bequest of David P. Kimball.
23.504

130*
Corner chair
1760-1790, probably Boston, mahogany with birch
and pine; H. 31⅞ in., W. 18⅛ in., DEPTH 18⅛ in.
Mr. and Mrs. Lewis T. Steadman

131
Side chair
1760-1790, probably Boston, mahogany with birch,
pine, and maple seat frame; H. 37⅞ in., W. 21⅜ in.,
DEPTH 17⅛ in.
Mr. and Mrs. Lewis T. Steadman

132*
Easy chair
Ca. 1750-1790, Boston area, mahogany with eastern
white pine and red maple; H. 47½ in., W. 36 in.,
DEPTH 28 in.
The Metropolitan Museum of Art, purchase, the
Friends of the American Wing Fund, 1967

133
Looking-glass
1755-1773, Boston, carved and gilded wood, hand-
written label on back: "A Variety of Pictures and,
Looking Glasses Sold by Stepⁿ Whiting Opposite
the Cornfield In Union Street Boston"; H. 34½ in.,
W. 17½ in.
Israel Sack, Inc.

134*
GAWEN BROWN, 1719-1801
Tall clock
1755-1775, Boston, mahogany with white pine;
H. 91¼ in., W. 22⅝ in., DEPTH 10¾ in.
Private collection

135*
JOHN HARRIS, active in Boston from 1768
Spinet
1769, Boston, mahogany with maple and pine,
labeled above keyboard: "John Harris, Boston,
New England fecit"; H. 32½ in., W. (rear edge) 73 in.
Mrs. Walter B. Robb

136*
WILLIAM BILLINGS, 1746-1800
PAUL REVERE II, 1735-1818
The New-England Psalm Singer
1770, Boston, line engraving, signed under picture
on frontispiece: "P Revere Sculp"; 6¼ x 8½ in.
Mrs. G. Gordon Olsen

137
JOSIAH FLAGG, 1737-1794
PAUL REVERE II, 1735-1818
Sixteen Anthems
1766, Boston, line engraving; 5¼ x 8¾ in.
American Antiquarian Society, Worcester, Mass.

138
JOSIAH FLAGG, 1737-1794
PAUL REVERE II, 1735-1818
A Collection of the Best Psalm Tunes
1764, Boston, line engraving, inscribed on title page:
"Engrav'd by Paul Revere . . ."; 5¼ x 8⅝ in.
Massachusetts Historical Society, Boston

139
Songbook
1782, Boston, music manuscript with flocked wallpaper cover, inscribed on front page: "Sukey Heaths
1st July 1782"; 6¾ x 8½ in.
Mrs. Clifford A. Waterhouse

140
SIMEON SNOW, active at least 1777-1784
Violin
1779, Lexington, Mass., probably pine, labeled:
"Simeon Snow Lexington March 29 1779";
L. 23½ in.
Lexington Historical Society, Lexington, Mass.

141
BENJAMIN CREHORE, 1765-1832
Bass viol
1780-1800, Milton, Mass., spruce belly with maple
sides, labeled on inside: "Baseviols made and sold
by Benjamin Crehore, in Milton."; L. 48⅝ in.,
L. (body) 28¾ in.
Mr. and Mrs. Charles Crehore Cunningham

142
Cittern
Ca. 1775-1800, England, spruce top, curly maple
sides, ebony fingerboard, ivory capastasto, nut and
string fasteners, inked perfling, end inlaid with holly
(?) and mahogany, brass rose with ivory bracelet;
L. 21⅛ in., W. 12 in.
Museum of Fine Arts, gift of Mrs. Arthur Holland
in memory of her husband. 36.343

143
THOMAS JOHNSTON, ca. 1708-1767
Coat of arms of Benjamin Lynde
Ca. 1760-1770, Boston, watercolor, signed lower
middle: "T. Johnston fecit"; 16⅜ x 16¾ in. (sight)
Andrew Oliver

144
CHRISTIAN REMICK, 1726-1773
Coat of arms of the James family
1772, Boston, watercolor, signed lower middle:
"Christⁿ Remich Del⁺"; 13⅝ x 10 in. (sight)
William A. Farnsworth Library and Art Museum,
Rockland, Maine

145
JOHN SINGLETON COPLEY, 1738-1815
Nathaniel Hurd (study), 1729-1777
Ca. 1765, Boston, oil on canvas; 28¾ x 24½ in.
Memorial Art Gallery of the University of
Rochester, Rochester, N.Y., Marion Stratton Gould
Fund

146*
THOMAS JOHNSTON, ca. 1708-1767
South Battery certificate
Before 1765, Boston, line engraving, signed under
picture of South Battery: "T. Johnston, Sculpᵗ";
7¾ x 10¾ in.
American Antiquarian Society, Worcester, Mass.

147*
PAUL REVERE II, 1735-1818
North Battery certificate
Ca. 1762, Boston, line engraving, signed lower right:
"P Revere Sculp"; 5⅞ x 8¼ in.
American Antiquarian Society, Worcester, Mass.

148
PAUL REVERE II, 1735-1818
Copperplate for the North Battery certificate
Ca. 1762, Boston, engraved copper, signed in
reverse in mid-left: "P Revere Sculp"; 6¼ x 8⅛ in.
(uneven)
Massachusetts Historical Society, Boston

149*
PAUL REVERE II, 1735-1818
A View of the Year 1765
Ca. 1765, Boston, line engraving, signed lower right:
"Engrav'd Printed & Sold by P • Revere • Boston";
6 x 7⅝ in.
American Antiquarian Society, Worcester, Mass.

150*
JOHN SINGLETON COPLEY, 1738-1815
The Deplorable State of America
1765, Boston, etching, inscribed in the hand of
Pierre Du Simitiere (ca. 1736-1784): "The Original
Print done in Boston by Jᵒ S. Copley.";
10¼ x 14⅞ in.
The Library Company of Philadelphia

151*
BENJAMIN BLYTH, 1746-1787?
John Adams, 1735-1826
1766, Salem, Massachusetts, pastel on paper;
23 x 17½ in.
Massachusetts Historical Society, Boston

152*
PAUL REVERE II, 1735-1818
A View of the Obelisk
1766, Boston, line engraving, signed lower right:
"Paul Revere Sculp"; 9½ x 13½ in.
The Boston Athenaeum

153
PAUL REVERE II, 1735-1818
*Copperplate for "A View of the Obelisk" and a
Masonic certificate*
1766 and 1773, Boston, engraved copper, signed on
Obelisk print lower left in reverse: "Paul Revere
Sculp"; on Masonic certificate lower left in reverse:
"Engraved Printed and Sold by Paul Revere.
Boston."; 10 x 13⅞ in.
National Gallery of Art, Washington, D.C.,
Rosenwald Collection

154*
CHRISTIAN REMICK, 1726-1773
*A Perspective View of the Blockade of Boston
Harbour*
Ca. 1768, Boston, watercolor, signed in shield upper
right: "Christian Remich"; 16⅛ x 64⅛ in.
Massachusetts Historical Society, Boston

155*
PAUL REVERE II, 1735-1818
*A View of Part of the Town of Boston in New
England and Brittish Ships of War Landing their
Troops!*
1770, Boston, line engraving, signed lower right:
"ENGRAVED, PRINTED & SOLD by PAUL REVERE
BOSTON"; 8⅝ x 15⅜ in.
The Boston Athenaeum

156*
PAUL REVERE II, 1735-1818
Liberty bowl
1768, Boston, silver, marked: "REVERE" in
rectangle slanted at right of center point on bottom,
inscribed in script below the rim: "Caleb Hopkins,
Nath¹ Barber, John White, Willm Mackay, Dan¹
Malcolm, Benjn Goodwin, John Welsh, Fortescue
Vernon, Dan¹ Parker, John Marston, Ichabod Jones,
John Homer, Willm Bowes, Peter Boyer, Benj^a
Cobb." Engraved on one side with circle with a
scroll and foliate frame topped by a Liberty Cap
flanked by flags inscribed respectively: "Magna/
Charta" and "Bill of/Rights," inside the circle
inscribed: "N° 45./Wilkes & Liberty/" over a torn
page labeled "Generall/Warrants"; inscribed on the
other side: "To the Memory of the glorious
NINETY-TWO: Members/of the Hon^bl House of
Representatives of the Massachusetts-Bay,/who,
undaunted by the insolent Menaces of Villains in
Power,/from a Strict Regard to Conscience, and the
LIBERTIES/of their Constituents, on the 30th of
June 1768/Voted NOT TO RESCIND."; H. 5½ in.
(uneven), DIAM. (base) 5¾ in. (uneven), DIAM. (lip)
11 in. (uneven)
Museum of Fine Arts, gift by subscription and
Francis Bartlett Fund. 49.45

157*
ATTRIBUTED TO JOHN BACON, 1740-1799
Figure of John Wilkes, 1727-1797
Ca. 1765, Derby, England, soft-paste porcelain,
H. 12⅜ in.
Museum of Fine Arts, bequest of Mrs. Martin
Brimmer. 06.2439

158
JOHN WILKES, 1727-1797
Letter to the Earls of Egremont and Halifax
1763, London, manuscript letter, signed by John
Wilkes; 9 x 7½ in.
Augustus P. Loring

159
PAUL REVERE II, 1735-1818
*Copperplate for "The Landing of the Troops" and
the 1775 seal of Massachusetts*
1770, Boston, engraved copper; 8 x 12½ in.
Archives Division, Office of the Secretary of the
Commonwealth of Massachusetts

160*
EDWARD TRUMAN, active 1741
Thomas Hutchinson, 1711-1780
1741, London, oil on canvas, signed lower left:
"Edward Truman 1741"; 27¼ x 22¾ in.
Massachusetts Historical Society, Boston

161
JOHN SINGLETON COPLEY, 1738-1815
Peter Oliver, 1713-1791
Ca. 1758, Boston, oil on copper; 5 x 4 in.
Andrew Oliver

162*
JOHN SINGLETON COPLEY, 1738-1815
Thomas Flucker, 1719-1783
Ca. 1770-1771, Boston, oil on canvas; 28⅞ x 24 in.
Bowdoin College Museum of Art, Brunswick,
Maine, bequest of Mrs. Lucy Flucker Knox Thatcher

163
JOHN SINGLETON COPLEY, 1738-1815
Ralph Inman, 1718-1788
Ca. 1770, Boston, pastel; 24 x 18 in.
The Boston Athenaeum

164
HENRY PELHAM, 1749-1806
*The Fruits of Arbitrary Power, or the Bloody
Massacre*
1770, Boston, line engraving; 11½ x 8¾ in.
American Antiquarian Society, Worcester, Mass.

165*
PAUL REVERE II, 1735-1818
The Bloody Massacre perpetrated in King Street
1770, Boston, line engraving, signed lower right:
"Engrav'd Printed & Sold by PAUL REVERE BOSTON";
signed bottom right: "Col^d by Christ^n Remich";
9⅝ x 8⅝ in.
Museum of Fine Arts, gift of Watson Grant Cutter.
67.1165

166
PAUL REVERE II, 1735-1818
*Copperplate for "The Bloody Massacre" and
Revolutionary Currency*
1770, Boston, engraved, copper, signed on obverse
lower left in reverse: "Engrav'd, Printed, & Sold by
Paul Revere, BOSTON"; 8¼ x 9¼ in.
Archives Division, Office of the Secretary of the
Commonwealth of Massachusetts

167*
JOHN JOHNSTON, 1753-1818
Green Dragon Tavern
1773, Boston, pen and ink with watercolor wash,
signed bottom center: "John Johnson";
8⅛ x 12¼ in.
American Antiquarian Society, Worcester, Mass.

168
Punch bowl
Ca. 1730-1770, Chinese, hard-paste porcelain;
H. 5⅛ in., DIAM. (base) 6 in., DIAM. (lip) 12⅛ in.
Massachusetts Historical Society, Boston

169
ANONYMOUS ARTIST
*The Able Doctor, or America Swallowing the
Bitter Draught*
1774, England, line engraving; 4½ x 6⅜ in.
Museum of Fine Arts, gift of the Estate of Lee M.
Friedman. 58.1058

170*
PAUL REVERE II, 1735-1818
*The Able Doctor, or America Swallowing the
Bitter Draught*
1774, Boston, line engraving, signed lower right:
"P Revere Sculp"; 7 x 4⅞ in.
Massachusetts Historical Society, Boston

171
PAUL REVERE II, 1735-1818
*A View of the Town of Boston with Several Ships of
War in the Harbour*
1774, Boston, line engraving; 6⅝ x 10⅜ in.
Museum of Fine Arts, the M. and M. Karolik
Fund. 1971.262

172*
JOHN SINGLETON COPLEY, 1738-1815
Samuel Adams, 1722-1803
Ca. 1770-1772, Boston, oil on canvas; 50 x 40½ in.
Museum of Fine Arts, deposited by the City of
Boston

173*
JOHN SINGLETON COPLEY, 1738-1815
John Hancock, 1737-1793
1765, Boston, oil on canvas, signed and dated lower
left: "J. S. Copley pinx 1765"; 49½ x 40½ in.
Museum of Fine Arts, deposited by the City of
Boston

174*
JOHN SINGLETON COPLEY, 1738-1815
Joseph Warren, 1741-1775
Ca. 1772-1774, Boston, oil on canvas; 50 x 40 in.
Museum of Fine Arts, gift of Buckminster Brown,
M.D., through Church M. Matthews, Jr., trustee.
95.1366

175*
AMOS DOOLITTLE, 1754-1832
The Battle of Lexington, April 19th 1775
1775, New Haven, Conn., hand-colored line
engraving, signed lower right: "A. Doolittle. Sculp^t";
13 x 17½ in.
The Connecticut Historical Society, Hartford

176
AMOS DOOLITTLE, 1754-1832
A View of the Town of Concord
1775, New Haven, Conn., hand-colored line
engraving, signed lower right: "A. Doolittle Sculp^t";
13 x 17½ in.
The Connecticut Historical Society, Hartford

177*
AMOS DOOLITTLE, 1754-1832
The Engagement at the North Bridge in Concord
1775, New Haven, Conn., hand-colored line
engraving, signed lower right: "A. Doolittle Sculp^t";
13 x 17½ in.
The Connecticut Historical Society, Hartford

178
AMOS DOOLITTLE, 1754-1832
A View of the South Part of Lexington
1775, New Haven, Conn., hand-colored line
engraving, signed lower right: "A. Doolittle. Sculp^t";
13 x 17½ in.
The Connecticut Historical Society, Hartford

179*
RICHARD WILLIAMS
*Plan of the Heights of Charles Town and Works
taken from the Rebels on the 17th June 1775*
1775, Boston, pen and ink, signed lower right:
"R^d Williams Lt R:W:Fuziliers"; 10¾ x 17½ in.
Mrs. Ellery Sedgwick

180*
BERNARD ROMANS, ca. 1720-1784
*An Exact View of the Late Battle at Charlestown
June 17th 1775*
1775, Philadelphia, Pennsylvania, line engraving,
signed lower right: "B. Romans in AEre incidit";
11⅛ x 16⅛ in.
Massachusetts Historical Society, Boston

181*
JOHN TRUMBULL, 1756-1843
The Battle of Bunker Hill
Ca. 1786-1820, London, oil on canvas; 20 x 29¾ in.
Private collection

182
COLONEL JOHN MONTRESOR, 1736-1799
A View of Charles Town and the back Ground as far as the narrow pass taken from the Beacon Hill
Before June 17, 1775, Boston, pen and ink;
5½ x 18⅜ in.
The Boston Athenaeum

183*
JOHN SINGLETON COPLEY, 1738-1815
Colonel John Montresor, 1736-1799
Ca. 1771, New York, oil on canvas; 30 x 25 in.
The Detroit Institute of Arts, Gibbs-Williams Fund

184
LT. WILLIAMS
A View of the Country round Boston
1775, Boston, watercolor, copied from a sketch of the original by Lt. Wood, signed on top of the second panel: "NB. These Views were taken by Lt Williams of the R:W:Fuziliers . . ."; four panels, each panel, 7 x 18½ in.
Massachusetts Historical Society, Boston

185
RICHARD WILLIAMS
A Plan of Boston, and its Environs
1775, Boston, colored line engraving, inscribed upper left corner: "The principal part of this Plan was Survey'd by Richard Williams. . . ."; published in London, 1776; 20 x 27 in.
Private collection

186*
GILBERT STUART, 1755-1828
Washington at Dorchester Heights
1806, Boston, oil on panel; 107½ x 71¼ in.
Museum of Fine Arts, deposited by the City of Boston

187
Declaration of Independence
1776, Boston, broadside, printed by John Gill and Powars and Willis; 20⅛ x 15⅝ in.
Massachusetts Historical Society, Boston

188*
HENRY PELHAM, 1749-1806
A Plan of Boston in New England
1777, London, line engraving, signed in ink lower right: "Henry Pelham"; 41½ x 29 in.
The Trustees of the Boston Public Library

189*
JOSEPH BOZE, 1744-1826
The Marquis de Lafayette, 1757-1834
1785-1789, Paris, oil on canvas; 36 x 28½ in.
Massachusetts Historical Society, Boston

190*
PIERRE OZANNE, 1737-1813
Boston, Capital of the United States
1778, Boston, pen and ink; 11⅝ x 24⅛ in.
The Metropolitan Museum of Art, gift of William H. Huntington, 1883

191*
HENRY DEBERNIERE
Plan of the Island Castle William
Ca. 1775, Boston, pen and ink with color wash, signed lower right: "Henry Debernire Fecit——";
28½ x 41½ in.
Private collection

192
JACOB HURD, 1702/3-1758
Creampot
Ca. 1740-1750, Boston, silver, marked: "HURD" in small rectangle at lip each side of handle, inscribed "ME" on bottom, engraved at left of handle with scene of Castle William flying British flag, at front with two swans swimming with gulls above, and at right of handle with house and trees with hill, field, and gate; H. 4 in.
Yale University Art Gallery, New Haven, Conn., the Mabel Brady Garvan Collection

193
PAUL REVERE II, 1735-1818
Note of May 25, 1775
1775, Boston, line engraving (pattern copy);
3⅛ x 7¾ in.
American Antiquarian Society, Worcester, Mass.

194
PAUL REVERE II, 1735-1818
Note of July 28, 1775
1775, Boston, line engraving; 3⅛ x 6⅝ in.
American Antiquarian Society, Worcester, Mass.

195
PAUL REVERE II, 1735-1818
Bill of August 18, 1775 (40 s.)
1775, Boston, line engraving; 3¾ x 3 in.
American Antiquarian Society, Worcester, Mass.

196
PAUL REVERE II, 1735-1818
Bill of October 18, 1776 (8d.)
1776, Boston, line engraving; 2½ x 2¾ in.
American Antiquarian Society, Worcester, Mass.

197
PAUL REVERE II, 1735-1818
Bill of October 16, 1778 (6d.)
1778, Boston, line engraving; 2½ x 2⅞ in.
American Antiquarian Society, Worcester, Mass.

198
PAUL REVERE II, 1735-1818
Rising Sun Bill of 1779 (2s)
1779, Boston, line engraving; 2⅞ x 2½ in.
American Antiquarian Society, Worcester, Mass.

199
Tavern sign
1789, Boston, carved wood with paint, inscribed on base: "Grand Turk Inne"; H. 31 in., w. 9½ in., DEPTH 7¼ in.
The Connecticut Historical Society, Hartford

200
PAUL REVERE II, 1735-1818
Billhead of Joshua Brackett
1771, Boston, line engraving, signed under head: "P. Revere Sc"; 6⅜ x 4 in.
American Antiquarian Society, Worcester, Mass.

201
Mug
Ca. 1790-1800, England, earthenware, decorated with transfer print bust of John Hancock and inscription "The Honourable John Hancock";
H. 6 in., DIAM. 4 in.
Peabody Museum, Salem, Mass.

202
Pitcher
Ca. 1790-1800, Staffordshire, England, earthenware, inscribed with transfer print "SUCCESS to the Crooked But interesting TOWN OF/BOSTON!";
H. 7½ in., w. 5½ in.
Peabody Museum, Salem, Mass.

203
JOHN EDWARDS, 1671-1746
Tankard
Ca. 1700, Boston, silver, marked: "IE," crowned, in cartouche on top below center point and at left of handle, engraved with Norton coat of arms on front;
H. 7 in., DIAM. (base) 5⅝ in., DIAM. (lip) 4⅞ in.
Massachusetts Historical Society, Boston

204
WILLIAM HOMES, 1716/17-1783
Punch bowl
1763, Boston, silver, marked: "HOMES" in italics in rectangle below center point over "W•H" in rectangle, engraved with Dawes coat of arms on one side, inscribed on the other in several letterings: "The Gift/of the Field Officers and/Captains of the Regiment/of the Town of BOSTON. to/THOMAS DAWES Esqr/for his past Services as Ad-/jutant to said Re-/giment Sept 13/1763."; H. 4⅞ in., DIAM. (base) 5¼ in., DIAM. (lip) 9⅞ in.
Museum of Fine Arts, gift of Mrs. Ambrose Dawes in memory of her husband. 13.381

205
PAUL REVERE I, 1702-1754
Strainer
Ca. 1730-1740, Boston, silver, marked: "P•Revere" in rectangle under end of each handle; L. 9½ in., DIAM. (bowl) 4¼ in.
Wilder Foote

206
PAUL REVERE II, 1735-1818
Ladle
1781, Boston, silver, marked: "•REVERE" in rectangle engraved with Morton crest on tip of handle and inscribed "PMS" on back of handle;
L. 14¾ in.
Miss Mary F. Thompson and Mrs. Louis Long, Jr.

207-208
PAUL REVERE II, 1735-1818
Pair of goblets
1782, Boston, silver with gilt-lined bowl, marked: "•REVERE" in rectangle at right of and facing monogram, inscribed near rim in script monogram "NMT"; H. (each) 5⅜ in., DIAM. (base) 3 in., DIAM. (lip) 3⅛ in.
Museum of Fine Arts, Pauline Revere Thayer Collection. 35.1769-1770

209
PAUL REVERE II, 1735-1818
Hoop'd cann
1792, Boston, silver, marked: "•REVERE" in
rectangle at left of handle, inscribed "SB" on
bottom, added on front is a coat of arms over
"BLAGGE"; H. 4¾ in., DIAM. (base) 4 in., DIAM.
(lip) 3⅛ in.
Museum of Fine Arts, Pauline Revere Thayer
Collection. 35.1762

210
PAUL REVERE II, 1735-1818
Wine quart cann
1787, Boston, silver, marked: "•REVERE" in
rectangle tangent to center point on bottom and at
left of handle, inscribed with script monogram
"TIL" on front; H. 6¼ in., DIAM. (base) 3⅞ in.,
DIAM. (lip) 3⅞ in.
Museum of Fine Arts, Pauline Revere Thayer
Collection. 35.1763

211-212
PAUL REVERE II, 1735-1818
Pair of beakers
Ca. 1800, Boston, silver, marked: "REVERE" in
rectangle with clipped corners on bottom of each,
inscribed with script "G" not quite opposite seam
on each; H. (each) 3½ in., DIAM. (base) 2¼ in.,
DIAM. (lip) 2¾ in. (uneven)
Museum of Fine Arts, gift of Eliot Wadsworth.
49.1788a, b

213
PAUL REVERE II, 1735-1818
Beaker
1803, Boston, silver, marked: "REVERE" in
rectangle on bottom, inscribed with script monogram "BSR" on front; H. 3½ in., DIAM. (base) 2⅝
in., DIAM. (lip) 3 in.
Private collection

214
*Broadside for procession in honor of George
Washington*
1789, Boston, hand-set type; 15½ x 10 in.
Massachusetts Historical Society, Boston

215*
SAMUEL HILL, active 1789-1803
View of the Triumphal Arch and Colonnade
1790, Boston, line engraving, signed lower right:
"Engraved by S. Hill"; 5 x 7⅜ in.
Massachusetts Historical Society, Boston

216*
CHRISTIAN GULLAGER, 1759-1826
George Washington, 1732-1799
1789, Portsmouth, N.H., oil on canvas; 29 x 24 in.
Massachusetts Historical Society, Boston

217*
JAMES B. MARSTON, active ca. 1800-1817
The Old State House and State Street
Ca. 1801, Boston, oil on canvas; 37½ x 52⅛ in.
Massachusetts Historical Society, Boston

218
JOHN SCOLES, active 1793-1844
*A View of the Bridge over Charles River
Massachusetts*
1789, Boston, line engraving, signed lower right:
"Scoles sc."; 4¼ x 7¼ in.
Massachusetts Historical Society, Boston

219*
BENJAMIN BURT, 1729-1805
Tankard
1786, Boston, silver, marked: "BENJAMIN/BURT"
in cartouche on body at each side of handle,
inscribed "RDE" on handle, engraved with view of
the Charles River Bridge on side opposite pourer,
on pourer's side inscribed: "Presented to/Richard
Devens, Esqr./by the Proprietors of/CHARLES
RIVER BRIDGE,/in Testimony of their entire
Approbation/of his faithful Services,/as a special
Director of that Work./begun A.D. 1785,/and
perfected/A.D. 1786."; H. 9⅛ in., DIAM. (base)
5¼ in., DIAM. (lip) 4¼ in.
Museum of Fine Arts, the M. and M. Karolik
Collection of Eighteenth Century Arts. 36.459

220*
MATHER BROWN, 1761-1831
Charles Bulfinch, 1763-1844
1786, London, oil on canvas, 30 x 25 in.
Harvard University Portrait Collection

221*
JOHN L. BOQUETA DE WOISERI, active in the U.S.
1797-1815
View of Boston
Ca. 1810, Boston, line engraving with watercolor;
22¼ x 34½ in. (sight).
Boston Public Library

222
SUSANNAH HEATH, 1795-1878
View of Boston from Heath Hill, Brookline
1813, Brookline, Mass., watercolor; 16 x 22 in.
Bertram K. and Nina Fletcher Little

223
JOHN RUBENS SMITH, 1775-1849
*Beacon Hill from the present site of the Reservoir,
between Hancock and Temple Streets*
1811-1812, Boston, watercolor; 10⅞ x 16⅝ in.
Boston Public Library, Print Department

224
JOHN RUBENS SMITH, 1775-1849
*Beacon Hill with Mr. Thurston's house from
Bowdoin Street*
1811-1812, Boston, watercolor; 11⅛ x 17¼ in.
Boston Public Library, Print Department

225
CHARLES BULFINCH, 1763-1844
*Elevation of four houses proposed to be built on
Park Street—39 feet each*
1800-1805, Boston, pen and ink, signed lower right:
"C. Bulfinch"; 7½ x 19⅝ in.
Massachusetts Historical Society, Boston

226
SIMEON SKILLEN, 1716-1778, and
JOHN SKILLEN, 1746-1800
Carved capital for the State House
1795-1797, Boston, carved and painted wood;

H. 32 in., W. 42 in., DEPTH 20½ in.
The Society for the Preservation of New England
Antiquities, Boston

227*
GEORGE BRIGHT, active 1750-1805
Armchair
1797, Boston, mahogany with original brass, iron,
and wood casters; H. 34 in., W. 22 in., DEPTH 24 in.
The Society for the Preservation of New England
Antiquities, Boston

228*
GILBERT STUART, 1755-1828
Harrison Gray Otis, 1765-1848
1809, Boston, oil on panel; 32 x 26 in.
The Society for the Preservation of New England
Antiquities, Boston
(On view June 1-September 1)

229
GILBERT STUART, 1755-1828
Sally Foster Otis (Mrs. Harrison Gray) 1770-1836
1809, Boston, oil on panel; 32 x 26 in.
Reynolda House, Winston-Salem, North Carolina

230*
CHARLES BULFINCH, 1763-1844
Front Elevation of the Harrison Gray Otis house
1795-1796, Boston, pen and ink with watercolor;
6⅛ x 5⅝ in. (uneven)
Massachusetts Historical Society, Boston

231*
JOSEPH CALLENDER, 1751-1821
Medal
1795, Boston, gold, engraved recto with relief picture
of the Boston Theatre, underneath which is
inscribed: "This MEDAL/entitles/CHARLES
BULFINCH, Esqr/to a Seat in the BOSTON THEATRE/
during Life;/Benefit Nights excepted"; inscribed
verso: "Presented/by the PROPRIETORS/of the
BOSTON THEATRE/To CHARLES BULFINCH, Esqr/For
his unremitted and liberal Attention/in the Plan
and Execution of/That Building;/The Elegance
of which is the/best Evidence of his/Taste and
Talents."; DIAM. 2½ in.
Private collection

232*
GILBERT STUART, 1755-1828
*Sarah Wentworth Apthorp Morton (Mrs. Perez),
1759-1846*
1802, Philadelphia, oil on canvas; 29¼ x 24 in.
Museum of Fine Arts, Juliana Cheney Edwards
Collection. Bequest of Hannah Marcy Edwards in
memory of her mother. 36.681

233
PAUL REVERE II, 1735-1818
Punch urn
1796, Boston, silver, marked: "REVERE" in
rectangle with clipped corners at right of handle,
to the left of the original inscription, engraved with
a facade of the Boston Theatre, and inscribed on the
opposite side: "The/Proprietors/of the/Boston
Theatre/to Genl Henry Jackson Esqr/one of their
Trustees/1796."; H. 10⅝ in., DIAM. (base) 4¼ in.,
DIAM. (lip) 5⅝ in.
Museum of Fine Arts, gift of Henry Davis Sleeper
in memory of his mother, Maria Westcote
Sleeper. 25.597

234*
GILBERT STUART, 1755-1828
Colonel James Swan, ca. 1750-1831
Ca. 1793-1798, New York or Philadelphia, oil on
canvas; 28¾ x 23½ in.
Museum of Fine Arts, bequest of Elizabeth Howard
Bartol. 27.538

235-236*
ATTRIBUTED TO PIERRE GOUTHIERE, 1732-1814
Pair of andirons
Ca. 1785-1800, France, ormolu (gilt bronze);
H. 19 in., W. 17⅞ in.
Museum of Fine Arts, Swan Collection. Bequest of
Miss Elizabeth Howard Bartol. 27.521

237
Fire screen
Ca. 1775-1790, France, wood with gesso and gilt,
silk lampas; H. 41⅝ in., W. 28⅜ in., DEPTH 16 in.
Museum of Fine Arts, Swan Collection. Bequest of
Miss Elizabeth Howard Bartol. 27.533

238*
GILBERT STUART, 1755-1828
Bishop Jean-Louis Lefebvre de Cheverus, 1768-1836
1823, Boston, oil on canvas; 36¼ x 28½ in.
Museum of Fine Arts, bequest of Mrs. Charlotte
Gore Greenough Hervoches du Quilliou. 21.9

239*
MATTHIEU DE MACHY, active 1770-1789
Coffee urn
1789, Paris, silver, maker's marks on front of plinth,
top of warmer, and bottom of urn, inscribed on
front over spigot: To CHARLES BULFINCH/
Esqʳ/Presented by the Catholics/OF BOSTON/
Janʸ 1.1806"; H. 16⅛ in.
Museum of Fine Arts, gift of Miss Ellen Susan
Bulfinch. 16.223

240*
ROBERT HASWELL, 1768-ca. 1801
*A Voyage Round the World Onboard the Ship
Columbia-Rediviva and Sloop Washington*
1787-1790, Boston, Oregon, Pacific Ocean,
manuscript logbook; 12⅞ x 8⅛ in.
Massachusetts Historical Society, Boston

241
ANONYMOUS ARTIST
Robert Haswell, 1768-ca. 1801
Ca. 1800, probably Boston, pastel on paper;
8⅝ x 6½ in.
Massachusetts Historical Society, Boston

242
Medal
1787, Boston, silver, inscribed recto: "COLUMBIA AND
WASHINGTON. COMMANDED BY J. KENDRICK" around
edge, with a ship and sloop under sail in center of
medal; inscribed verso: "*FITTED AT BOSTON
N. AMERICA FOR THE PACIFIC OCEAN" around edge,
in center: "BY/J. BARRELL,/S. BROWN, C.
BULFINCH,/J. DARBY, C. HATCH,/J.M. PINTARD./
1787"; DIAM. 1⅝ in.
Massachusetts Historical Society, Boston

243*
Punch bowl
1790, China, hard-paste porcelain, inscribed:
"Boston. N. 75/These are to Certify that CAPᵀ
JAMES MAGEE/was by a Majority of Votes regularly
admitted a Member/of the BOSTON MARINE
SOCIETY at a Meeting held the/5th day of Novemʳᵇ
1782. Given under my hand and the/Seal of the
Society this 9th day of Febʸ Annoque Domini/
1789 SAMᴸ BLAGGE Secʸ Mungo Mackay President,"
and under this: "Presented to the/BOSTON MARINE
SOCIETY/by James Magee"; H. 5⅞ in., DIAM.
(rim) 14⅜ in.
Boston Marine Society, Boston

244*
Jug
1790, China, hard-paste porcelain, inscribed:
"Boston. N. 75/These are to Certify that CAPᵀ
JAMES MAGEE/ was by a Majority of Votes regularly
admitted a Member/of the BOSTON MARINE SOCIETY
at a Meeting held the/5th day of Novemʳᵇ 1782.
Given under my hand and the/Seal of the Society
this 9th day of Febʸ Annoque Domini/1789 SAMᴸ
BLAGGE Secʸ Mungo Mackay President," and under
this: "Presented to the/BOSTON MARINE SOCIETY/by
James Magee"; H. 8⅞ in., DIAM. (lip) 4¾ in.,
DIAM. (base) 4½ in.
Boston Marine Society, Boston

245*
Covered tureen
1790-1800, China, hard-paste porcelain, inscribed:
"JA" in script monogram; H. 6⅜ in., L. 5¾ in.
Museum of Fine Arts, gift of the Winfield
Foundation. 51.1153a, b

246
Teapot
1790-1800, China, hard-paste porcelain, decorated
with Sargent crest; H. 5 in., DIAM. (base) 4⅜ in.,
L. 8½ in.
Miss Aimée Lamb

247*
JOHN MASON FURNESS, 1763-1809
John Vinall, 1736-1823
Ca. 1785, Boston, oil on canvas; 50 x 40⅝ in.
The Brooklyn Museum, Dick S. Ramsay Fund

248
JOHN VINALL, 1736-1823
The Preceptor's Assistant, or Student's Guide
1792, Boston, printed by P. Edes for Thomas &
Andrews; 7 x 4⅜ in.
The Boston Athenaeum

249
SAMUEL H. DEARBORN, active 1796-1825
*Perspective View, on the Northward of Mr.
Dearborn's School*
1796, Boston, watercolor, inscribed across top:
". . . taken by Samuel H. Dearborn June 21st, 1796";
8 x 12½ in.
The Boston Athenaeum

250
SAMUEL F. B. MORSE, 1791-1872
Jedidiah Morse, 1761-1826
Ca. 1810, Charlestown, Mass., oil on millboard;
28¾ x 22⅞ in.
Yale University Art Gallery, New Haven, Conn.,
gift of Miss Helen E. Carpenter

251*
SAMUEL F. B. MORSE, 1791-1872
The Morse Family
1811, Charlestown, Mass., watercolor; 12 x 15 in.,
Smithsonian Institution, National Museum of
History and Technology, Washington, D.C.

252
JEDIDIAH MORSE, 1761-1826
*Geography Made Easy, Being an Abridgment of the
American Geography, Second Edition, Abridged by
the Author*
1790, Boston, Printed by Isaiah Thomas and
Ebenezer T. Andrews; 7¼ x 4½ in.
Massachusetts Historical Society, Boston

253
NOAH WEBSTER, 1758-1843
*The American Spelling Book: Containing an Easy
Standard of Pronunciation. Being the First Part of a
Grammatical Institute of the English Language.*
1789, Boston, Printed by Isaiah Thomas and
Ebenezer T. Andrews; 6¾ x 4¼ in.
Massachusetts Historical Society, Boston

254*
GERRIT SCHIPPER, 1775-ca. 1830
Isaiah Thomas, 1749-1831
1804, Boston or Worcester, pastel on paper;
7⅜ x 5¾ in.
American Antiquarian Society, Worcester, Mass.

255
PAUL REVERE II, 1735-1818
Bookplate of Isaiah Thomas
1790's, Boston, line engraving; 3⅞ x 2⅞ in.
Massachusetts Historical Society, Boston

256
POSSIBLY BY JOHN SEYMOUR, 1738-1818, or
THOMAS SEYMOUR, 1771-1848
Work box
Ca. 1814, Boston, bird's-eye maple with curly maple;
H. 5¼ in., W. 14¼ in., DEPTH 10¼ in.
Private collection

257*
JOHN RITTO PENNIMAN, 1783-1837, painter
Work box
Ca. 1800, Boston, satinwood with bird's-eye maple
veneer and mahogany bottom, satin lining, shell
painting on top signed: "J.R.P."; H. 3½ in., W. 8 in.,
L. 10⅝ in.
Private collection

258*
Work table
1790-1805, Boston, satinwood with rosewood and
mahogany; H. 29¼ in., W. 21¼ in., DEPTH 17 in.
Richard S. duPont

259
Work table
1790-1810, Boston, maple with curly maple, satin-
wood and mahogany inlays, and painted decoration;
H. 30 in., W. 20 in., DEPTH 16 in.
Vernon Stoneman

260
SARAH EATON BALCH, 1782-1850, painter
Work table
Ca. 1810, bird's-eye maple with pine, and painted
decoration; H. 29 in., W. 17 in., DEPTH 17 in.
Bertram K. and Nina Fletcher Little

261*
NANCY LEE, 1788-1865
Embroidered picture
1804, Dorchester, Mass., silk yarns and watercolor
on silk, signed on glass: "Wrought by Nancy Lee, at
Mrs. Saunders & Miss Beach's Academy Dor-
chester," signed on back: "Wrought in 1804, 16 yrs.
Nancy Lee born 1788, died 1865"; 18 x 14 in.
Bertram K. and Nina Fletcher Little

262*
SARAH CHANDLER
Embroidered sampler
1808, Boston, silk yarns on linen, signed upper
left and upper right: "Executed by Sarah Chandler
In The Year 1808 At Mrs Dobls Seminary In
Boston"; 21⅞ x 20¼ in.
New England Historic Genealogical Society, Boston

263
THOMAS SHERATON, 1751-1806
*The Cabinet-Maker and Upholsterer's
Drawing-Book*
1791-1793, London, printed book in 2 vols.,
inscribed on flyleaf of vol. 1: "Thomas Seymour";
H. 10⅝ in., W. 8⅜ in.
Museum of Fine Arts, gift of the William N. Banks
Foundation. 1971.330a, b

264*
ANONYMOUS ARTIST
Memorial picture
1818, Boston area, watercolor on paper, inscribed
on tomb: "IN MEMORY OF Mr JOHN COGSWELL Who
died 30 Jany 1818 AE 80 Yr's"; 18 x 22 in.
Bertram K. and Nina Fletcher Little

265*
JOHN COGSWELL, 1738-1818
Chest-on-chest
1782, Boston, mahogany with white pine, inscribed
on top of the lower section: "Made By John
Cogswell in middle Street Boston 1782"; H. 97 in.,
W. 44¼ in., DEPTH 23½ in.
Museum of Fine Arts, William Francis Warden
Fund. 1973.289

266*
STEPHEN BADLAM, 1751-1815
Side chair
1790-1800, Dorchester, Mass., mahogany, secondary
woods unexamined, stamped: "S. BADLAM" on out-
side back seat rail; H. 38⅜ in., W. 21½ in.,
DEPTH 21½ in.
Mr. and Mrs. Bertram D. Coleman

267
BENJAMIN FROTHINGHAM, JR., 1734-1809
Side chair
1790-1809, Charlestown, Massachusetts, mahogany
with beech and maple, signed on underside of rear
seat rail: "Mr. Benjan. Frothingham Charlestown";
H. 33 in., W. 22 in., DEPTH 18 in.
Toms Memorial Collection, Craighead Jackson
House, Knoxville, Tenn.

268*
JACOB FORSTER, 1764-1838
Side chair
1790-1800, Charlestown, Massachusetts, mahogany
with satinwood inlay and birch, labeled on inside
rear seat rail: "J. Forster, Charlestown: Massa. 179";
H. 37½ in., DEPTH 20¾ in.
Private collection

269
Military commission of Stephen Badlam
1776, Philadelphia, printed commission with
autograph, signed lower right: "John Hancock,
President"; 12¾ x 16¼ in.
Israel Sack, Inc.

270
STEPHEN BADLAM, 1751-1815
Card table
1790-1800, Dorchester, Massachusetts, stamped:
"S. BADLAM" and "WH" on top side of gate;
H. 28½ in., W. 36 in., DEPTH 17½ in.
Ginsburg & Levy, Inc., New York

271*
THOMAS FOSTER
Card table
1790-1800, Boston, mahogany, mahogany veneer on
pine, maple gate, labeled on back: "Thomas Foster
Cabinet-maker BSOTON"; H. 29 in., W. 35½ in.,
DEPTH (closed) 17 in.
Mr. and Mrs. George M. Kaufman

272
STEPHEN BADLAM, 1751-1815
Tray
Ca. 1800, Dorchester, Massachusetts, mahogany
with satinwood inlay, stamped on reverse: "S. BAD-
LAM," and "A.W."; H. 1¼ in., W. 20¼ in., L. 31¾ in.
Mrs. Charles G. Milham

273*
BENJAMIN FROTHINGHAM, JR., 1734-1809
Slant-top desk
1785-1800, Charlestown, Massachusetts, mahogany
with pine, labeled on inside interior drawer with fan
inlay: "Benjn Frothingham Cabbinet Maker
Charles-Town. N.E."; H. 43 in., W. 40⅞ in.,
DEPTH 21⅜ in.
The Currier Gallery of Art, Manchester,
New Hampshire

274
JEAN-JACQUES LE VEAU, 1729-1785 (after I. Belle)
*Membership certificate in the Society of the
Cincinnati for Benjamin Frothingham, Jr.*
1784, Philadelphia, Pennsylvania, line engraving,
certificate signed by George Washington and Henry
Knox, engraving signed lower left: "Aug. I, Belle,
Del.," and lower right: "J. J. Le Veau, Sculp.";
14 x 21 in.
Ginsburg & Levy, Inc., New York

275
JAMES DOULE, working in Boston ca. 1790-1820
Tall clock
1790-1810, Charlestown, Mass., mahogany, ma-
hogany veneer and pine with satinwood inlay, face
inscribed: "James Douel, Charlestown"; H. 112 in.,
W. 20¼ in., DEPTH 9¾ in.
Mr. and Mrs. Edward Johnson III

276*
PAUL REVERE II, 1735-1818
Clock label for Aaron Willard
Ca. 1781, Boston, line engraving, 6⅝ in. x 4⅞ in.
American Antiquarian Society, Worcester, Mass.

277*
AARON WILLARD, 1757-1844
Tall clock
1806, Boston, mahogany, mahogany and satinwood
veneers and inlay, with pine, face inscribed:
"Warranted for Mr. Joshua Seaver 1806 Aaron
Willard Boston"; H. 94 in., W. 19 in., DEPTH 19½ in.
Private collection

278*
AARON WILLARD, 1757-1844
Shelf clock
1817, Boston, mahogany with pine, brass, painted
glass, inscribed on upper glass panel in gold on red
ground: "Aaron Willard BOSTON"; H. 36 in.,
W. 13½ in., DEPTH 5⅞ in.
Museum of Fine Arts, gift of Mrs. Anna R. B.
Wilson in memory of Charles H. Wilson, of
Hingham, Mass. 64.1601

279*
JOHN DOGGETT, 1780-1857
Looking-glass (one of a pair)
1800-1815, Roxbury, Mass., carved and gilt pine,
reverse painting on glass, label on back reads: "John
Doggett, Gilder, Looking Glass & Picture Frame
Manufacturer. Roxbury. Constantly for sale a large
assortment of Looking Glasses"; H. 57 in., W. 25 in.
Mrs. Charles L. Bybee

280
THOMAS SEYMOUR, 1771-1848
JOHN RITTO PENNIMAN, 1783-1837
Commode
1809, Boston, mahogany with mahogany veneer,
satinwood veneer, bird's-eye maple, rosewood
veneer, white pine, maple, and chestnut, and painted
top, H. 41½ in., W. 50 in., DEPTH 24⅝ in.
Museum of Fine Arts, the M. and M. Karolik Collection of Eighteenth Century American Arts. 23.19

281-284*
ATTRIBUTED TO JOHN SEYMOUR, ca. 1738-1818 or
THOMAS SEYMOUR, 1771-1848
Nest of tables
1800-1815, Boston, painted curly maple, H. 29¼ in.,
W. 7¾ in., DEPTH 12¾ in.
Mr. and Mrs. George M. Kaufman

285
JOHN RITTO PENNIMAN, 1783-1837
Family Group
1798, Boston, oil on canvas, signed on back of
canvas: "Painted by J.R. PENNIMAN 1798"; 15⅞ x
12½ in.
Museum of Fine Arts, gift of Mr. and Mrs. Stuart
P. Feld. 1974.584

286*
ATTRIBUTED TO THOMAS SEYMOUR, 1771-1848
Pedimented tambour desk
1790-1810, Boston, mahogany with mahogany
veneer and satinwood veneer and pine, portrait of
man in pencil on rear boards; H. 65½ in., W. 36 in.,
DEPTH 18½ in.
Mr. and Mrs. George M. Kaufman

287*
Gaming table
1790-1805, Boston, mahogany with satinwood veneer, H. 30 in., W. 20 in., DEPTH 30 in.
Mr. and Mrs. George M. Kaufman

288*
PAUL REVERE II, 1735-1818
Teapot
1783, Boston, silver with replaced wooden handle, marked: "• REVERE" in rectangle on bottom, inscribed on pourer's side in script monogram "MRH"; H. 6½ in., DIAM. (base) 4¼ in., DIAM. (lip) 3 in.
Private collection

289*
PAUL REVERE II, 1735-1818
Creampot
1783, Boston, silver, marked: "• REVERE" in rectangle at left of handle, inscribed in script monogram "MRH" under spout; H. 5¼ in., DIAM. (base) 2⅜ in.
Private collection

290-293
PAUL REVERE II, 1735-1818
Set of four goblets
1792, Boston, silver, marked: "REVERE" in rectangle above the engraving, inscribed with script monogram "MRH" on front; H. (each) 5½ in., DIAM. (base) 3¼ in., DIAM. (rim) 3⅛ in.
Private collection

294-295
PAUL REVERE II, 1735-1818
Pair of sauceboats (from a set of four)
Ca. 1790, Boston, silver, inscribed "Hays" on each front; marked: (a) "REVERE" in rectangle with clipped corners, on bottom, (b) "• REVERE" on bottom; L. (each) 8 in., H. (each) 5½ in.
Peter W. Eliot

296*
PAUL REVERE II, 1735-1818
Waiter
1797, Boston, silver, marked: "REVERE" in rectangle with clipped lower corner and uneven lower line on bottom, inscribed "EHD" on face; W. 13¼ in., L. 17 in.
Yale University Art Gallery, New Haven, Conn., the Mabel Brady Garvan Collection

297*
DENIS COLOMBIER, active in Paris, 1776-1809
Cup (from a set of four)
1789, Paris, silver, maker's marks on bottom; H. 2¾ in., DIAM. (base) 2 in., DIAM. (rim) 2¾ in.
Sheldon Arpad

298-299*
PAUL REVERE II, 1735-1818
Two cups (from a set of eight)
1795, Boston, silver, marked: "REVERE" on bottom; H. 2¾ in., DIAM. (rim) 2¾ in.
Sheldon Arpad (no. 298)
David Saltonstall (no. 299)

300
PAUL REVERE II, 1735-1818
Sauceboat
1783, Boston, silver, marked: "• REVERE" in rectangle upside down below initials in center of base, inscribed just above center between legs: "EHᴰE," added below "1761"; H. 5¼ in., L. 7⅜ in.
Museum of Fine Arts, gift of Mary P. Scott and Robert E. Peabody in memory of their father, Robert Swain Peabody. 66.207

301
PAUL REVERE II, 1735-1818
Sauceboat
1783, Boston, silver, marked: "• REVERE" in rectangle centered between legs and above initials, inscribed just above center between legs "EHᴰE," added below "1761"; H. 5⅛ in., L. 7⅝ in.
Museum of Fine Arts, gift of Mary P. Scott and Robert E. Peabody in memory of their father, Robert Swain Peabody. 67.951

302*
JOHN SCHOFIELD, active 1778-1796
Urn
1786, London, silver, maker's marks under plinth and three on bezel of cover, inscribed monogram on front "OAW"; H. 20½ in., W. 11¼ in.
Museum of Fine Arts, bequest of Mrs. M. A. Elton. 88.291

303
PAUL REVERE II, 1735-1818
Coffee urn
1793, Boston, silver with ivory spigot handle, marked: "• REVERE" in rectangle at edge of plinth in back, inscribed in ellipse in back: "BAC"; H. 18 in., W. (base) 4⅝ in., DIAM. (lip) 4¼ in.
Museum of Fine Arts, gift of Henry Davis Sleeper in memory of his mother, Maria Westcote Sleeper, by exchange. 60.1419

304*
PAUL REVERE II, 1735-1818
Urn
1800, Boston, silver with ivory spigot handle, marked: "REVERE" in rectangle on side of plinth, inscribed on front: "TO PERPETUATE/The Gallant defence/Made by/Capt GAMALIEL BRADFORD./in the Ship Industry on the 8th July 1800/when Attacked by four French Privateers/in the Streights of Gibralter./This URN is Presented to him/by/SAMUEL PARKMAN"; H. 19 in., W. 10¼ in., DIAM. (rim) 6½ in.
Massachusetts Historical Society, Boston

305*
CHARLES BALTHAZAR JULIEN FEVRET DE SAINT-MEMIN, 1770-1852
Paul Revere, 1735-1818
Ca. 1800, Philadelphia, chalk on paper; 20¼ x 14¼ in.
Museum of Fine Arts, gift of Mrs. Walter Knight (Patricia Riddle Knight). 47.1055

306*
GILBERT STUART, 1755-1828
Joseph Warren Revere, 1777-1868
Ca. 1813, Boston, oil on panel; 27¼ x 21¾ in.
Private collection

307*
THOMAS CLARKE, active in Boston ca. 1800-1801
Restrike of trade card of Paul Revere and Son
1944, probably Boston, line engraving, signed bottom center: "T. Clarke Sc."; 3¼ x 4¾ in.
Museum of Fine Arts, gift of the American Antiquarian Society. M36095

308
THOMAS CLARKE, active in Boston ca. 1800-1801
Steel Plate for Revere and Son trade card
Ca. 1796-1803, probably Boston, engraved steel, signed bottom center in reverse: "T. Clarke Sc."; 3⅜ x 5 in.
Massachusetts Historical Society, Boston

309*
WILLIAM LYNN, active ca. 1800-1818, and ABEL BOWEN, 1790-1850
U.S. Frigate Constitution, of 44 Guns
Ca. 1813, Boston, etching and aquatint, touched, signed lower left: "Drawn by Wᵐ Lynn," signed lower right: "A. Bowen Sc."; 17⅝ x 22⅛ in.
Museum of Fine Arts, bequest of Charles Hitchcock Tyler. 33.791

310
ANONYMOUS ARTIST
Captain Isaac Hull, 1773-1843
1813, Philadelphia, mezzotint, state II, published by Freeman and Pierie; 14⅞ x 13¾ in.
Boston Public Library, Print Department

311*
PAUL REVERE II, 1735-1818
Teapot and stand
1799, Boston, silver with wooden handle, marked: "REVERE" in rectangle with clipped corner on inside bottom and twice on bottom of teapot and in center of bottom of stand, inscribed with script monogram "EH" on pourer's side, and on the other side: "To/Edmund Hartt/Constructor of the Frigate BOSTON/Presented by a number of his fellow citizens as a/Memorial of their sense of his Ability, Zeal, and Fidelity/in the completion of that Ornament/of the AMERICAN NAVY./1799"; H. teapot 7¼ in., L. (base) 5 in., OVERALL LENGTH 12⅜ in., H. (stand) 1 in., L. 6⅜ in.
Museum of Fine Arts, gift of James Longley. 96.1 and 96.4

312*
PAUL REVERE II, 1735-1818
Creampot
1799, Boston, silver, marked: "REVERE" in rectangle with clipped edge upside down on edge of plinth, inscribed with script monogram "EH" on front; H. 7 in., W. (base) 2⅝ in.
Museum of Fine Arts, gift of James Longley. 96.2

313*
PAUL REVERE II, 1735-1818
Sugar bowl
1799, Boston, silver, marked: "REVERE" in rectangle with clipped edge on edge of plinth, with inscription the same as on teapot; H. 9⅜ in., W. (base) 3 in.
Museum of Fine Arts, gift of James Longley. 96.3

314*
GILBERT STUART, 1755-1828
Paul Revere, 1735-1818
1813, Boston, oil on panel; 28½ x 23¼ in.
Museum of Fine Arts, gift of Joseph W., William B., and Edward H. R. Revere. 30.782

315*
GILBERT STUART, 1755-1828
Rachel Walker Revere (Mrs. Paul), 1745-1813
1813, Boston, oil on panel, signed on the back: "Painted by G. Stuart Esqr. For Joseph W. Revere In the Spring of 1813"; 28½ x 23¾ in.
Museum of Fine Arts, gift of Joseph W., William B., and Edward H. R. Revere. 30.783

316
PAUL REVERE II, 1735-1818
Copperplate for Paul Revere bookplate
1758, Boston, engraved copper; 3⅞ x 2⅞ in.
Massachusetts Historical Society, Boston

317
ATTRIBUTED TO JOSEPH DUNKERLY, active in Boston 1784-1785
Rachel Walker Revere (Mrs. Paul), 1745-1813
Ca. 1784, watercolor on ivory with gold frame; 1¾ x 1⅜ in.
Museum of Fine Arts, Pauline Revere Thayer Collection. 35.1850

318
PAUL REVERE II, 1735-1818
Wedding ring
1773, Boston, gold, inscribed on the inside: "[L]IVE Co[n]tented"; DIAM. ¾ in.
Museum of Fine Arts, gift of Mrs. Henry B. Chapin and Edward H. R. Revere. 56.585

319
PAUL REVERE II, 1735-1818
Thimble
Ca. 1805, Boston, gold, inscribed on side: "Maria Revere Balestier"; H. 1¼ in., DIAM. (base) ⅝ in.
Museum of Fine Arts, gift of Mrs. Henry B. Chapin and Edward H. R. Revere. 56.113

320*
PAUL REVERE II, 1735-1818
Covered porringer
Ca. 1773, Boston, silver, inscribed with monogram: "PRR" away from bowl; H. (body) 1⅞ in., DIAM. (lip) 5⅝ in., L. (handle) 3 in.
Museum of Fine Arts, Pauline Revere Thayer Collection. 35.1758

321
PAUL REVERE II, 1735-1818
Sugar urn
1790, Boston, silver; H. 10⅛ in., w. (base) 3¼ in., DIAM. (at points of flutes) 4¼ in.
Museum of Fine Arts, Pauline Revere Thayer Collection. 35.1759

322*
PAUL REVERE II, 1735-1818
Pitcher
Ca. 1800, Boston, silver, marked: "REVERE" in rectangle with uneven bottom line, engraved with script *R* below spout, added on base: "Paul and

Rachel Revere./Charter Street"; H. 7⅛ in., DIAM. (base) 4¼ in., DIAM. (lip) 4 in.
Museum of Fine Arts, gift of Joseph W. R. Rogers and Mary C. Rogers. 42.462

323
Plate
Ca. 1750-1770, China, hard-paste porcelain with blue, red, and gold underglaze (Imari pattern); DIAM. 9⅛ in.
Museum of Fine Arts, bequest of Mrs. Pauline Revere Thayer. 35.1849

324*
Pole screen
1760-1790, Boston, mahogany with pine, embroidered panel of wool and silk yarns and paint on linen; H. 64½ in., H. (screen) 27¾ in., w. 22½ in.
Museum of Fine Arts, bequest of Mrs. Pauline Revere Thayer. 35.1845

325
Chest of drawers
1780-1800, Boston area, mahogany with mahogany veneer and white pine; H. 32¼ in., w. 41¼ in., DEPTH 21⅝ in.
Museum of Fine Arts, bequest of Mrs. Pauline Revere Thayer. 35.1844

326*
Tambour desk
1790-1805, Boston, mahogany, mahogany veneer, and satinwood inlay, with pine; H. 43⅜ in., w. 41¾ in., DEPTH 18¾ in.
Private collection

327*
A view of Canton Dale
Undated, Canton, Mass., pen and ink sketch; 5½ x 11⅜ in.
Massachusetts Historical Society, Boston

328
PAUL REVERE II, 1735-1818
Untitled poem
Ca. 1810, Canton, Mass., manuscript copy; 14½ x 5⅞ in.
Massachusetts Historical Society, Boston

329
EBENEZER CLOUGH, 1767-1848(?)
Wallpaper panel
Ca. 1800, Boston, printed paper, inscribed on pedestal: "SACRED TO WASHINGTON"; 44¼ x 22⅞ in.
Mrs. Clifford A. Waterhouse

330
ISAIAH THOMAS, 1749-1831
The Constitutions of the . . . Free and Accepted Masons
1792, Worcester, printed book; 9½ x 7½ in.
Massachusetts Historical Society, Boston

331*
PAUL REVERE II, 1735-1818
Notification for the Lodge of Saint Andrew
1767, Boston, line engraving, certificate signed by Paul Revere as secretary of the lodge, engraving signed lower right: "Engrav'd, Printed & Sold by Paul Revere, Boston"; 7⅝ x 6 in.
Mrs. Frances Brooks

332-333*
PAUL REVERE II, 1735-1818
Pair of ladles
1762, Boston, silver with wooden handles, marked: "•REVERE" in rectangle on inside of bowl, inscribed on reverse of bowl (a) "No 1/The Gift of/Br Saml Barrett to/St Andrew.s Lodge/No 82/1762"; (b) "No 2/The Gift of/Br Saml Barrett to/St Andrew.s Lodge/No 82/1762"; L. (a) 15 in., (b) 14⅛ in.
Lodge of Saint Andrew, Boston

334
PAUL REVERE II, 1735-1818
General Masonic certificate
Ca. 1773, Boston, line engraving, signed lower right: "Engraved Printed & Sold by Paul Revere•BOSTON," signed by Revere in 1779 as Master, lower right; 15 x 10¾ in.
American Antiquarian Society, Worcester, Mass.

335*
Armchair
1765-1785, Boston area, mahogany with maple and gilding, original webbing, liner, and horsehair cover; H. 50½ in., w. 25½ in., DEPTH 19½ in.
Private collection

336
Armchair
1780-1790, England or France, painted beech; H. 51 in., w. 25⅞ in., DEPTH 25 in.
The Grand Lodge of Masons in Massachusetts, Boston

337
WOOD AND CALDWELL MANUFACTORY
Pitcher
1790-1805, Staffordshire, England, earthenware, transfer-printed on bottom with view of the factory and inscribed: "The South View of the Earthenware Manufactory of WOOD and CALDWELL Burslem"; inscribed on side under lip: "CORN Benjamin Emmons Born in Boston May the 10th 1762"; H. 13¾ in., DIAM. (base) 6½ in., DIAM. (lip) 6¾ in.
The Grand Lodge of Masons in Massachusetts, Boston

338*
PAUL REVERE II, 1735-1818
Urn
1800-1801, Boston, gold, inscribed: "This URN incloses a Lock of HAIR/of the Immortal WASHINGTON/PRESENTED JANUARY 27, 1800,/to the Massachusetts GRAND LODGE/by HIS amiable WIDOW./Born Feby 11th 1732/Obt Decr 14. 1799."; H. 3¾ in., DIAM. (base) 1½ in.
The Grand Lodge of Masons in Massachusetts, Boston

339
PAUL REVERE II, 1735-1818
Cup (one of a pair)
Ca. 1795, Boston, silver, marked: "REVERE" in rectangle with clipped corners below center point, inscribed with script monogram "SSE" on upper curve opposite handle; H. 5⅛ in., DIAM. (base) 2¾ in., DIAM. (lip) 4¾ in.
Museum of Fine Arts, gift of Mrs. Guy Lowell in memory of Professor and Mrs. Charles S. Sargent. 50.2344

340*

PAUL REVERE II, 1735-1818
Teapot and stand
1787, Boston, silver with wooden handle and finial on teapot, marked: on teapot, first stroke of "•REVERE" visible under "J•AUSTIN" stamped over in opposite direction on bottom, on stand, "•REVERE" on bottom, inscribed with script monogram "HC" in ellipse on pourer's side; teapot, H. 5½ in., L. 10¾ in., stand H. 1 in., L. 6¾ in.
Museum of Fine Arts, gift of the estates of the Misses Eunice McLelland and Frances Cordis Cruft. 42.377-378

341

PAUL REVERE II, 1735-1818
Sugar basket
Ca. 1798, Boston, silver, marked: "REVERE" in rectangle on top of bail handle, inscribed script monograms on one side: "ET/to /EHT"; H. 6¾ in., L. 6⅛ in.
Museum of Fine Arts, Helen and Alice Colburn Fund. 39.39

342

PAUL REVERE II, 1735-1818
Skewer
1796, Boston, marked "REVERE" slightly lower than the initial and on other side, inscribed with script "B" on blade beneath circle; L. 9¼ in.
Museum of Fine Arts, Pauline Revere Thayer Collection. 35.1793

343-344

PAUL REVERE II, 1735-1818
Pair of salts
Ca. 1760, Boston, silver, marked: "PR" in small rectangle above and below center point on bottom; H. 1½ in. (each), DIAM. (rim) (a) 2½ in., (b) 2⅜ in.
Miss Jane Pray

345-348

PAUL REVERE II, 1735-1818
Set of four salt spoons
1786-1787, Boston, silver, marked: "PR" in rectangle on reverse of stem, engraved with Swan crest on handles; L. 4⅛ in. (each)
Miss Mary S. Thompson and Mrs. Louis Long, Jr.

349

PAUL REVERE II, 1735-1818
Two-handled bowl
Ca. 1785, Boston, silver, marked: "•REVERE" in rectangle twice on side, inscribed front and back in medallion: "T O"; H. 7 in., W. (handles) 8¾ in., DIAM. 5⅜ in., DIAM.(foot) 3½ in.
Museum of Fine Arts, gift of Mrs. Henry Lyman in memory of her father, Samuel Cabot (1850-1906). 1970.646

350

ATTRIBUTED TO PAUL REVERE II, 1735-1818
Seal
Ca. 1782, Boston, silver set in wood; H. 1¾ in., L. 2 in.
Massachusetts Medical Society, Boston

351

PAUL REVERE I, 1702-1754
Saucepan
1740-1750, Boston, silver with wooden handle, marked: "P. REVERE" in rectangle above center point on bottom; H. (bowl) 2⅞ in., DIAM. (base) 2¾ in., DIAM. (lip) 2½ in., L. (handle) 6⅛ in.
Museum of Fine Arts, gift of Talbot Aldrich. 53.2081

352

THOMAS REVERE, 1739/40-1817
Ladle
Ca. 1790-1800, Boston, silver, marked: "TR" in rectangle on reverse of handle, inscribed "HT to ST" with ellipse on tip; L. 14¼ in.
Private collection

353

PAUL REVERE II, 1735-1818
Teaspoon
Ca. 1785, Boston, silver, marked: "PR" in script in rectangle on back of handle, inscribed "NAG" at tip; L. 5 in.
Museum of Fine Arts, gift of the Paul Revere Insurance Company. 63.466

354-355

PAUL REVERE II, 1735-1818
Pair of sauceboats
1780-1800, Boston, silver, marked: "•REVERE" on bottom, near center point, of each, engraved with crest of lion's head issuing from crown on pourer's side and inscribed with script monogram "JES" on the other; H. 4⅞ in., L. 7¾ in.
Museum of Fine Arts, Pauline Revere Thayer Collection. 35.1773-1774

356

PAUL REVERE I, 1702-1754
Cann
1740-1750, Boston, silver, marked: "P. REVERE" above center point on bottom, inscribed: "Edes" in script on bottom; H. 5 in., DIAM. (base) 3⅜ in., DIAM. (lip) 3⅛ in.
Museum of Fine Arts, gift of Mr. and Mrs. Henry Herbert Edes. 36.47

357

PAUL REVERE II, 1735-1818
Cann
1766, Boston, silver, marked: "•REVERE" in rectangle at left of handle, inscribed: "ZIE" on the handle; H. 5⅜ in., DIAM. (base) 3½ in., DIAM. (lip) 3¼ in.
Museum of Fine Arts, gift of Henry Davis Sleeper in memory of his mother, Maria Westcote Sleeper. 25.601

358

PAUL REVERE I, 1702-1754
Teapot
Ca. 1740, Boston, silver with wooden handle and part-wood finial, marked: "P. Revere" in rectangle at center point on bottom; H. 5 in., DIAM. (base) 3⅜ in.
Museum of Fine Arts, gift of Mrs. George P. Montgomery. 1972.122

359

PAUL REVERE II, 1735-1818
Teapot
1760-1765, Boston, silver with wooden handle, marked: "•REVERE" below center point and script "PR" in rectangle upside down above center point on bottom, engraved with Ross crest on pourer's side, inscribed "RBS" on bottom at left of center point; H. 5⅞ in., DIAM. (base) 3¼ in.
Museum of Fine Arts, Pauline Revere Thayer Collection. 35.1775

360

PAUL REVERE I, 1702-1754
Porringer
Ca. 1740-1750, Boston, silver, marked: "PR" in shield in center of bowl and on rim at left of handle, inscribed on handle: "B/E to C/C" over "A•C"; H. 1⅞ in., DIAM. (lip) 5 in.
Mr. and Mrs. Howland Warren

361

PAUL REVERE II, 1735-1818
Porringer
1769, Boston, silver, marked: "•REVERE" in rectangle on back of handle and through center point in bowl, inscribed: "TPS" away from bowl; H. 2¼ in., DIAM. (lip) 5⅝ in.
Museum of Fine Arts, bequest of Mrs. Beatrice Constance (Turner) Maynard in memory of Winthrop Sargent. 61.1161

362

PAUL REVERE I, 1702-1754
Caster
1740-1750, Boston, silver, marked: "PR" in shield with line above and below on bottom, inscribed "DT" under foot; H. 5¼ in., DIAM. (base) 1¾ in.
Museum of Fine Arts, bequest of Charles Hitchcock Tyler. 32.403

363

PAUL REVERE II, 1735-1818
Caster
Ca. 1765, Boston, silver, marked: "•REVERE" in rectangle near rim, engraved with crest of cross crosslet, "Trusty to the end" inscribed in scroll above added to side; H. 5⅞ in.
Private collection

364

PAUL REVERE I, 1702-1754
Spoon
Ca. 1725, Boston, silver, marked: "PR" in shield on back of stem, inscribed: "ITs" on back; L. 7½ in.
Museum of Fine Arts, the H. E. Bolles Fund. 54.661

365

PAUL REVERE II, 1735-1818
Tablespoon
Ca. 1760, Boston, silver, marked: "•REVERE" in rectangle on back of stem, engraved on back of handle with Johonnot crest on torse, script monogram "HJ" inscribed below; L. 7⅞ in.
Museum of Fine Arts, gift of Henry Davis Sleeper in memory of his mother, Maria Westcote Sleeper, by exchange. 56.1150

366

PAUL REVERE II, 1735-1818

Tablespoon

1772, Boston, silver, marked: "•REVERE" in rectangle on back of stem, inscribed with script monogram in cartouche on tip "TAH"; L. 8½ in.
Museum of Fine Arts, Pauline Revere Thayer Collection, by exchange. 39.60

367

PAUL REVERE I, 1702-1754

Creampot

Ca. 1750, Boston, silver, marked: "P. REVERE" in rectangle on bottom; H. (lip) 4¼ in.
Private collection

368

PAUL REVERE II, 1735-1818

Creampot

1755-1760, Boston, silver, marked: "•REVERE" across center point on bottom, inscribed "HM" above mark and "RO" below mark; H. 3⅞ in.
Museum of Fine Arts, gift of Talbot Aldrich. 53.2080

369

PAUL REVERE I, 1702-1754

Tankard

Ca. 1750, Boston, silver, marked: "P. Revere" in italics in rectangle at left of handle and on bottom, inscribed: "BBM" on handle; H. 7⅞ in., DIAM. (lip) 4⅛ in., DIAM. (base) 5⅜ in.
Robert, David, and Edward Tappan

370

PAUL REVERE II, 1735-1818

Tankard

Ca. 1765, Boston, silver, marked: "•REVERE" in rectangle at left of handle, engraved initials erased from handle; H. 8⅞ in., DIAM. (base) 5½ in., DIAM. (lip) 4⅛ in.
Museum of Fine Arts, gift of Henry Davis Sleeper in memory of his mother, Maria Westcote Sleeper. 25.596

371-372

PAUL REVERE I, 1702-1754

Pair of strainer spoons

Ca. 1730, Boston, silver, marked: "PR" in rectangle on back of each spoon; L. 5 in. (each)
First and Second Church in Boston (Second Church Collection), Boston

373

PAUL REVERE II, 1735-1818

Dish

1796, Boston, silver, marked: "REVERE" in rectangle, inscribed on rim: "Given by SUVIAH THAYER in testimony of her/respect for the FIRST CHURCH OF CHRIST IN/BOSTON. A.D. 1796."; DIAM. 12⅞ in.
First and Second Church in Boston (First Church Collection), Boston

374

PAUL REVERE II, 1735-1818

Standing cup

1758, Boston, silver, marked: "•REVERE" on rim, inscribed on one side of bowl in beaded medallion:

"The Gift of the Revd Mr Thos Prince to the South Church in Boston who was Ordained Pastor of said church Oct. 1st 1718 & died Oct = 22.1753 A E 72"; H. 10 in., DIAM. (base) 5⅝ in., DIAM (rim) 3⅞ in.
Old South Church, Boston

375

Chalice

1692, France, silver, inscribed: "The gift of Mr. Anthony Bracket to the South Church in Boston, 1758"; H. 10½ in., DIAM. (base) 5⅝ in., DIAM. (rim) 3¾ in.
Old South Church, Boston

376

PAUL REVERE II, 1735-1818

Flagon

1773, Boston, silver, marked: "REVERE" at left of handle and on cover, inscribed: "Humbly Presented/ to the Church of CHRIST in Hollis Street/ under the Pastoral Care of/the Revd MATHER BYLES D.D./for the Communion Table/by ZACHARIAH JOHONNOT Esqr 1773"; H. 13⅜ in., DIAM. (base) 7⅜ in.
First and Second Church in Boston (From Hollis Street Church), Boston

377

PAUL REVERE II, 1735-1818

Baptismal bowl

1761, Boston, silver, marked: "•REVERE" in rectangle on bottom, engraved with Johonnot arms on rim and inscribed in script: "Presented to the Church of CHRIST in/Boston, under the Pastoral Care of the Revd MATHER BYLES, D.D./by ZACHARIAH JOHONNOT Esqr/Decr 1761"; H. 5 in., DIAM. 14½ in.
First and Second Church in Boston (From Hollis Street Church), Boston

378

PAUL REVERE II, 1735-1818

Creampot

Ca. 1795, Boston, silver, marked: "REVERE" in rectangle on front edge of plinth, inscribed monograms in three cuttings on front: "FPI [or "J"]/MAE/JAE"; H. 7⅛ in., W. (base) 2½ in.
Museum of Fine Arts, Pauline Revere Thayer Collection. 35.1787

379

PAUL REVERE II, 1735-1818

Creampot

Ca. 1800, Boston, silver, marked: "REVERE" in rectangle on flat bottom, inscribed nineteenth century monogram on front: "FAB"; H. 5 in., L. (base) 2½ in.
Museum of Fine Arts, Pauline Revere Thayer Collection. 35.1788

380

PAUL REVERE II, 1735-1818

Creampot

1795-1800, Boston, silver, marked: "REVERE" in rectangle on rim of base at pourer's side inscribed with script monogram "SI," scratched "D" twice on bottom; H. 5½ in., L. (base) 3⅝ in.
Museum of Fine Arts, Pauline Revere Thayer Collection. 35.1783

381

PAUL REVERE II, 1735-1818

Coffee pot

1781, Boston, silver with wooden handle, marked: "•REVERE" in rectangle on bottom near center point, engraved with Sargent coat of arms and crest on pourer's side; H. 12⅞ in., DIAM. (base) 4½ in.
Museum of Fine Arts, gift of Mrs. Nathaniel Thayer. 31.139

382

PAUL REVERE II, 1735-1818

Copper bookplate

1764, Boston, engraved copper, signed lower right corner in reverse: "P Revere Sculp," engraved in reverse with Sargent coat of arms and crest and inscribed below "Epes Sargent"; 3½ x 2¾ in.
Museum of Fine Arts, Annie A. Hawley Bequest. 59.517

383

PAUL REVERE II, 1735-1818

Coffee pot

Ca. 1795, Boston, silver with wooden handle, marked: "REVERE" in rectangle with clipped corners upside down on vertical edge on foot, inscribed with script monogram on pourer's side: "HCS"; H. 13⅞ in., DIAM. (base) 4½ in.
Museum of Fine Arts, bequest of Arthur D. Fay. 1972.56

384

ATTRIBUTED TO PAUL REVERE II, 1735-1818

Teapot

1785, Boston, silver with replaced wooden handle and finial, unmarked, engraved with Warren coat of arms, and inscribed with script monogram "JAW"; H. 5¾ in., L. 11 in., L. (body) 5½ in.
Mr. and Mrs. Howland Warren

385

PAUL REVERE II, 1735-1818

Sugar bowl

Ca. 1785, Boston, silver, marked: "•REVERE" in rectangle on bottom, engraved with Warren coat of arms and inscribed with script monogram "JAW" in ovals on sides; H. 10⅛ in., base 3 in. square, DIAM. (rim) 4 in.
Mrs. Mary W. Murphy

386-387

PAUL REVERE II, 1735-1818

Pair of teaspoons

Ca. 1770, Boston, silver, marked: "•REVERE" in rectangle on back of stem, inscribed on back of tip in small letters: "EB to EBC"; L. (each) 5⅝ in.
Dr. Richard Warren

388

PAUL REVERE II, 1735-1818

Teapot

1789, Boston, silver with wooden handle and finial, marked: "•REVERE" in rectangle on bottom, inscribed in ellipse on both sides: "MB"; H. 4⅛ in., L. 11⅛ in., L. (body) 5⅜ in.
Museum of Fine Arts, Pauline Revere Thayer Collection. 35.1777

389

PAUL REVERE II, 1735-1818

Teapot

1795-1800, Boston, silver with replaced wooden handle, marked: "REVERE" on bottom, inscribed in script monogram "OEG" in ellipse over center angle of each side; H. 6 in., L. 11¼ in., L. (base) 5⅝ in.

Museum of Fine Arts, bequest of Mrs. Elizabeth Goodwin Chapin. 68.431

390

PAUL REVERE II, 1735-1818

Sugar urn

Ca. 1795, Boston, silver, marked: "REVERE" in rectangle with lower corners cut, inscribed with script monogram "OEG" in dotted elliptical medallions on body and cover; H. 9 in., W. (base) 3⅛ in.

Museum of Fine Arts, gift of Eliot Wadsworth. 48.1355

391

PAUL REVERE II, 1735-1818

Sugar tongs

1780-1785, Boston, silver, marked: "•REVERE" in rectangle inside one arm; L. 5 in.

Museum of Fine Arts, Pauline Revere Thayer Collection. 35.1792

392

PAUL REVERE II, 1735-1818

Slop bowl

Ca. 1785, Boston, silver, marked: "•REVERE" in rectangle on each side of and facing center point on bottom, inscribed on side: "TIL"; H. 3⅜ in. (uneven), DIAM. (base) 3⅝ in., DIAM. (lip) 6½ in.

Museum of Fine Arts, Pauline Revere Thayer Collection. 35.1766

393

GILBERT STUART, 1755-1828

Hepzibah Clark Swan (Mrs. James), 1756-1825

Ca. 1806-1810, Boston, oil on panel; 32½ x 26½ in.

Museum of Fine Arts, Swan Collection. Bequest of Elizabeth Howard Bartol. 27.539

On view April 18-June 1, and September 1-October 12

394

ANONYMOUS ARTIST

Privateer ship Bethell

Ca. 1745, probably Boston, oil on canvas; 34¼ x 44 in.

Massachusetts Historical Society, Boston

395

PAUL REVERE II, 1735-1818

Deposition

1775, Boston, manuscript, in Revere's hand; 12¼ x 7¾ in.

Massachusetts Historical Society, Boston